"*Ottawa and Empire* is an import
scholarly research that exposes the bourgeois lie about Canada's benign internationalism, and it is capped off with a stimulating discussion of the radical political implications of the country's marauding imperialist agenda."

— Thom Workman, professor of political science, University of New Brunswick

"We have lived through a very long period of myth-making about Canada's place in the world as peacekeeper and promoter of human rights and democracy. *Ottawa and Empire* is a punchy, compelling, and utterly myth-busting account of Canada's role in 'building democracy' in Honduras. No one reading this book will ever jump on the 'support the troops' bandwagon again."

— Greg Albo, professor of political science, York University

"Canada's growing economic involvement in Honduras has had devastating implications for human rights, democracy, and the health and safety of the population. Shipley raises important questions about this new Canadian imperialism and provides a much needed examination of the rise of Canadian interests in Central America and elsewhere in the world."

— Lynn Holland, Josef Korbel School of International Studies, University of Denver, Colorado

"*Ottawa and Empire* is a major contribution to the study of Canadian foreign policy and political economy. By combining rich historical materials with astute political theory and substantive empirical evidence, Shipley demonstrates convincingly that Canada's role in Honduras has been exploitative and violent—a case study of imperialism in action."

— Jerome Klassen, author of *Joining Empire: The Political Economy of the New Canadian Foreign Policy*

"The overthrow of Honduras's elected government in 2009 was a swift, brutal reminder of the limits of freedom that a small country is allowed. The murders of pro-democracy activists in the years since have ensured that low-key terror is a part of political life. Based on close engagement with the people struggling for their rights in Honduras, *Ottawa and Empire* tells the story of the coup and the regime that followed. It reveals the continuity between Canada's role in the coup and its foreign policy from Haiti to Afghanistan. Tracing the profits flowing to Canadian corporations and describing the bizarre colonial fantasies of "Charter Cities," Shipley's book will dispel any illusions readers may hold on to about Canada's benevolent role in the world."

— Justin Podur, author of *Haiti's New Dictatorship*

"Tyler Shipley's well-researched and probing work focuses on Canadian involvement in the overthrow of the reformist liberal President of Honduras Manuel Zelaya. In doing so, Shipley has produced an illuminating case study of the new Canadian imperialism in Latin America and elsewhere."

— Henry Heller, author of *The Birth of Capitalism: A 21st Century Perspective*

"Based upon meticulous fieldwork, including dozens of interviews with activists in resistance communities, this book is a compelling account of the nefarious effects of Canada's foreign policy in Central America and elsewhere. Shipley shatters the illusion that the Canadian government is dedicated to keeping 'peace.' This book is a must-read for activists and academics interested in international relations, international development, and social movements."

— Susan Spronk, associate professor of international development and global studies, University of Ottawa

"Remarkably well-researched, cogently argued, and engagingly written, *Ottawa and Empire* is obligatory reading for all interested in Canadian foreign policy, and not only in the shameful conduct of our government and corporations in Honduras. Shipley sets his analysis into historical perspective and provides us with a first-hand account of the ways in which Canada has buttressed the Washington-led reversal of progressive change in the proverbial 'banana republic.'"

— Liisa L. North, professor emeritus, York University

"Shipley gives a devastating critique of Canada's support for the violent oppression that accompanies the process of making Honduras 'right' for Canadian capital. *Ottawa and Empire* contributes to the critique of modern neoliberal globalization as an essentially neocolonial process that perpetuates and deepens the misery of much of the world for the profit of others."

— James Phillips, assistant professor of anthropology and international studies, Southern Oregon University

"The 2009 coup in Honduras in which the military overturned the elected government of President Manuel Zelaya has been followed by years of popular unrest and widespread human rights violations. Based on extensive interviews with a wide range of Hondurans, Shipley recounts the events leading up to and following the coup and the surprising support for the post-coup regime by the Canadian government. Shipley's analysis presents an important critique of Canadian economic interests in Honduras and the implications for understanding Canada's role in the hemisphere."

— Laura Macdonald, professor of political science and political economy, Carleton University

OTTAWA AND EMPIRE

Canada and the Military Coup in Honduras

TYLER A. SHIPLEY

Between the Lines
Toronto

Ottawa and Empire

First published in 2017 by
Between the Lines
401 Richmond Street West
Studio 277
Toronto, Ontario M5V 3A8
Canada
1-800-718-7201
www.btlbooks.com

Library and Archives Canada Cataloguing in Publication

Shipley, Tyler, author
Ottawa and empire : Canada and the military coup in Honduras / Tyler Shipley.

Includes bibliographical references and index.
Issued in print and electronic formats.
ISBN 978-1- 77113-314- 2 (softcover).-- ISBN 978-1- 77113-315- 9 (EPUB).-- ISBN 978-1- 77113-316- 6 (PDF)

1. Honduras-- History-- Coup d'état, 2009. 2. Canada-- Foreign relations-- Honduras. 3. Honduras-- Foreign relations-- Canada. 4. Honduras-- Politics and government-- 1982-. I. Title.

F1508.3 S54 2017 972.8305'38 C2016-907426- 9
C2016-907427- 78

Cover and text design by Maggie Earle
Printed in Canada

We acknowledge for their financial support of our publishing activities the Government of Canada through the Canada Book Fund, the Canada Council for the Arts, which last year invested $153 million to bring the arts to Canadians throughout the country, and the Government of Ontario through the Ontario Arts Council, the Ontario Book Publishers Tax Credit program, and the Ontario Media Development Corporation.

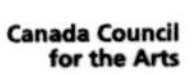

Conseil des Arts du Canada

CONTENTS

Acknowledgements vii

INTRODUCTION 1
"Our Job is to Kill People"

1 IMPERIAL LEGACIES 5
Five Centuries of Foreign Domination in Honduras

Civilizations Lost 6
Haughty Defiance 8
The Bells of Freedom? 10
The Banana Republic 14
1954 and the Fountain of Honduran History 17
Agrarian Struggles Emerge 19
The USS Honduras 22
The Imposition of Neoliberalism 24
Maras and Vigilantes 29
Glimmers of Resistance 32

2 THE PRESIDENT IN HIS PYJAMAS 34
The June 2009 Coup d'Etat

The Genealogy of a Social Movement 35
Manuel Zelaya and the CNRP 38
Constituyente 42
Sunset on the Zelaya Era 45
Golpe de Estado 47
La Resistencia 51
Pantomime Elections 57

3 THE VIEW FROM OTTAWA **65**
Seeing and Unseeing the Demise of Democracy

Canada and the Coup 65
Breaking the Social Movement 72
Truth and Reconciliation? 78
The Cartagena Accord 84
The Movement and the Party 87
The FNRP Persists 91

4 A FRUITFUL PARTNERSHIP **95**
Canadian Investments in the Banana Republic

Extracting Profits 95
Condemned to Death 99
Workshops of Canadian Capital 103
The Banana Coast 109
Making Honduras "Right" for Ottawa 115
The Insecurity State in Honduras 120
Grand Strategies 124

5 MIDDLE POWER OR EMPIRE'S ALLY? **130**
Canada's Place in the World Today

Capitalism and Imperialism 131
A Helpful Fixer? 134
Holding the Bully's Coat? 138
A Short History of Canadian Foreign Policy 143
The Contemporary Turn: Militarism and Imperialism 148
Reorganizing the Imperial Machine 154
A Very Canadian Engagement 157

6 CONCLUSION **161**
Mythologies Old and New

¡Berta Vive! 161
Don Cherry and Canadian Militarism 163
Support the Troops 165
"We're Better than You" 168
Colonial Past, Imperial Present 171

Notes **174**

Index **214**

ACKNOWLEDGEMENTS

It is only due to the enormous generosity and support I received over the past decade that this book has seen the light of day. I owe more thanks than can be fit in the space I have and, as such, this list is far from exhaustive and has no particular order. But, since Marx begins his study of capital with the commodity form, I will start by thanking Amanda Crocker and everyone at Between the Lines for helping me transform this research into an actual book, a physical commodity which I hope will be purchased, read, marked up, dog-eared, celebrated, denounced, loaned, and borrowed by many.

There are a few people whose influence on this work was indispensable and to whom I am deeply thankful. My doctoral supervisor, David McNally, has been a mentor in the best possible way. His impact on my work has always been positive and productive, and his moral support and guidance over the past ten years has been a major component of everything I have achieved. Greg Albo's rigorous work is one of the most important intellectual influences behind this book and he has also been a kind and supportive friend over many years of academic and activist pursuits. Across my eight years of research in Central America, I have had no greater ally than Liisa North, who is as generous with her time and energy as she is committed to truth and justice. I also owe a particular note of thanks to my good friend and comrade, Josh Moufawad-Paul, for reading an early draft of the book and offering detailed and helpful editorial feedback.

This book is a product of much circulation and exchange of ideas, and the final work benefited greatly from many years of dialogue, debate, and collaboration with Abigail Bakan, Warren Bernauer, Annie Bird, Raul Burbano, Sandra Cuffe, Anthony Fenton, Todd Gordon, Jasmine Hristov, Dhruv Jain, Angela Joya, Rebecca Granovsky-Larsen, Simon Granovsky-Larsen, Ricardo Grinspun, Tanya Kerssen, Kole Kilibarda, Don Kingsbury, Michael Kirkpatrick, Jerome Klassen, Rodney Loeppky, Laura Macdonald, Geoff McCormack, Rajiv Rawat, Grahame Russell, Riaz Sayani-Mulji, Greg Shupak, Mike Skinner, Jessica Stites-Mor, Iselin Strønen, Caren Weisbart, and Anna Zalik.

I am also grateful to the many friends who may not have had a direct impact on this particular work but have shaped my thinking in broader ways that, inevitably, come across in a variety of unintended ways throughout this work. Among them, I would especially thank Julian Ammirante, Hulya Arik, Peter Braun, Jesse Carlson, Sarah Hornstein, Joel Irwin, Cory Jansson, Kurt Korneski, Renee Lung, Matt McLennan, Ryan McVeigh, Victoria Moufawad-Paul, Adrie Naylor, Nathan Nun, Anne Quigley-Rowley, Marc Roy, Parastou Saberi, Dale Shin, Carmen Teeple-Hopkins, Ryan Toews, Chris Webb, Jude Welburn, and Gareth Williams. I was fortunate early in my academic career to find myself among a cluster of supportive and critical scholars at the University of Manitoba. Much credit is owed to them, especially Mark Gabbert, Henry Heller, Tina Chen, David Churchill, and V. Ravi Vaithees, for first nudging me in the direction that my work has now taken. Thanks also to my many students at York University and Humber College who have embraced the critical spirit and encouraged me to continue teaching and learning every day.

I would like to acknowledge the support of the Social Sciences and Humanities Research Council for their financial contribution to the research that informs this book. I would also like to thank the Chr. Michelson Institute for commissioning a report on civil-military relations in Honduras, which gave me further opportunities to develop this research. I would also offer my gratitude to the many colleagues in CUPE 3903, past and present, whose efforts over many years produced working conditions for me as a graduate student and adjunct professor which, while not perfect, were much better than those of my colleagues at other institutions. Financial support won by CUPE 3903 helped me conduct research in Honduras and present my work at conferences across the Americas, which would otherwise have been beyond my economic means.

To those closest to me, a note of appreciation for putting up with the more-than-occasional rants that are an inevitable by-product of this kind of work. I am grateful for the support of my partner, Tina Benigno, and her family, and I am thankful to my mother, Brenda Shipley, for the example of strength that she has so often demonstrated. Along with my sister, Vanessa, and my brothers, Gavin and Chris, we said goodbye to our father last year. One of my strongest recent memories of my dad was when, in 2010, he came to Central America to visit me on one of the research trips that informs this book. What I remember most was the respect with which he listened to every person we met, and I like to think that this book is written in a similar spirit.

Indeed, it is to the hundreds of people in Honduras I have met, talked with, and listened to that this book is dedicated. Though they gained little by talking to me, every person who took the time to share their histories, experiences, and analyses made this book infinitely stronger. In particular, I would like to mention Juan Almendares, Tomás Andino, Jari Dixon, Pedro Landa, Luis Mendez, Victor Meza, Felix Molina, Berta Oliva, Gilberto Ríos, Nectali Rodezno, Raul Valdivia, and, especially, Berta Cáceres, to whose memory this work is dedicated. Their willingness to make time for me, under sometimes very difficult circumstances, is a testament to the commitment of so many Hondurans to make their country—and the world—a better place, despite all the forces stacked up against them. It is also a reflection of the faith they place in Karen Spring, a Canadian activist who relocated to Honduras in 2009 and has been a trusted ally to the social movement ever since.

It is through Karen that I was able to meet and connect with so many people in the movement; not only did Karen arrange interviews and translate along the way, she helped me to identify who I wanted to talk to, who would be willing to share, and how the various individuals, factions, and organizations related to one another. If that wasn't enough, she and her partner Edwin Espinal also became great friends to me and even allowed me to stay with them in Tegucigalpa. Without Karen's help, I could not possibly have navigated the extremely complicated and dangerous social terrain of contemporary Honduras. Over many days and nights, in hotels and offices and homes, over coffees and dinners and drinks, I was introduced to the social movement in Honduras, in all of its beauty and complexity. The experience has changed me, offering a window into both the richness of lives dedicated to social justice, and also the suddenness with which those lives can be taken away. Thus, while I acknowledge and dedicate this work to the activists whose struggles inform it, I also plead with readers to understand and heed the urgency of their calls to action.

INTRODUCTION
"Our Job is to Kill People"

In 2005, four years into the Canadian occupation of Afghanistan, Canadian Forces General Rick Hillier surprised a gathering of reporters by reminding them that the job of the Canadian military was "to kill people."[1] The frankness of this admission suggested that dramatic changes were afoot in a country that had long imagined itself a great peacekeeper. By 2009, Canada was deeply implicated in the torture of detainees in its Afghan occupation. In the same year, the then-ruling Conservative government supported the violent military overthrow of the democratic government of Honduras, placing Canada at odds with almost every other state in the western hemisphere. This decision, which is the primary concern of this book, stood in sharp contrast to the noble mythology of "Canada" that is touted by its leaders. And yet, a brief scan of Canada's recent engagements in the world suggests that it is quite representative of the new Canada.

In 2013, a journalist at *The Globe and Mail* reported on Canadian involvement in Africa and concluded that it did not look dissimilar to British and French colonialism:

> What do we call the thing Canada is doing in Africa? It involves our largest corporations, the federal government, public- and private-sector aid agencies, and sometimes the military. And their activities are increasingly connected, sometimes by choice, often by force of circumstance ... Canada is no longer simply "doing business" or "providing aid" in Africa ... [it has] become something like a colonial government.[2]

The Globe and Mail is anything but a leftist news source; that it offered critical comment on emergent Canadian imperialism signals a serious shift in thought.

Canadians—like their southern neighbours—have long been encouraged to believe that their state is a beacon of freedom and democracy. While that discourse has been hard to sustain in the United States, it has stubbornly refused to disappear from the Canadian mainstream, where popular media and public perception still seem to reflect the belief that Canada is, more or less, one of the "good guys" in international affairs. Canada, according to this narrative, is a state that has perfected the arts of democracy and good governance, offers freedom to its citizens and refuge to foreigners, and promotes peace, stability, and human rights in the rest of the world. An astonishing 94 percent of Canadians think their country is well-liked internationally and 84 percent believe Canada is a force for good in the world,[3] in spite of the increasing mobilizations of popular protest in foreign countries against Canadian policy.[4] In fact, the changes that have marked Canadian foreign policy over the past decade appear, to many Canadians, to reflect simply an increased sense of Canadian "self-confidence," as though Canada finally feels comfortable going out and asserting its good values in the world. The irony of a politics whereby "goodness" is militarized and hammered down upon the "less good" is, regrettably, lost in most of these assessments.

Michael Ignatieff, political scientist and former leader of the now-governing Liberal Party of Canada, is among the most articulate Canadian imperial cheerleaders. In a program for Canadian foreign policy written in 2003, Ignatieff waxed poetic about "Canadian values" like democracy, federalism, and pluralism. He then claimed that those values give Canada a "responsibility to protect" people living in "failed states," explaining that Canada has a "comparative advantage in the politics of managing divided societies," and must "intervene, if necessary, with military force."[5] His celebration of Canada's commitment to good government would likely raise a few eyebrows—from Indigenous people, for instance—but he nevertheless implores Canada to intervene militarily when it feels that others are not meeting Canadian criteria for good government.[6] His program, self-described as "muscular multilateralism," would see Canada take such pride in its purported successes that it would impose them on others. Indeed, the Canadian public is consistently presented with a version of Canada that imagines itself an enlightened and benevolent force that would help the rest of the world replicate its own success. Increasingly, however, the reality of Canadian policy looks radically different from the popular picture presented.

In fact, despite coming to power on a wave of progressive rhetoric, Canada's newest government quickly pronounced peacekeeping dead: "the terminology of peacekeeping is not valid at this time … those peacekeeping days do not exist now."[7] Arguably, Canada's peacekeeping pedigree was always an exaggeration. During the Cold War, while peacekeeping dressed the windows, the Canadian state gradually took on the role of a secondary imperial power in the global capitalist world order. This process has accelerated since the 1980s, and as Canadian capital has looked outward in search of new profits, the Canadian state has used its considerable resources to support that expansion, successfully carving out considerable space for its economic interests. That space, and the profits that come with it, has often been taken directly from communities in the Global South. Canadian capital is now heavily invested in the world's poorest countries, where it takes advantage of weak states that cannot—or will not—protect their citizens from dispossession and exploitation. Honduras is paradigmatic of this development, and Canada's reaction to the 2009 coup d'état, in particular, is among the most compelling cases of the new Canadian imperialism.

This book will document Canada's role in supporting the coup in Honduras and protecting the dictatorship that has ruled the country ever since. In the process, it will explode several of the cherished myths that Canadians are taught about their country. It will begin by providing an overview of the history of Honduras where, after centuries of foreign domination, working people were mobilizing to take back control over their destiny. But before that process could get off the ground, as the second chapter will demonstrate, it was stamped out by force. The perpetrators of the coup quickly found their closest ally was the government in Ottawa, the subject of chapter three. In exchange for Canada's political support, the new dictatorship reasserted the conditions for foreign companies' exploitation of Honduran land and labour and cracked down brutally on any dissent. The crackdown, which has culminated in Honduras becoming the most dangerous country in the world—with the highest homicide rate by a massive margin—was conducted with Canada's blessing. As chapter four will document, this process has given a major boost to the profits of Canadian companies like Goldcorp, Gildan, and Life Vision Properties.

In a fitting irony, the current president of Honduras has changed the Constitution to allow himself to run for re-election; this was precisely the ambition that former president Manuel Zelaya was falsely accused of to justify his abduction and overthrow in 2009. The experience of Honduras is significant because it demonstrates that Canada has constructed a foreign policy wherein imperialism and injustice are not just potential incidental factors but, rather, are at its heart. Such an understanding grows increasingly urgent as Canada's foreign policy becomes ever more deeply enmeshed and committed to its new role as an emerging imperial power. The final substantive chapter of this book will make explicit the connection between Canada's behaviour in Honduras and its broader foreign policy trajectory. After all, if Honduras was an isolated case, we might be justifiably upset about it but we could not conclude that Canada was an imperialist state. However, as the book will demonstrate, Honduras is not unique; rather, it fits into the pattern that Canada has established in the twenty-first century, which has already included armed military interventions in Haiti, Afghanistan, Libya, Mali, and, most recently, Syria and Iraq. Canada, it would seem, is deeply committed to the imperial path.

At the same time, I do not believe that this political situation is static or unalterable; politics can always be contested by organized social movements, a theme that runs throughout these pages. This book is partly motivated by the need to rebuild the capacities of people and movements to contest the current direction of the Canadian state. Hence, it represents both a critical intervention in the understanding and analysis of Canadian foreign policy at a crucial moment of transformation, and also a call to action for Canadians. Honduras has been thrust into the spotlight in Central America precisely because of the activist networks that built a movement capable of pushing back against the dominant neoliberal world order. The victories they won in the mid-2000s demonstrated the possibilities that can still be unleashed by collective action, and Canadians would do well to learn from the Honduran social movement that is, even now, struggling to build a better world.

In keeping with that theme, this book is informed and inspired by many long hours of conversations with activists in Honduras—teachers, electricians, taxi drivers, parents, children, artists, lawyers, farmers, feminists, socialists, democrats—who have found themselves struggling for justice against a constellation of powerful forces that includes Canadian businesses and the Canadian state. Those conversations instilled in me the gravity and urgency of building a coherent and committed opposition to Canadian imperialism; it is my hope that their voices will speak the loudest in the pages that follow, and will help to inspire the resurgent opposition that is so desperately needed.

1 IMPERIAL LEGACIES
Five Centuries of Foreign Domination in Honduras

There is no place in the western hemisphere where history wasn't irrevocably changed by the voyages of conquest launched by Europe in the late fifteenth century. The contemporary memory of the apocalyptic genocide that changed the fate of the world varies remarkably; north of the Rio Grande, Christopher Columbus is often presented as a hero; south of it, he is usually a villain.[1] Canada's relationship to its own bloody heritage remains marred in denial and misdirection, with former prime minister Stephen Harper declaring that Canada "has no history of colonialism,"[2] in spite of the damning and widely publicized Truth and Reconciliation report in 2015 detailing Canada's participation in the genocide.[3] Indeed, Canada's colonial past speaks quite directly to its imperial present, a point I will return to in the final chapter of this book. Suffice it to say, for now, that the legacy of the conquest still looms heavily over all the Americas.

In Honduras, that colonial legacy is ever-present. The word "Honduras," which translates from Spanish as "the watery depths," was given by none other than Columbus himself,[4] as he and his crew thanked their god in 1502 for delivering their ships from the depths off the north coast of the Central American isthmus.[5] The Honduran currency, the *lempira*, is named after an Indigenous Lenca leader who led a great rebellion against the Spanish *conquistadors* in the sixteenth century. And nearly all of Honduran history has been forged in the fires of colonial occupation and interference: from the catastrophic enslavement of Indigenous people by the Spanish, to the stunting of Honduran infrastructure by rapacious British financiers, to the occupation of the country as a launch pad for war by the US military, to the contemporary plunder of wealth from Honduran land and labour by Canadian mining and manufacturing companies.

There are continuities across the various threads of Honduras' five-century encounter with empire. But there have also been significant shifts, often sparked by popular resistance, which altered the direction of the small country's history. The presence of radical and committed workers' movements on the banana plantations compelled the Honduran elite to band together behind the dictator Tiburcio Carías in the 1930s, while the mobilization of the entire country in a general strike in 1954 forced the state to back down and adopt several reformist policies. The destruction of the organized left in the 1980s made it easy to impose neoliberal austerity measures, but the resurgence of popular resistance in the late 1990s changed the game entirely. It was precisely the growth of a sustained and defiant social movement in the 2000s, which rejected colonialism and its associated impositions, that led to the dramatic events of 2009 that are at the heart of this book. History weighs heavily in Honduras and, to understand the present crisis, we must be conscious of its roots.

CIVILIZATIONS LOST

Long before there was a "Honduras," there were thousands of years of social, political, and cultural history, with records of human civilization dating as far back as the second millennium BCE, including civilizations like the Maya, Lenca, Pipil, Nahuatl, Jicaque, Paya, Chorotega, and Sumu.[6] Mayan civilization, at its height around 500 CE, was among the most complex tributary societies in the world. One of its greatest city-states was Copán, located near Honduras' western border with Guatemala, where some of the great Mayan accomplishments took place, including the development of detailed calendars and numerical systems, the construction of courts and arenas that could host over 50,000 people, and the nurturing of the study of astronomy that allowed Mayan priests to predict solar eclipses and calculate the revolutions of the planet Venus.

These accomplishments are often portrayed as archaeological oddities. Consider the 2012 feature exhibit *Maya: Secrets of their Ancient World* at the Royal Ontario Museum (ROM) in Toronto, which presented Mayan civilization as ancient and mysterious, a relic of an era of mysticism and superstition so backward and irrational that it may hold the key to primeval secrets about the nature of humanity or the meaning of life, long forgotten by the fast-moving modern society constructed by European civilization.[7] In fact, these religious, artistic, and scientific advances were not the product of some vaguely alien mystical force but, rather, of a complex social and political system that was able to sustain a large population and create the conditions under which some people could pursue a variety of activities that were not directly related to survival.[8] The Mayan civilization constructed complicated agricultural systems, which many Eurocentric historians had previously deemed impossible given the supposed backwardness of their society. These systems incorporated intensive irrigation and drained field agriculture, and only went into decline following Spanish invasion and "scorched Earth" tactics.[9] But the ancient and mystical framing, exemplified by the ROM exhibit but ubiquitous in Eurocentric scholarship and popular culture, serves only to undermine the actual complexity of Mayan society, and to turn attention away from the fact that the Mayan civilization was all but destroyed by the catastrophic European conquest.

The creation of what would be called Honduras was part of the seismic transformation of the world precipitated by the establishment of capitalist social relations and the modern state form in Europe. While much inter-oceanic travel had taken place prior to 1492, what distinguished the European arrival was the emphasis it placed on the accumulation of precious metals, which was a major piece of what Marx described as the "so-called primitive accumulation" that was an important component of the establishment of the material basis for the expansion of global capitalism.[10] Spanish *conquistadors'* greed for gold and silver was often matched by a terrifying savagery towards the people they encountered, who would often be forced into immediate slavery for the Spanish or, if they resisted enslavement, slaughtered. Indeed, without slipping into the Leyendra Negra—the exaggeration of Spanish brutality by Northern Europeans claiming their own colonial projects to be more civilized—it is worth noting that many of the *conquistadors* were veterans of the vicious wars with the Moors and did not hesitate to use extreme violence to accomplish their goals.[11]

The Spanish colonizers quickly established themselves in what is now Mexico and Panama, and moved into Central America largely from those flanks.[12] Indigenous people living in what became Honduras were seized and set to work either in gold and silver mines or sent on ships to the Spanish colonies in the Caribbean, especially Cuba, to work on sugar plantations. Some were even sent to be slaves in Spain itself.[13] Meanwhile, the Spanish conquerors were furnished with a *requerimiento*—a statement of "requirement" for Christian conversion—which they were to read to so-called Indians before they attacked, captured, and enslaved them. The *requerimiento* was designed in 1513 and explained that the only way for Indigenous people to avoid this violent fate was to immediately submit to conversion and to the Christian god. As Honduran historian Longino Becerra notes, the *requerimiento* was established after Spanish brutality had already begun, and was set up only out of "the necessity of justifying the manner of their conduct."[14] Bartolomé de las Casas, a Spanish missionary famous for his critique of Spanish brutality in the Americas, considered the *requerimiento* an absurdity wherein people were expected to convert on the spot to a faith they knew nothing of, and whose emissaries appeared as "cruel, pitiless and bloodthirsty tyrants."[15] Furthermore, Las Casas described a variety of occasions in which the *requerimiento* was read to Indigenous villages at night, quietly, from afar, in order to justify a murderous invasion the following morning.[16]

HAUGHTY DEFIANCE

Spanish conquest of Central America was more or less consolidated by the 1520s, and the areas that came to be Honduras were used primarily for the capture and transport of Indigenous slaves.[17] By mid-century, the Indigenous population in Honduras had been catastrophically reduced. As Spanish control tightened, the conquering authorities set to work establishing more permanent dominion over the remaining people whose labour they would need to extract wealth from the earth, the fields, the mines, and the ranches.[18] Three primary strategies were used to obtain Indigenous labour during the period of Spanish rule: the *encomienda,* the *repartimiento,* and, eventually, "free" capitalist wage labour. In the first, Indigenous people were "granted" to one or another Spanish colonizer, and they functioned as servants for the individual *encomendero*. In 1549, the Spanish Crown banned almost all *encomiendas* (exceptions were made for government officials and clergy) in the hopes of creating a free labour market, through which all Spanish colonists would be able to exploit Indigenous labour, but this plan did not account for the possibility that Indigenous people might choose anything—even death—over working for the Spanish.[19]

Hence, the creation of a system of forced labour called the *repartimiento*, under which Indigenous villages would be expected to give a certain quantity of tribute and labour to various Spanish enterprises at fixed wages under the supervision of one or another Spanish colonist. These conscripted labourers would be kept in a constant rotation so that Spanish colonists could count on a regular supply of labour, and employers of *repartimiento* workers were supposed to be responsible for providing food and decent treatment to their workers. However, overwork, malnourishment, and injury were regular parts of the work experience, and even the fixed wages set by the Crown were regularly ignored.[20] This super-exploitative semi-feudal arrangement amounted to slavery by another name, and it was to be a fixture of the colonial relationship throughout the three centuries of Spanish dominion, especially in mining and agriculture. Nevertheless, the *repartimiento* would be gradually replaced by capitalist forms of free labour, whereby Spanish landowners would hire Indigenous workers outside of the *repartimiento* at slightly higher wages and with large advances for housing and food, in an effort to draw Indigenous people into a form of debt-slavery.[21]

Given the shock, dislocation, and disarray that Spanish conquest had beset upon Indigenous people and their own political and economic structures, the prospects for survival outside of the newly imposed Spanish infrastructure were increasingly bleak. As a result, Spanish colonists hoped they would find a relatively steady supply of Indigenous labourers prepared to enter into profoundly unfair waged labour relations—which would perhaps be better described as debt peonage—in which the Indigenous workers would be expected to work in order to pay back the debt that they incurred when they accepted their employers' advances.[22] These "free" labour arrangements first appeared in the late 1500s, but they failed to attract many Indigenous workers. Following the historical pattern of most impositions of capitalist social relations, people chose almost any option over entering into the wage relationship, and even as the *repartimiento* system faltered and Spanish employers offered higher wages to draw people in, they still complained of their inability to find willing Indigenous workers.[23]

The imposition of Spanish rule in Central America was not accepted without resistance. As early as 1515, Indigenous people, enslaved and sent to work in the Caribbean, were considered "unsatisfactory workers" in large part due to their refusal to accept enslavement; one group of slaves seized a ship in Cuba and sailed it back to their home on the Bay Islands.[24] On the mainland, resistance first mounted in the west, where in the 1530s it was co-ordinated by an Indigenous leader named Cocumba; pitched battles were fought in the Ulúa Valley, ending in a brutal massacre at the hands of the Spaniards led by Pedro de Alvarado.[25] The resentment sown by Alvarado blew up again in 1537–39, when a Lenca leader called Lempira—whose name is now given to the Honduran currency—raised an army 30,000 strong, refused the *repartimiento*, and made a dramatic stand at the Peñol de Cerquín.[26] This inspired Indigenous revolts across the province, centred around Comayagua and San Pedro, on such a scale that the Spanish administration had to send for help from neighbouring colonial centres. One account of Lempira's uprising cites him calling upon all Indigenous people to drive the Spaniards out, declaring it "shameful, that so many valiant men should be held in bondage by so few."[27]

When even a siege of Lempira's stronghold at Cerquín could not defeat the uprising, the Spanish turned to trickery in order to kill Lempira and dishearten the rebellion. Lempira was lured into false peace negotiations and then shot by a hidden gunman. English historian Robert S. Chamberlain describes the events, emphasizing Lempira's "haughty defiance" and his followers' fanaticism, leaving the implication that the Indigenous rebels were irrational and backwards, and that they needed to be defeated in order to be brought into "civilization."[28] These colonial assumptions remain present even in the way Canada speaks about Honduras today, as we will see. The Indigenous civilizations in Honduras did not welcome this violent "civilizing" and continued to resist Spanish occupation.[29]

Nevertheless, after the fall of Lempira, few uprisings would achieve significant success against the firmly planted Spanish colonial apparatus. Especially in the west, rebellions were quickly and violently repressed by colonial forces, and it was only in the eastern provinces, where Spanish settlement took place more gradually, that resistance could be sustained. From 1542 to 1546, for instance, there were a number of loosely connected uprisings in Olancho and Gracias a Dios, many of which united both Indigenous and recently arrived African slaves against the Spanish.[30] Nonetheless, with their own societies crumbling under the weight of the genocidal Spanish conquest, by the late 1700s, Indigenous people could find fewer and fewer alternatives to working for the Spanish. Those who survived were increasingly shifted away from the *repartimiento* system, which went into relative decline as dynamics in Spain led to a diminished capacity to govern its own empire.[31]

Prior to the Spanish invasion, Indigenous peoples had relied upon complex social-agricultural systems for their survival,[32] but Spanish colonization forced Indigenous people—either by direct coercion or by the de-population of their communities and subsequent impossibility of survival by traditional means—to offer their labour to the new Spanish occupiers, who dramatically reoriented the economy, over three centuries, away from subsistence production towards the production of exports in order to bring wealth to themselves and the Spanish Crown.[33]

THE BELLS OF FREEDOM?

While the Spanish rulers of Honduras used violence and terror to maintain their dominion over Indigenous peoples, they quarrelled among themselves over the various territories of their American empire, which would be gradually taken over by the increasingly powerful Great Britain. Having never intended Honduras to be a genuine settler colony, the Spanish made little attempt to advance local capitalist development or industry; instead, they used various forms of slavery to extract natural resources—especially precious metals—from the earth to be shipped for sale in European markets. Honduran urban development was to be shaped by the boom and bust cycles of particular non-renewable exports, a dynamic that still resonates today. Rapid development around the village of Gracias was halted when the gold ran out. Tegucigalpa initially expanded as a base for silver mining, but as the silver became difficult to extract, the city fell into stagnation.[34] Spanish attempts to impose production of other exports, from balsam to sarsaparilla to cacao, all proved ineffectual and unsuccessful. These dynamics were similar in most of the Central American countries (with the exception of Costa Rica) and many historians trace the deep social disparities of today back to the mismanagement of the Spanish colonial system.[35] These conditions were particularly acute in Honduras, a fact that would have significant consequences in the twentieth century.

When independence from Spain finally arrived, it was under the auspices of moderate liberal reformers from the *criollo* elite (of Spanish ancestry but born in Central America) who were looking to imitate the American Revolution and separate themselves from the Spanish Crown while leaving the fundamental class structure intact. Indeed, it was the profound "absence of the masses" that was notable in this transition,[36] since they were viewed as a threat to the Honduran elite, especially in light of the recent popular uprisings in Mexico and Haiti.[37] With the Spanish empire crumbling and the newly independent Mexico threatening to annex all of Central America, the landed elite in the Central American provinces organized a tenuous union to declare their own independence from both Spain and Mexico, writing the region's first constitution in 1824. This was a document modelled after those in Mexico and the United States, though, notably, the United Provinces of Central America banned the practice of direct slavery some nineteen years prior to Great Britain and forty-one years before the United States.[38]

While the ruling classes in Central America squabbled among themselves over how power should be divided in their new union, they actively discouraged any popular mobilization, lest it lead to demands for more radical change. As journalist Alison Acker notes, the governor of Honduras "prohibited the ringing of bells to celebrate Central American independence, in case it should generate mass enthusiasm."[39] In fact, it was a Honduran—a privileged *criollo* from Tegucigalpa named Francisco Morazán—who would lead an army to Guatemala City to consolidate the union of Central American states in 1827. Morazán is canonized in official Honduran histories as a hero of liberty and democracy, but his project was similar to that of Símon Bolívar in South America, insofar as he dreamt of a union of liberal capitalist republics, modelled after those in Europe, that would carry on business-as-usual from a position of political equality with the European states from whence, according to this narrative, they came.

Morazán's vision of liberty contained all the contradictions of the states he emulated; when peasants and priests refused to submit to a poorly co-ordinated cholera quarantine in 1837, he marched in with the military.[40] This was one of twenty-one such military ventures in his eleven years of unelected presidency, most of them directed at poor Indigenous people. Many such Hondurans were conscripted to build "more humane" prisons, and could hardly be blamed for questioning this kind of freedom.[41] It is unhelpful, then, to imagine that the Morazán era was idyllic for the majority of the people who were now considered independent Hondurans. Nonetheless, the failure of a United Central America under the Honduran-born Morazán, within fifteen years of its birth, left Honduras in an even more precarious position vis-à-vis the rapacious new colonizers from Britain and especially the United States.[42]

With the Honduran elite weakened by the failure of the union, it had little will or capacity to resist the English-speaking adventurers hoping to cash in on Honduras' weakness. In 1853, American tycoon Ephraim George Squier signed a charter with Honduran president José Trinidad Cabañas to build a trans-isthmus railroad across Honduran territory, using forced Honduran convict labour.[43] The charter gave Squier 1,000 square miles of Honduran land at no cost and guaranteed rights to US citizens to travel in Honduras without a passport and to work in Honduras without paying taxes. Despite the onerous conditions placed on Honduras, North American bankers lost interest in the railroad project,[44] and it sat simply as an illustration of the extent to which Honduran governments were willing to prostrate themselves to the needs of foreign capital.

The railroad debacle—the first of many—set the tone for the century of North American interference that was to follow; direct colonization was a thing of the past but distinct forms of neo-colonialism were taking shape and would profoundly affect all aspects of Honduran life, as they still do today. After the failure of Central American unity, Honduras sank into political chaos as successive governments were pushed and pulled by the whims of British and American foreign policy, which routinely collaborated with various factions of the weak and divided Honduran ruling class in its internecine conflicts. From 1824 to 1900, the country went through no less than ninety-eight changes of government, each lasting, on average, less than one year.[45] Most of these governments were established in military coups, as one *caudillo* after another gained the support of the foreigners and tried his hand at ruling the country.

The cycle of internal weakness and external interference reinforced itself. As William I. Robinson describes, "the weakness of Honduran social forces and the state allowed for the vulgar domination of the country by foreign companies, making Honduras the quintessential 'Banana Republic.'"[46] Undaunted by the first failure to build a trans-isthmus railroad, for instance, the "modernizing" liberal government of Marco Aurelio Soto—enamoured as it was with the spirit of enterprise and the dream of a modern, capitalist Honduras—borrowed nearly six million pounds from British moneylenders from 1867 to 1870 to try again. The project, and its one and only completed bridge, promptly collapsed in 1872 with only fifty miles of track laid. It was a swindle from the start, allowing Soto and his allies to live large while British bankers cashed in for decades to come. Without the means to pay off the debt, successive Honduran governments left it to collect interest, so that by the 1920s Honduras' external debt had grown to over thirty million pounds, leaving the country at the mercy of international capital.[47]

And this was just the beginning. In 1880, President Soto joined with financiers from New York to form the Rosario Mining Company; within twenty years, Rosario would come to dominate the Honduran gold and silver mines, which had originally been dispersed by the state to 276 different companies.[48] Rosario, which controlled 87 percent of Honduran mining, was completely exempt from Honduran taxes and paid next to nothing in wages to its local workers. After a series of calamitous accidents at Rosario mines near San Juancito in 1909, workers went on strike for better pay and protection; police and military were brought in by President Miguel Dávila to attack the strikers, quickly ending the standoff.[49] The company continued to extract wealth from the ground and the people, and made riches for its foreign owners, along with a handful of Honduran oligarchs and a scattering of Arab, French, and German businessmen who gradually formed a small merchant class. But when the market for silver dropped off around the turn of the century, the mines were closed and most of the money was taken out of

Honduras.[50] Over as quickly as it had begun, the mini-boom in mining left, as Alison Acker describes, little more than "unemployment, ravaged hillsides and an empty national treasury."[51]

THE BANANA REPUBLIC

The banana companies came next, led by the infamous United Fruit Company. By the turn of the century, they dominated Honduras and routinely tore up its physical and social geography, raising armies of Hondurans into deadly conflicts with other Hondurans for the right to exploit other Hondurans. Naturally, back in North America, these exploits were described as the romantic hustle-and-bustle of modern industry.[52] But on the plantations, the reality was deplorable conditions, coercive intimidation, and legal manipulation and trickery, all marshalled for the benefit of foreign owners. The work itself was hyper-exploitative and, between overcrowded, unsanitary living conditions and hard days of supervised physical labour, it is easy to see why workers quickly came to view the plantation, as per Ramón Amaya Amador's description, as a *prisión verde* (green prison). Workers typically lasted an average of just twelve years before their bodies succumbed and they ceased to be useful to the banana empires.[53]

As the new export industry grew, Honduran governments tried to learn from the mistakes they had made with earlier foreign concessions and moved to enact laws that would bring some of the banana profits back to the Honduran treasury and improve the prospects for local growers. A tax levied in 1893 sought to impose two cents on every banana stem exported, and laws passed in 1897 would structure foreign land purchases in such a way as to discourage the consolidation of major estates.[54] But the mostly American banana growers did not want their profits diverted. The 1897 laws to prevent consolidation were easily sidestepped by a combination of legal trickery and naked force, which was especially easy when it was small farmers the companies were up against, who relied on US suppliers for irrigation equipment and pesticides. As for the tax on banana stems, it would be repealed after a 1911 US-led coup installed Manuel Bonilla—in the employ of the Cuyamel Fruit Company—as president.[55] This was but one of the many military interventions and occupations that the United States would effect in Honduras during this period; in a now-infamous confession in 1935, US General Smedley D. Butler acknowledged that his work in the US Marine Corps had amounted to being "a racketeer for capitalism" and that he and his troops had "helped make Honduras 'right' for American fruit companies in 1903."[56]

Whatever development took place in Honduras was for the benefit of the fruit companies alone; Daniel Faber notes that "the railroads built by these companies led directly from the coastal ports to the banana plantations and failed to integrate the rest of the country."[57] The railroad situation was perhaps one of the best indications of the dominance of foreign interests in Honduran development; a US newspaper in 1921 mused whimsically about the absurdity and backwardness of the country, pointing to the fact that Tegucigalpa was "the only capital in the North American continent that has never echoed to the more or less musical blast of the railroad locomotive and [was] one of the few railroadless capitals in the western hemisphere."[58] In fact, Tegucigalpa would never be served by a railroad; the north coast rail network wasn't even connected to the capital by anything more than a "cart path" until US military engineers completed a highway in the 1940s.[59] This example was but one of the myriad ways that state infrastructure reflected Honduras' continued colonial subjugation.

However willing the Honduran elite may have been to mortgage their country to foreign capital, the majority of Hondurans were not. Beginning in 1916, just as the struggle between the various banana companies was heating up, the workers on the plantations began to resist the dreadful conditions imposed on them. Over 600 workers struck at a Cuyamel plantation that year, and while the company could rely on the support of a compliant Honduran state to break the strike eventually, it discovered with some surprise that local policing agencies were not wholly sympathetic; the commander of the prison at Omoa released the workers who were brought there, insisting that their demands were legitimate.[60] A major strike at Standard Fruit saw over 1,000 workers walk off the job in 1920 and another in 1925 at Cuyamel demonstrated that workers were not going to suffer in silence. In both cases, armed forces were brought to bear against the strikers, and the strikes were blamed on "foreigners" infected with "anti-Americanism," with the intent of keeping the urban working class skeptical of those on the plantations.[61]

But despite efforts by the banana empires to divide urban and rural workers, organizing continued and, by the late 1920s, there were two major workers' federations. The Federación de Sindicatos de Honduras (Honduran Federation of Unions, FSH) was the more radical of the two and organized not only against workplace injustice but also against capitalism at large. FSH unions were concentrated in the north, among the banana workers, but as their strikes grew in size and frequency, and in the scale of the repression they evoked, workers in other industries in the north began to join and support them. In 1932, strikes broke out on the plantations and at the ports where the bananas were to be shipped out; railroad workers joined in solidarity and the strikebreakers hired as scabs quickly joined the strike.[62]

When full-scale armed assault seemed unlikely to break the will of the strikers, US officials and banana company representatives used a combination of bribery and coercion to acquire names of union or strike leaders, who would then be rounded up individually and deported or imprisoned. And by the mid-1930s, they had found their man in Honduras. Tiburcio Carías, Honduran *caudillo* who ruled from 1932 to 1948, was quick to demonstrate his commitment to the success of the banana empires, shutting down all unions, closing all newspapers, and banning public demonstrations.[63] Those who disobeyed these laws were punished severely, as when over 100 peaceful protestors were killed by the military in San Pedro Sula in 1944.[64] His entire presidency was marked by strict and terroristic repression. He established complete National Party dictatorship over the country, with local party officials set up as regional *comandantes de armas* who governed by force, celebrating the most vicious among them. Speaking of Carlos Sanabria, who was accused of wiping out entire villages in the department of Colón, Carías said, "… would that I had seventeen Sanabrias, one for every department of Honduras."[65] His Ley Fernanda empowered the armed forces to arrest untold hundreds on suspicion of aiding communism, and he even moved to ban baseball, lest people should turn their bats against his regime.[66]

Carías cultivated the friendship and mutual support of neighbouring dictators—Generals Ubico and Martínez in Guatemala and El Salvador respectively—and considered the support of the United States his most important asset. As such, he ensured that his policies largely satisfied US interests as, for instance, when he established an internal passport and spy network with the support of United Fruit, whose management was keen to confront workers' organizing drives.[67] In particular, Carías invited the United States to help him build, train, and equip an air force; by the 1930s and 1940s, no other Central American dictator relied so heavily on air power and none could challenge its supremacy. Between 1933 and 1947, US colonels ran the aviation school, and four of the six instructors at the school were American. Their position guaranteed that they virtually commanded that wing of the military. One US captain reported in 1940 that he was "in absolute command of the Air Force" and reported directly to President Carías. The eight planes which made up the fleet—including heavy bombers and gunners—were all sold to Carías by the United States, and were used in many of his brutal campaigns, "sowing panic and death" in the words of his War Ministry.[68]

1954 AND THE FOUNTAIN OF HONDURAN HISTORY

Nevertheless, worker militancy, especially in the context of continued labour shortages, was not defeated. While many labour organizations were disbanded, unofficial ties remained, especially those established within or around the communist parties, accustomed as they were to operating clandestinely.[69] After Carías stepped down in 1948, and the political system reopened somewhat, organizing was reinvigorated and the ensuing period of mobilization would lead to the general strike of 1954, which Dana Frank has described as "the fountain from which all of modern Honduran history flows."[70]

The strike began on the banana plantations, with workers at United Fruit demanding double-time pay for work during the Sunday of Holy Week. Port and hospital workers were the first to actually strike, after a worker was fired for dropping—as the story goes—a single stem of bananas at Puerto Cortés. Soon, all of the stevedores at the docks at Tela were on strike, and the banana plantations near El Progreso and La Lima were next; by May 5, 1954, all of the workers of the two primary banana empires—United Fruit and Standard Fruit—were on strike. A week later, they were joined by workers at Rosario Mining, the Honduras Brewery, and British American Tobacco Company, such that the total number of strikers was somewhere near 50,000.[71] As Alison Acker describes, "peasant families fed the strikers, telegraph workers cut the line to Tegucigalpa, students, teachers and small tradesmen contributed to the strike fund. The campaign became an unprecedented show of worker solidarity."[72]

The outcome of the strike—both its victories and defeats—was to have enormous consequences for Honduras. The 50,000-strong strike was able to demand significant, though certainly not adequate, pay increases and secured the creation of an official union for United Fruit workers, the curiously named Sindicato de Trabajadores de La Tela Railroad Company (Union of Tela Railroad Company Workers, SITRATERCO),[73] as well as gaining a number of specific terms of employment. The strike and its aftermath also paved the way for the creation of the first Honduran labour code in 1959, with all the contradictory advantages and disadvantages such legislation typically brings.[74] But those contradictions were even more acute in the Honduran case because of the conditions under which the strike was ended. As the US began to rapidly increase its presence in Honduras to counter the reforming Arbenz government in Guatemala, it encouraged hysteria among the Honduran elite and even labour activists themselves about the dangers of a communist takeover. This hysteria would be stoked by US trade unionists ostensibly brought in to demonstrate solidarity with the strike and assist with logistics.[75]

The year 1954 was a watershed for Honduras and for Central America at large, with the CIA-orchestrated overthrow of Guatemalan president Jacobo Arbenz playing a crucial role. As the US worked to up the pressure on Arbenz, it made no secret of using Honduras as its launching pad, and when the general strike broke out in April 1954, it was immediately framed as part of an Arbenz-led communist conspiracy; after all, Arbenz and the strikers had a common enemy in the United Fruit Company. When, in May, a Swedish ship arrived in Honduras with a shipment of arms destined for Arbenz's government, US president Eisenhower and Secretary of State Foster Dulles discussed the prospect of dropping 4,000 marines into Honduras to intervene.[76] Instead, on May 20, an agreement was signed with Honduran president Juan Gálvez for major military assistance from Washington—organization, equipment, and training for a new, professional infantry unit—for which materials began arriving just five days later in a very public demonstration of American power in the region.[77] The US ambassador, Whiting Willauer, demanded that the new infantry unit be prepared for action by October to oversee the Honduran elections, which featured former dictator Tiburcio Carías and liberal candidate Ramon Villeda Morales (whom Willauer incorrectly believed to be loyal to Arbenz) in order to keep the Honduran government "in line."[78]

A snapshot of 1954, then, demonstrates the way that the Honduran ruling elite relied more heavily than any in the region on the support of imperial power, even while its subordinate classes were less organized and defiant than elsewhere. Unlike in Guatemala, El Salvador, or Nicaragua, Honduras did not have a functional, autonomous, and unified national military force until it was established by the United States in the 1950s.[79] Nor did it have the massive social dislocations associated with intensive export-oriented capitalist development as experienced elsewhere, and, as a result, social movements of peasants and working classes rarely came together in unified action before the general strike of 1954.[80] The response to collective action was typically a combination of accommodation and repression—in contrast to the swift and brutal repression experienced in other parts of Central America—and meant that much of the hyper-violence of the regional civil wars of the 1960s, '70s, and '80s was to be avoided in Honduras. Nevertheless, Honduran politics after the 1954 strike came to be dominated by a constellation of social forces—the foreign-owned banana companies, the office-seeking *políticos*, an emerging Honduran oligarchy, the church, and, to a much lesser extent, the peasantry and working classes—all under the watchful eye of the newly professionalized and increasingly autonomous Honduran military and its closest allies in the US state department.

AGRARIAN STRUGGLES EMERGE

No chief of the Honduran armed forces retired between 1954 and 1981 without first serving a stretch as Honduran president, as the military became the institution responsible for managing class conflict in Honduras. The primary conflict this new military apparatus would have to navigate was the sudden scarcity and struggle over land, and the ensuing process of agrarian reform, which some have argued was crucial in forestalling the kind of guerrilla struggles that emerged elsewhere in the region.[81] Beginning in the 1950s and accelerating in the 1960s, the fruit companies began to mechanize, shedding workers and expanding the size of their plantations. They—alongside an emerging Honduran oligarchy—also began to diversify their operations into more land-intensive crops, like cotton and sugar, or into cattle ranching.[82] Combined, this meant that many plantation workers, who had formerly been peasants, went back to their communities to find their traditional holdings under attack. As ranchers and increasingly large landowners began a new round of enclosures—in some cases literally erecting barbed-wire fencing around formerly peasant-held land—the number of evicted peasants and laid-off plantation workers swelled and, over several decades, was amplified by an influx of up to 300,000 peasant refugees fleeing the same policies, imposed with even more aggression, in neighbouring El Salvador.[83]

For the first time, land scarcity had become a serious problem in Honduras. Peasant organization followed quickly, given the experiences of many former plantation workers with organizing in the unions. The Federación Nacional de Campesinos de Honduras (National Federation of Honduran Peasants, FENACH) was the largest and most militant organization and had close ties with the various communist movements that had persisted in the face of repression throughout the early twentieth century. A rival group, the Asociación Nacional de Campesinos Hondureños (Association of Honduran Peasants, ANACH), was created under the auspices of the Organización Regional Interamericana de Trabajadores (Inter-American Regional Organization, ORIT), set up by the US-based American Federation of Labour (AFL) to manage and contain labour militancy in Central America. ANACH, with the support of its North American allies, used all manner of underhanded tactics to undermine FENACH and seize control of the peasant movement.[84] With both large landowners and peasant organizations demanding that the government protect their access to contested land, the Honduran military often became the arbiter between the various classes, allowing certain presidents to enact limited agrarian reform while cutting them off—generally by effecting a military coup—if they took the process far enough to significantly alienate the foreign and local oligarchy.[85]

In general, a limited degree of land reform had the support of the military and its allies in the United States as a way of avoiding the perceived communist-inspired social struggles in neighbouring countries. But there was no way to satisfy the demands of both the banana companies and landed oligarchy on the one hand, and the increasing numbers of landless peasants on the other. The military government of Oswaldo López Arellano, for instance, was installed in a coup in 1972 and proceeded with a program that James Dunkerley called "progressive Bonapartism," which included land redistribution, the establishment of a minimum wage, and strengthened labour laws.[86] Nevertheless, the role of the military as arbiter should not lead to the assumption that it acted with restraint; it generally still sided with the landowners and used violence to keep the peasant movements at bay.

In 1963, the military cracked down on FENACH, destroying offices and imprisoning leaders—many of whom were tortured—at El Progreso. The organization would be wiped out for good in 1965 when troops were sent to El Jute to kill FENACH leader Lorenzo Zelaya and many other key members of the group.[87] In 1972, eight peasants were massacred at Talanquera during an attempted land occupation, who had asked for the presence of a Catholic priest; Father Luis Henas, shaken with terror after discovering the bodies and hearing first-hand accounts of the attack, offered a full testimony of his experience, but, like many of his brethren, was too intimidated to offer continued direct support to the peasant movements.[88] The clergy themselves, originally strong supporters of the peasant land occupations, began to be targeted in the mid-1970s.

In a particularly gruesome attack, two priests were murdered in Olancho in 1975: Father Iván Betancur and Father Jerome Cypher were kidnapped and taken to the estate of José Manuel Zelaya (the father of José Manuel Zelaya Rosales, elected president in 2005 and overthrown in the 2009 coup):

> Both priests were stripped and beaten. Cypher was castrated and shot. Betancur had his eyes gouged out, his fingernails, tongue and teeth pulled out, his hands, feet and testicles slashed off. The bodies of the two men were thrown down a well with those of the five peasants [killed in a related attack] and the two women [kidnapped with Betancur] were thrown in alive. The soldiers sealed the well off with a blast of dynamite. The landowners and military went on to pillage every church, convent and parish house in the Department of Olancho, arresting or expelling 32 priests and nuns.[89]

The attack had been initiated by the largest landowners' association—which had put a price on the two priests' heads—and carried out with military support, leaving the two priests and seven peasants who had been grabbed at a Unión Nacional de Campesinos (National Union of Campesinos, UNC) training centre dead; nine others were found buried in the walls or burned to death in bread ovens at a ranch near Juticalpa.[90] Though some of the officers involved in this attack were charged and sentenced to prison terms, many church groups were intimidated away from supporting peasant movements and the attacks continued with frightening regularity. Just two years later, when the Las Isletas peasant banana co-operative ran afoul of Standard Fruit, the military, led by soon-to-be-infamous, then-colonel Gustavo Alvarez, intervened to dismantle the co-operative, jailing and torturing hundreds of peasants who had been members.[91]

This period of military-directed corporatism, then, was far from idyllic, and framing it that way, as some historians do, is deeply misleading. It is true that Honduras was able to avert the collapses into genocide and horror that befell its neighbours, but it did not resolve Honduras' land crisis nor did it eliminate the growing tensions between insurgent subordinate classes and recalcitrant foreign and local oligarchs. It did serve to ease those tensions and to allow certain outlets for them, but by the end of the 1970s, military rule was discredited and all social classes were dissatisfied. This pressure was finally starting to boil over into significant social unrest, as some 68 percent of Hondurans were unable to meet their basic daily needs.[92] And yet, despite widespread dissatisfaction with military rule, Honduras was about to become central to US aims in the region, as Washington sought to defeat the revolution in Nicaragua and the guerrilla struggles in Guatemala and El Salvador. As such, between 1978 and 1980, the US spent some $10 million beefing up the Honduran armed forces.[93] The invasion of Guatemala in 1954 from Honduras would be a model for Honduras' role in America's wars in Central

America in the 1980s, during which the country would come to be disparagingly dubbed the "USS Honduras."

THE USS HONDURAS

In 1980, the Honduran military peacefully relinquished political power, a move that was designed—by the military and its allies in the US—to forestall more dramatic civil unrest. Certainly, the peaceful transfer of nominal power was remarkable in contrast to the rest of Central America; fearing a civil war that could undermine the strength of the armed forces, the military chose to hand over power peacefully rather than risk its own destruction in the effort to hold on. As Honduras became the base of American operations against revolutionary movements in Central America, it became the focal point of military spending and training. As a result, just as political power was supposedly being transferred to civilian authorities, the military was growing in size and strength and so, not surprisingly, the head of the armed forces, Col. Gustavo Alvarez Martínez, became the *de facto* head of Honduras, exercising more real power than the president or Congress.[94]

Between 1980 and 1992, the US spent some $1.6 billion in military and economic aid to Honduras, intended to establish the apparatus of repression, buttress the institutions of political power, and infiltrate and co-opt the civil society organizations that were best positioned to harness social unrest.[95] This project was undertaken with the consent and co-operation of much of the Honduran ruling class, and the massive influx of USAID funding—and the interference in civil society organizations that came with it—derailed the nascent revolutionary organizations that were emerging from the workers' and peasants' organizations in the 1970s.[96] It is of much significance to contemporary problems that this period first established what has been called a "national security state" in Honduras. The presence of the US military itself, along with the counterrevolutionary Nicaraguan Contra forces, were a major part of that; hundreds of thousands of US soldiers were involved in military exercises in Honduras, and some 20,000 Contra fighters were trained and based in Honduran territory. The US established a number of its own military bases, airstrips, training centres, and other facilities, and it used massive exercises as both demonstrations of its power and as cover for arms transfers to the Contra fighters.[97]

Meanwhile, US ambassador John Negroponte worked closely with Gen. Alvarez, and from 1982 to 1984 the two men were, for all intents and purposes, the highest authorities in Honduras.[98] Upon his election in 1982, President Suazo Córdova was given a twelve-point list of "suggestions" by Ambassador Negroponte, which he was to follow during his term if he wanted to benefit from the US occupation.[99] In 2012 I spoke with Juan Almendares, a medical doctor and former director of the Universidad Nacional Autónoma de Honduras (National Autonomous University of Honduras, UNAH) and a prominent and critical member of Honduran civil society in the early 1980s. He described Negroponte's power in Honduras by telling this anecdote:

> I had a meeting with Negroponte because he said he wanted to meet some of the personalities in the country. He invited me to dinner with him at the embassy. When I arrived, some other political advisor attended to me; Negroponte was at the table with me, but he was seated at a higher level, we were down below. He didn't say anything, Negroponte, for twenty minutes—he just looked at me. And I didn't say anything either. And after twenty minutes, he said, "Are you going to be re-elected at the university?" And I said, "When are you going to pull out American military bases in Honduras, because we don't want you here." And he replied, "When you are re-elected." And I understood what he meant.[100]

Almendares was not re-elected, and the US occupation of Honduran territory was a major factor in the militarization of the country, as the Honduran military co-operated with the occupation and sought to strengthen its own position through it. Between 1976 and 1984, the Honduran military doubled in size and established a framework of internal control that began to look more like those that were established under the dictatorships elsewhere in the region. Civilian branches of governance, like immigration, customs, and telecommunications, were increasingly militarized, new installations and facilities were built across the country, and counterinsurgency units were established.[101]

The most notorious of these counterinsurgency units would be Battalion 3-16, a clandestine organization that would function as an unofficial death squad for the state—the first of its kind in Honduras.[102] Battalion 3-16 kidnapped, tortured, and killed hundreds of Honduran civilians in the early 1980s, with particular emphasis on the leaders of the incipient guerrilla movements, which were largely wiped out.[103] This new repressive apparatus, facilitated by the US occupation, targeted the burgeoning social movements that had grown in the 1960s and 1970s, and sought to ensure that these movements would not develop into significant revolutionary struggles. Though limited in size and scope and nowhere near the level of Guatemala,

El Salvador, or Nicaragua, opposition groups had begun to form some small guerrilla factions, and although some of the organizations were muted by the reintroduction of civilian rule, others grew bolder in opposition to US occupation.[104] Demonstrations grew larger, their sentiment well expressed by a peasant leader who said: "There is plenty of money to build military airports, construct ports and buy arms. Here you have the spectacle of military manoeuvres that cost millions of dollars in the very zones where peasants are dying of hunger."[105]

Although Honduras had suffered foreign domination in multiple forms for centuries, the US occupation in the 1980s was unique both in its totality and its publicity. Honduran authorities—on behalf of their American overlords—denied the presence of the Contras in spite of widespread knowledge of their whereabouts in the international press,[106] prompting editorial mockery of Honduras as a "puppet" of the US and accusations by other regional leaders that Honduras had completely surrendered its autonomy and sovereignty to "Yankee imperialism."[107] All the while, the Reagan administration demanded compliance from Honduran leaders—using the USAID funding upon which many of its institutions had become dependent as leverage—whenever it needed support for one or another aspect of its regional war.

By the late 1980s, public discontent with the US occupation was widespread, even among the ruling classes, who recognized that the growing popular rebellions were significantly disrupting business-as-usual. As the US war itself was winding down, it was clear that change was coming. But the Honduras that emerged after the US occupation was severely transformed: what social peace had existed was now deeply ruptured, and the trauma of extreme violence had left a permanent impression. And it was at precisely this moment in the history of world capitalism that the crisis of over-accumulation, stagnation, and declining profitability in the advanced industrial centres was compelling the painful shift to neoliberal globalization.[108] In Honduras, the military occupation facilitated American oversight of this transition so that, by the early 1990s, the capitalist classes had undergone a major transformation and Honduras no longer looked like the "banana republic" of old.

THE IMPOSITION OF NEOLIBERALISM

Much of the architecture of neoliberalism that is today the subject of social struggle in Honduras had its foundation laid during US occupation. For instance, in 1984, a temporary import law was passed so that foreign capitalists could bring materials and equipment into Honduras exempt from duties, provided that the products were to be exported, and could avoid paying tax on their profits for up to ten years.[109] Full-scale *maquiladora* laws were established in 1987, and these industrial processing zones were legally designed as public service industries, making it easier to clamp down on attempts by workers to organize.[110] For the Honduran oligarchy, linking up with circuits of capital that originated in the Global North was to be the strategy going forward and those factions that succeeded in doing so would become the most powerful in the country. Nonetheless, the ongoing violent conflict in the 1980s was such that neoliberalism in Honduras was stillborn; the free port established at Puerto Castillo was empty, and lack of taxation did not stop some $100 million per year from fleeing the country, for a total of nearly $1.5 billion in capital flight by the end of the 1980s.[111] It wasn't until the fall of the Sandinistas in Nicaragua in 1990, with the resultant departure of the US military and the gradual regional demobilization and peace process, that the neoliberal reforms had any major effects.

Counterrevolution had won in Central America—just as global capitalism had been imposed upon the former communist blocs—and the new capitalist classes needed an efficient and compliant local elite who could rule without the cumbersome disruptions of ongoing conflict and military domination and who could, instead, guarantee a state of security for profitable investments.[112] A small but determined faction of Honduran capital was ready to lead the country through that transformation, in the hopes that it could plug into neoliberal globalization and gain access to its rewards. By the mid-1990s, the military's role in governance had been significantly reduced. Emblematic of this shift, after the military was seen to have bungled its response to Hurricane Mitch in 1998, the civilian government rebuked the military and dismissed its highest officers.[113] As the neoliberal project took hold, it was no simple matter to back out, as discipline could be enforced by the agencies of international capital without any need for significant military interruption.

As a result, successive Honduran governments capitulated to the neoliberal project with a greater or lesser degree of structural coercion. In March 1990, the government of Rafaél Callejas (1990–1993) launched the *paquetazo*, a "grand package" of economic reform that put several billion dollars of IMF and USAID money into maintaining stability through the first major structural adjustment policies (SAPs). These included painful austerity measures ranging from crackdowns on labour to the elimination of price controls, with simultaneous tax hikes on consumption, as well as moves towards privatization of state enterprises, reductions or eliminations of tariffs on exports, and a

50 percent devaluation of the *lempira*.[114] Further austerity measures included 100 percent increases in water, electricity, fuel, and telephone rates and significant layoffs of public employees.[115]

A second set of SAPs was undertaken by the Carlos Roberto Reina administration (1994–1997), called El Gran Proyecto de Transformación Nacional or "The Great National Transformation Project," which sought to insert Honduras more intensely into globalization by promoting non-traditional exports and marketing the country as a tourist destination. This entailed establishing more and larger free trade zones and spending public funds on energy and transportation megaprojects that would facilitate the expansion of business.[116] This represented massive public infrastructure development that was openly intended to serve only private capital's interests; as Roger Marin, a representative of the Reina government, described, "the primary objectives are designed to satisfy the needs of the international community and not the needs of the domestic market."[117] The Carlos Flores Facussé administration (1998-2001), which was made up of many of the architects of the earlier SAPs, established a third round of such adjustments in the early 2000s.

The effects of neoliberal adjustments like these are well-documented in much of the critical political economy tradition, and Honduras followed many of the predictable patterns. Devaluation of the currency meant that anyone whose savings were held in local currency saw rapid and dramatic drops in the value of those savings, plunging people deeper into poverty and making them increasingly desperate for work of any kind, even when it paid less than living wages. The shifting of tax regimes away from taxing imports and exports and towards taxing consumption meant that while big firms got a break, the tax burden was shifted to those who were reliant on the local market for their survival; that is, ordinary people who needed to buy food, pay for services, use public transportation, and so on. Austerity measures and privatization meant that services formerly provided by the state at low or no cost, ranging from health and education to provisioning of water and telecommunications, were subject to funding cuts (reducing both the number of people who worked in these industries and the quality and quantity of the services provided) or were sold to private firms who would run these services for profit, such that people would have access to less services for higher cost. The free trade zones, of course, were havens for capital to exploit labour at higher-than-usual rates, taking advantage of existing inequality to foster even greater inequality. The net result of such policies was a deeper polarization of wealth between those at the top, who benefited from enhanced structural conditions for exploitation and capital accumulation, and those at the bottom, whose bodies and resources were squeezed ever harder and forced to survive on less and less. Extreme wealth and extreme poverty were fostered together. This pattern was as evident in Honduras in the 1990s as anywhere.

The Honduran economy was to see rapid and profound changes as a result of the SAPs and the introduction of neoliberalism. Among other things was the immediate maturation of the mostly foreign-owned *maquiladora* industries, especially in electronics and apparel, which grew from 26 factories in 1990 to nearly 200 in 1996. In that same time, the number of workers in this highly exploitative sector grew from 9,000 to over 75,000, with some $112 million in clothing exports alone, making the *maquiladora* industry the third largest generator of foreign exchange in the country.[118] Tourism also grew rapidly, especially along Honduras' North Coast and the Bay Islands, which fostered new and similarly exploitative job markets in service provision, as did large-scale agriculture, often in new fruits and vegetables grown for export. These emerging sites of exploitation and accumulation were increasingly serviced by private sector organizations that worked with the state to promote the new industries and exports, usually financed by USAID and IMF money.[119] Privatization pressures led to the sale of Honduran airports and energy industries, and an attempt to sell the Empresa Hondureña de Telecomunicaciones (Honduran Telecommunications Company, HONDUTEL).[120]

Of crucial importance in all of this was the escalation of the process of proletarianization of Honduras' peasant classes. Given the importance attributed to peasants' access to land in the period prior to the conflicts of the 1980s, and the role that access played in forestalling the worst of the violence of the 1980s, it should be emphasized that the neoliberal turn in Honduras actively and aggressively undermined the remaining spaces of non-capitalist production in the country. Following the uprooting of peasant communities, which reached high points prior to the so-called "Futbol War" in the late 1960s and the Contra conflicts of the 1980s, a variety of structural forces were set into motion under neoliberalism to tear remaining peasants from the land and force them onto the capitalist labour market, in the hopes that they would fill up the *maquiladoras* and the service sectors, or enter into wage labour on large-scale agricultural or mining operations. The shift from political to economic strategies of proletarianization relied on the initial uprooting of peasants by the military conflict, but was increasingly characterized by structural reform that included the deeper commodification of land, and the privatization of credit mechanisms, which effectively ratcheted up interest rates and left *campesino* communities at the mercy of a market that had been forcibly opened up to transnational capital.

Using economic levers recommended or imposed by the IMF and USAID, the Honduran state uprooted peasants from the land to an extent hitherto unseen in the country. As such, the process of land reform that had proceeded with more or less energy since the 1950s ground to a halt in the 1980s and was formally terminated in 1992, when the Callejas government passed the Ley de Modernización Agrícola (Agricultural Modernization Law). Drafted in consultation with USAID and the World Bank, the "modernization" law reversed land reform and facilitated the transfer of land into private commercial hands. The state body responsible for land reform, the Instituto Nacional Agraria (National Agrarian Institute, INA), was made largely redundant and lost its autonomy, effectively ending state intervention and expropriation of land, while the new package of laws strengthened private property rights and converted all titled land into marketable property. Co-operative lands were converted into individual parcels, which gave powerful oligarchs greater opportunities to buy up formerly co-operative lands, as the state withdrew most of its support for *campesinos*. This was especially evident in the privatization of the Banco Nacional de Desarrollo Agrícola (National Agricultural Development Bank, BANADESA), the sell-off of—and subsequent rate increases for—state infrastructure like grain storage facilities, and the concurrent abandonment of low-interest loans for peasant farmers, all of which served to leave individual families and co-operatives so desperate for cash that they sold their land for infinitely less than its market value. The Lourdes Sugar Cooperative, for instance, sold for 3 million *lempiras* in July 1991, though its book value was estimated at 30 million.[121] The Ley de Modernización Agrícola represented a thorough overhaul of the land system in Honduras and ensured that there would be no further tolerance of non-capitalist *campesino* land co-operatives.

The result, not surprisingly, has been a massive migration from rural to urban areas, a shift from self-sufficient, non-capitalist agricultural production to dependence on waged labour and intensified competition for existing wage work leading to decreases in those wages. It was an all-out assault on Honduras' poor and the effects were dramatic. Between 1990 and 1992, per capita income plummeted by more than half, dropping from $534 to $204 in that time.[122] All the while, prices continued to rise, and by 2003, over 75 percent of Hondurans lived in poverty and could not meet their basic daily needs.[123] Environmental destruction that had increased under the US occupation was exacerbated by the neoliberal adjustments of the 1990s, and deforestation and soil erosion continued, making the effects of Hurricane Mitch in 1998 particularly devastating: some 11,000 Hondurans were killed and as many as two million people—almost one-third of the population—were left without homes.[124] Not surprisingly, many of these people were the suburban poor, former peasants who had been forced by neoliberal policies to move to the cities to find work. The storm devastated the hillsides surrounding Tegucigalpa, where so many of the new migrants had set up flimsy shantytown dwellings on recently deforested areas; the vulnerable soil was easily washed away, wiping out homes and ruining crops.[125] Agriculture was devastated and, all told, the storm did upwards of $4 billion in damage.

MARAS AND VIGILANTES

Hurricane Mitch can be understood as a kind of litmus test for the neoliberal transition; its utterly devastating effects and the social and economic mess that it left in its wake was a clear indication that the neoliberal project had created a nightmare for poor Hondurans who now made up an overwhelming majority of the country. The already endemic poverty of the 1990s was deepened by the storm's destruction, which fell hardest on those who could least afford it, and the perception of the hurricane as having "punished" people who were already so poor sent impoverished communities into a tailspin of violent crime.[126]

By the year 2000, murder rates in Tegucigalpa and San Pedro Sula had risen to make Honduras one of the most violent countries in the western hemisphere.[127] The increase in violence was often linked to street gangs, or *maras*, themselves usually connected to narco-trafficking; by the turn of the millennium, there were an estimated 500 *maras* in the country with over 100,000 members, mostly drawn from Honduras' urban poor.[128] Gang violence became a central theme of the 2001 elections and the winner, Ricardo Maduro, won on a platform that promised to fight a "war on crime," which would only exacerbate the already bad situation.

In the period between Hurricane Mitch and the election of Maduro, Honduras experienced a spate of extrajudicial killings of children, almost all of them boys who appeared to have connections to the *maras*. The killings were carried out by vigilante groups, usually made up of off-duty police or ex-paramilitaries, who patrolled poor neighbourhoods, shooting youths who had tattoos or wore clothing that fit into the stereotypical image of gang members, which, not surprisingly, was closely linked to the image of the urban poor.[129]

Between 1998 and 2002, somewhere between 1,500 and 4,500 youths were killed without any legal process, neither an investigation connecting them to criminal activity in the first place nor a juridical hearing sentencing them to any kind of punishment.[130] Few attempts were made to even investigate the killings, which took place with the tacit approval of the state and the mainstream media, which was by this point largely owned and controlled by the Honduran oligarchy. Ministers in the Flores government criticized the "irresponsible parenting" of street children and repeated sensationalized stories of youths who raped their mothers—fabrications dreamt up by corporate tabloid journalists who contributed to the victim-blaming process—in order to focus attention on the supposed criminality of the youths, rather than the extraordinary extension of impunity to vigilantes who were committing murder.[131]

Despite a special UN report that highlighted both the social and economic causes of the growth of *maras*, and the fact that vigilante assassinations of street youth only deepened the violent crisis in Honduras, President Maduro launched his "War on Crime" with the emphasis entirely on a militarized crackdown on criminals rather than any effort to reverse the neoliberal project that was producing such dramatic inequality and poverty.[132] Initially, while violence had been largely kept within poor communities, there was rarely cause for notice from the state, beyond campaign rhetoric. But as crime increasingly targeted prominent businessmen and officials, *maquiladora* owners began relocating out of Honduras and crime became a primary state concern; once again, the needs of foreign capital figured prominently in the actions of the Honduran state.[133] The Maduro administration and the corporate media encouraged Hondurans to both fear and police one another; criminality was constructed as a "traditional" characteristic of the poor and emphasis placed on this "innate" criminal nature of poor people. Poverty and violence became ideologically connected, such that the causal chain—i.e., that the violence of poverty encourages other forms of violence—could be reversed to suggest that poverty was a *result* of a criminal nature.[134] The victims of neoliberal structural violence were to be blamed for their own poverty.

Legislation introduced in Maduro's Ley Antimara (Anti-Gang Law) strengthened the powers of the military and police to deal with suspected gang members, establishing laws that could sentence gang members to up to twenty years of incarceration and empowering the armed forces to patrol the slums in much the same way that the vigilantes had been doing for years.[135] It put some 10,000 new police and military officers in the streets; made the armed forces "untouchable," describing an attack against an officer as an attack "against Honduras"; and extended the powers of the police to arrest, question, and detain people on suspicion alone.[136] When two deadly fires broke out at Honduran prisons in 2003 and 2004, over 170 "suspected gang members" were killed, though dozens had only been imprisoned for "illicit association" and dozens more had been charged with no crime whatsoever.[137] These fires were part of what some observers have described as an "invisible genocide" against Honduras' poor; assassinations were carried out at an average rate of sixty killings per month in 2003.[138]

As for the gangs themselves, their numbers were only increased by the extrajudicial killings and Maduro's offensive, which made Honduras a more dangerous place for young males, pushing many more youths into groups like the Mara Salvatrucha and the Mara 18, which seemed to offer some protection from the myriad forms of violence that beset Hondurans on a daily basis. As Adrienne Pine argued in 2007, "while it is important not to romanticize gang solidarity, over the past two decades, gangs provided one of the few spheres in which poor young Hondurans had an opportunity to construct a defiant, positive, class-based self-image," significant in a society where poverty was being cast as criminal and reflective of innate inferiority.[139] Given these conditions, it is not surprising that participation in gangs was widespread, despite the violence that it, too, entailed. Bolstered in numbers, the *maras* fought back against Maduro's so-called *mano dura* (iron fist) policies, as in 2004 when a bus was bombed in San Pedro Sula in retaliation for the possible reimposition of the death penalty.[140] Meanwhile, the street gangs were gradually incorporated into the broader narco-trafficking circuits, themselves closely affiliated with corrupt state institutions. In the early 2000s, around 30 percent of the Honduran police participated in and profited from the drug trade, and even the general of the armed forces, Romeo Vásquez, was himself implicated with the cartels.[141]

Real violence and perceived violence reinforced one another in a terrible feedback loop. By 2006, the homicide rate in Honduras had reached 46.2 per 100,000. The deepening of poverty created by the introduction of neoliberalism and the devastation of Hurricane Mitch had led to an expansion of physical violence—both in terms of the growth of *maras* and vigilante death squad activity—that had its roots in the violence carried out in the 1980s. This dynamic was intricately connected to Honduras' full incorporation into neoliberal capitalist globalization, oriented as it was to benefit the few—mostly in the Global North—at the expense of the many. This polarization of wealth also expanded the scope of structural, social, and economic violence, which was inflicted on Honduras' poor in the slums, the factories, and the fields.

Nevertheless, Maduro sought to intensify the neoliberal apparatus upon which this new Honduras was constructed. In consultation with the IMF, he proceeded with the dismantling of social funding and state-run enterprises, pushing a number of new privatization schemes and reducing the workforce in the state bureaucracy.[142] With conditions getting worse in Honduras, many workers sought relief by plugging into the vast migratory networks that saw workers from Central America moving north—with or without papers—to work in the United States and Canada.[143] The worsening situation in Honduras produced a growing supply of cheap migrant labour in North America and remittances sent back by those workers became an increasingly crucial source of income for many Honduran families. Remittances grew from $400 million in 2000 to $1.8 billion in 2006 and reached $2.7 billion by 2008, accounting for 20 percent of Honduras' GDP and acting as a lifeline for some 20 percent of Honduran families who were only spared from extreme poverty by the remittance money they received.[144]

GLIMMERS OF RESISTANCE

Despite the mounting difficulties facing all but the wealthiest Hondurans, there continued to be strength in the organizations committed to resisting class domination. The 1980s had been a decade of rupture; the movements that had been building from the strikes of the 1950s to the peasant movements of the 1970s were largely squashed by the repressive apparatus of the 1980s.[145] New movements, however, were built out of the difficulties of that period—often in response to the violence ushered in by the US occupation—and they continued to resist imperial impositions in the form of neoliberal restructuring by a comprador elite through the 1990s and 2000s.

Organizations like the Comité para la Defensa de los Derechos Humanos en Honduras (Human Rights Committee of Honduras, CODEH) and the Comité de Familiares de Detenidos Desaparecidos en Honduras (Committee of the Families of the Disappeared and Detained in Honduras, COFADEH) emerged in response to the repression of the 1980s and became important participants in contemporary struggles. *Maquiladora* workers increasingly engaged in acts of individual and organized resistance—ranging from sabotage and stealing to union drives and demonstrations—often bringing well-developed feminist networks into the sphere of production to fight against both capitalist exploitation and the complicated gendered dynamics that helped sustain it.[146] Urban professional classes, civil servants, and trade unionists became increasingly defiant in the 2000s in the face of privatization and the dismantling of social services, leading protests of some 25,000 people in 2003 in response to Maduro's plans to privatize water.[147]

Peasant movements, undeterred by the violence brought upon them, continued to demand access to land, organizing massive land reoccupations throughout the 1980s and 1990s, including a movement of over 100,000 peasants in the northwest in 1987.[148] Although proletarianization weakened the peasant movement, *campesino* groups increasingly organized alongside workers in other sectors, Indigenous communities, women's organizations, and other resistance networks. In 1989 many of these groups came together to form the Plataforma de Lucha Hondureña (Platform of Struggle) and, later, the Consejo Cívico de Organizaciones Populares y Indígenas de Honduras (Civic Council of Popular and Indigenous Organizations of Honduras, COPINH). These types of broader co-operative networks would become the legacy of the organizing that took place in response to the neoliberal push: as the capitalist class pooled its resources to consolidate a common class project, so, too, subordinate classes built movements that would cut across many traditional divides. The joining of many of these struggles would, ultimately, be the strength of the resistance networks in the 1990s and 2000s. It was precisely this new wave of activism that led to the 2009 coup, and it was these networks that emerged as a national resistance movement in its aftermath.

2 THE PRESIDENT IN HIS PYJAMAS
The June 2009 Coup d'Etat

On the morning of June 28, 2009, Honduran president Manuel Zelaya was awakened at 5:15 a.m. to find his home under military lockdown, as masked soldiers fired warning shots into the walls and held him at gunpoint. The pre-dawn raid whisked Zelaya out of the presidential palace in his pyjamas and bare feet to the Soto Cano air force base, from which the US operates its Joint Task Force Bravo, and then on to Costa Rica.[1] Dramatic live video footage, broadcast internationally on Venezuela-based Telesur, showed people in the early hours of the day coming out to vote in a referendum and finding the military in the streets, confiscating the ballots.[2] In the capital city, a crowd gathered at the presidential palace, and Telesur ran a video clip of outraged women who slammed their fists into the chests of soldiers while scattered crowds elsewhere held impromptu demonstrations and performed spontaneous street theatre in defiance of the coup.[3]

With Zelaya removed, the military cut off electricity, phone service, international cable TV, and even water to many neighbourhoods in Tegucigalpa and other major cities, and took all pro-Zelaya local TV stations off the air. Even some international news stations were cut off, including CNN and Telesur,[4] and ambassadors from Venezuela, Nicaragua, and Cuba all reported that they were detained and beaten by the Honduran armed forces.[5] Police and military violence escalated in the streets, targeting anyone who dared to participate in the public demonstrations, using tear gas, batons, water cannons, rubber bullets, and even live rounds. On several occasions, hundreds of heavily armed officers launched sudden charges against unsuspecting crowds, who would be hammered on their backs as they tried to flee the scene.[6]

The coup subverted the already limited democratic process in Honduras and undermined the progress that had been made in the protection of human rights since the disasters of the 1980s and '90s. Indeed, it was precisely designed to undercut those forces in the country seeking to reverse the dramatic decline in the conditions of life that had beset the majority of Hondurans in the previous two decades. The coup was a violent response to a growing and credible threat from popular social movements to the neoliberal capitalist order, and the conflict that emerged around this event laid bare the continued power that imperialist powers possess in Honduras. While it was the Honduran oligarchy that carried out the coup itself, it did so knowing that it had the support of the United States and Canada. This chapter will document the events surrounding the 2009 coup, picking up where the previous chapter left off, while the next will trace Canada's role in facilitating the coup and protecting its perpetrators. But to understand the coup, we must understand the movement it was seeking to break, so it is there that we begin.

THE GENEALOGY OF A SOCIAL MOVEMENT

Observers of the Honduran coup who only first tuned in during the drama of June 2009 often fail to understand that the coup was the key piece in *transforming* Manuel Zelaya into a popular figure in Honduras. He was elected president in 2005 as a member of the Liberal Party, which has traditionally functioned—along with the National Party—as one of the two competing parties of the oligarchy, neither known for any history of radicalism. Zelaya himself was a junior member of the oligarchy, a wealthy landowner from the eastern department of Olancho whose father, José Manuel, was implicated in the murder of two Catholic priests who were supporting escalations of *campesino* activism in 1975. José Manuel avoided any culpability in the massacre, and his son's political career was unaffected.

The younger Zelaya's career did not initially show any signs of significant divergence from the standard trajectory of Honduran politics. In fact, the only thing that distinguished Manuel Zelaya from someone like Roberto Micheletti—the tremendously unpopular figure who emerged as *de facto* president after the coup—was that he recognized the growing strength of the movements for social reform and learned to work with them. Zelaya's presidency became increasingly responsive to the sharp demands for change from trade unions, *campesinos*, women, Indigenous, Garífuna, and other marginalized communities. But, in spite of the way that he was later characterized by many observers from a variety of political stripes, Zelaya was not a hero to Honduras' poor; his presidency and his role in the social movement were, instead, complicated and inconsistent. In fact, after winning by an exceptionally narrow margin in the 2005 elections, Zelaya was immediately subjected to a show of strength and defiance from many of those who had supported his campaign, facing some 200 protests in just his first year in office.[7]

These strikes and mobilizations did not materialize out of thin air, nor were they spontaneous expressions of discontent; they were a manifestation of the growing strength of the new social movements that had begun to coalesce in the late 1980s and 1990s. The militarization of Honduras under the US occupation in the 1980s, and the repression and death-squad activity that accompanied it, significantly weakened or even snuffed out much of the radical left and the impressive *campesino* organizing that had characterized the period from the 1950s to the 1970s. As a result, there was limited capacity to muster opposition to the imposition of neoliberalism in the 1990s, especially as the Callejas government was setting up alternative parallel structures to existing social organizations in order to weaken and divide the movement. So, the hammer of structural adjustment, privatizations, foreign concessions, theft of *campesino* and Indigenous land, cuts to social and state services and infrastructure, and other austerity measures fell hard on Hondurans who were already reeling from the violence and insecurity of the 1980s. The devastating social consequences of Hurricane Mitch in 1998 were as clear a signal as any that conditions in Honduras had become intolerable.

Not surprisingly, it was around this time that a new generation of social movements was beginning to consolidate itself, first in regional organizations based loosely around the different departments, or provinces, of the country. These included, but were not limited to: the Asamblea Popular Permanente (Permanent Popular Assembly, APP) in El Progreso, the Movimiento Ambientalista de Olancho (Environmental Movement of Olancho, MAO) in Olancho, Coordinadora de Organizaciones Populares de Valle Aguán (Coordinated Popular Organizations of the Aguán Valley, COPA) in Atlántida, Patronato Regional de Occidente (Regional Council of the West, PRO) in the west, Consejo Cívico de Organizaciones Populares y Indígenas de Honduras (Civic Council of Popular and Indigenous Organizations of Honduras, COPINH) in Intibucá, and the Bloque Popular (Popular Bloc, BP) in Tegucigalpa and the southern departments. Most of these groups were, themselves, unions of smaller organizations that had been coming together around particular issues and gradually connecting up with larger pockets of struggle. For instance, the Bloque Popular—one of the key groups—was "a union of unions, anti-poverty groups, and *juntas de agua*," activist networks organized around the protection of public access to clean water, and it also encompassed a number of small socialist and communist parties, including the

Movimiento Democrático Popular (Popular Democratic Movement, MDR), a Marxist-Leninist party, the Tendencia Revolucionaria (Revolutionary Tendency, TR), made up of disaffected and increasingly radicalized government workers, and Los Necios (The Fools), a Marxist student organization that continues to have an important presence in the resistance.[8]

The larger regional groups, like the Bloque Popular and COPINH, began linking up in the late 1990s and organized co-ordinated actions in the early 2000s, including a dramatic blockade of the four main highways into Tegucigalpa in 2003. The blockade was held from 4:00 a.m. until 2:00 p.m., at which point it proceeded to the National Congress to confront then-President Maduro directly; the success of this demonstration encouraged further co-operation, and thus was created the Coordinadora Nacional de Resistencia Popular (Coordinated National Popular Resistance, CNRP). This organization would be converted into the Frente Nacional de Resistencia Popular (National Front of Popular Resistance, FNRP) immediately following the 2009 coup and remains the central institution of the resistance. The CNRP rotated its leadership between its different member groups, and I interviewed Juan Barahona, who was the co-ordinator of the Bloque Popular and became one of the central leaders of the FNRP after the coup: "The social movement was not born with the coup," he explained, "but strengthened by it. We had been mobilized for a decade, we had fought against Mel Zelaya for two years."[9]

Indeed, Zelaya's inauguration as president in 2006 was met—just a few months later—by one of Honduras' largest pre-coup demonstrations; tens of thousands of people participated in a national strike, led by the teachers' unions, that shut down many of the country's major highways and was met by swift and violent repression from Zelaya's government, which, according to Los Necios' Gilberto Rios, only further emboldened the CNRP to redouble its pressure against Zelaya.[10] A few months later, in May 2006, Zelaya reached out to the CNRP in an effort to bring the wave of strikes to an end and to ask for CNRP support in his plan to join the Venezuelan-led alliance Alternativa Bolivariana para los pueblos de nuestra América (Bolivarian Alternative for the Peoples of Our America, ALBA) in order to participate in the PetroCaribe project to significantly reduce energy costs. Launched by the Venezuelan government in 2005, PetroCaribe offers member countries the option of purchasing Venezuelan oil for reduced prices, with long-term payment options set at low interest rates. While this ended the strike in question, it did little to satisfy the growing demands for change from the increasingly well-organized and active movements that had emerged from the wreckage of the 1990s.

The reforms pursued by Zelaya's government, then, were concessions made in order to appease the growing social movements; it would be wrong to give complete credit for them to Zelaya, but similarly inaccurate to understate the significance of these reforms and his shift to the left. Though Zelaya began as a traditional politician who emerged at the height of the neoliberal push, his presidency was markedly different from the outset, because, as Honduran sociologist Tomás Andino explained to me, Zelaya came from a fraction of the Honduran oligarchy—the traditional landowning classes—that was being left behind by the embrace of neoliberalism and transnational capital.[11] The structural adjustment policies imposed in the 1990s had the effect of attracting more foreign capital and reorienting the Honduran economy towards the production of exports, especially in industrial manufacturing. In addition, Hurricane Mitch in 1998 hit the traditional landowner sector—of which Zelaya was a part—much harder than the growing *maquiladora* sector. According to Andino, Zelaya came to represent a disaffected section within the oligarchy that was less connected to foreign capital and was not reaping the rewards of neoliberalism in the same way, especially under the government of Ricardo Maduro.[12]

As such, when Zelaya succeeded Maduro, he brought a different agenda to the front of the Liberal Party. In a deeply divided party, Zelaya represented a centrist, reforming faction that was less committed to neoliberalism and saw social democratic reform as a viable avenue out of the deep economic and social crisis in Honduras.[13] While Zelaya initially tried to bridge the divides in the party, he gradually established an administration that reflected the centrist position and as he became increasingly alienated from the most powerful elements of the Honduran oligarchy—even within his own party—he needed to cultivate relationships with other elements of Honduran society in order to maintain his position. This would prove to be of critical importance because it explains Zelaya's openness to building a less oppositional relationship with the social movements that had coalesced into the CNRP.

MANUEL ZELAYA AND THE CNRP

Zelaya's presidency was pulled—albeit gradually and inconsistently—towards the social movements, and that shift is reflected in the series of reforms it enacted. One of these reforms, an increase of approximately 60 percent in the monthly minimum wage from the equivalent of $157 to $289, was to provide some immediate, if inadequate, relief for Honduras' poorest workers in the non-*maquiladora* sectors.[14] Under pressure from trade unions and the CNRP, Zelaya imposed the wage increase by decree when the Honduran Congress refused to co-operate and, not surprisingly, the move elicited an angry response from the oligarchy and most of the larger media outlets they own, not to mention those foreign companies that do not fall under *maquiladora* laws, including the banana plantations and mining companies. The exemption for *maquiladora* zones is, of course, part of the broader capitulation of the Honduran state to foreign capital, but it is also worth noting that *maquiladora* workers are generally better paid than average working-class Hondurans, so the wage increase was still targeted to assist some of Honduras' poorest people.[15]

Closely related were a series of reforms designed to reduce the overall cost of living for Honduras' poor and working classes. Zelaya's move towards ALBA, though often read in the North American media as part of a nefarious pact with former Venezuelan president Hugo Chávez, is better understood as a policy option that would allow him to make good on promises to improve conditions for Honduras' poorest communities, upon whose support his political position was increasingly reliant. After all, Zelaya's realignment towards ALBA included signing onto the PetroCaribe initiative—of which a large majority of Central American and Caribbean countries are participants—under which Venezuela provides oil and gas to those countries at 40 percent of market price on a 25-year financing plan at just 1 percent interest. This decision had immediate benefits for Hondurans, in terms of lower energy costs, but of course it also made life easier for the Honduran oligarchy whose businesses were much more reliant on energy than the average household, which may explain why the same people who later accused Zelaya of being a puppet of Chávez were actually rather supportive of the initiative when it was introduced.[16] Nevertheless, Zelaya also used the $100 million in Honduran bonds purchased by Venezuela to lower the rate that low-income families paid in energy costs, to reduce interest rates on housing, and to provide subsidies for single mothers, for equipment for small farmers, and for meals in schools across the country.[17]

With each new reform measure pursued, and with the social movement growing increasingly defiant and demanding, the internal tensions in the Liberal Party grew ever more difficult to reconcile. The acrimonious process by which Honduras joined ALBA was a particularly instructive example that may have been a critical turning point in Zelaya's relationship with the oligarchy, both outside and within his own party. In order to secure enough votes in Congress to approve the decision to join ALBA, Zelaya needed the support of the right wing of the Liberal Party, which was not easily gained. Roberto Micheletti, who led the right-wing faction and would later lead the coup d'état, agreed to support the joining of ALBA on the condition that Zelaya endorse him for president in 2009.[18] Zelaya would go on to break this promise, choosing to endorse neither Micheletti nor his vice-president, Edwin Santos, whose loyalties were with the right wing, and instead endorsing a leader in the social movement who was running as an independent candidate. These events illustrate the mutually reinforcing relationship between Zelaya's concessions to the social movement and his tenuous position in his own party: each concession hastened and intensified his isolation from large sections of the party, and that isolation only encouraged him to tilt even further towards the social movement, until he found his position entirely dependent on the movement's support.

Nevertheless, Zelaya's calculations shouldn't lead us to downplay the significance of his concessions for poor and working people in Honduras. In legislation passed in 2007, Zelaya's government also took action to reduce the environmental consequences of deforestation by designating nearly 90 percent of Honduran territory to be protected against logging, and he resisted pressure from the oligarchy to privatize the state electrical company, Empresa Nacional de Energía Eléctrica (National Electrical Energy Company, ENEE), and the national telecommunications firm, Empresa Hondureña de Telecomunicaciones (Honduran Telecommunications Company, HONDUTEL).[19] Though both enterprises have been mired in corruption for decades, the experience of privatizations in Honduras clearly indicates that handing those industries directly to the oligarchy would have only deepened the extent to which the wealth of the many would be diverted to the pockets of the few. These initiatives were complemented by a plan to convert sections of the US/Honduran military base at Palmerola into a commercial airport to reduce Hondurans' reliance on Toncontín airport in Tegucigalpa, long recognized as one of the world's most dangerous international airports, given the complicated mountainous approach and short runways.[20]

One of Zelaya's actions that bore much significance for Canadian capital was his enforcement of a moratorium on the granting of new mining concessions to foreign firms. Like many of Zelaya's reformist positions, it had contradictory impulses: it was at once designed as a gesture to appease the social movements and, as per Tomás Andino's analysis above, as a wedge against the dominant transnational capitalists in favour of his own faction of the Honduran oligarchy. Nevertheless, it was a significant step, and it cannot be considered apart from the pressure Zelaya was facing from the CNRP in the context of social and environmental crises caused by mining operations, notable among them the San Martín mine in the Siria Valley, owned by the Canadian firm Goldcorp.

Pedro Landa, of the anti-mining organization Centro Hondureño de Promoción para el Desarrollo Comunitario (Centre for the Promotion of Community Development in Honduras, CEHPRODEC), recalled that the moratorium was actually first imposed in August 2004, when upwards of 4,000 anti-mining activists converged on Tegucigalpa in a seven-day Marcha por la Vida (March for Life) and then-President Maduro decreed a temporary suspension of approvals of new mining concessions, to take effect at the end of 2005 when his term would be over. Zelaya thus inherited the moratorium and had thirty days to approve it; otherwise all outstanding concessions would have been granted—a canny move on Maduro's part that forced Zelaya to take a strong position one way or the other.[21] CNRP-affiliated anti-mining groups like CEHPRODEC held meetings with Zelaya and convinced him to not only enforce Maduro's decree but, furthermore, to add that there could be no consideration of any additional concessions until such time as a new set of laws governing mining in Honduras could be written and approved. It is worth noting that, while this was a step in the right direction, mines already in operation continued functioning unabated.[22] Nevertheless, since the new mining code was not prepared during Zelaya's term in office, the moratorium remained in effect until the coup.[23]

In another significant move, Zelaya applied a presidential veto to a law in May 2009, passed by the Honduran Congress a month earlier, which would have criminalized the use of the "morning-after pill" at the request of the ultra-conservative Christian movement.[24] The "morning-after pill" has taken on particular significance in Honduran feminist circles because, as Andrea Nuila, a lawyer with the group Feministas en Resistencia (Feminists in Resistance), explained, "All forms of abortion are criminalized in Honduras," making the pill an important exception to the rule of careful regulation of female bodies by the state.[25]

The proposed law was presented by a member of Zelaya's Liberal Party, Martha Lorena Alvarado, and was enthusiastically endorsed by John Smeaton, the director of the US anti-abortion organization Society for the Protection of Unborn Children.[26] Acknowledging that the president had the right to veto the bill, Smeaton encouraged his readers to write to Roberto Micheletti in his role as president of Congress to support its decision. Under pressure from

Honduran and international feminist groups, notably the Comité de América Latina y el Caribe para la Defensa de los Derechos de la Mujer (Committee for the Defense of the Rights of Women in Latin America and the Caribbean, CLADEM), Zelaya vetoed the bill after it was passed in Congress. When, just over a month later, his government was overthrown, the coup government waited only one day to pass a bill into law that banned the pill and the two congresswomen who introduced the law in the first place were promoted to high-ranking positions in the coup government.[27]

CONSTITUYENTE

By far the most significant initiative taken by Zelaya's increasingly reform-oriented government was its decision to support the social movements' call for striking a constituent assembly—a *constituyente*—to rewrite the Honduran Constitution along more equitable lines. Indeed, it is no coincidence that this was the project that ultimately provoked the full, militarized ire of the Honduran oligarchy. The push for constitutional reform came out of the determination, on the part of leading activists in the struggle, that the existing legal structures in Honduras severely restricted the possibility of more significant reform. The present Constitution was ratified in 1982, under the auspices of the US-sponsored military dictatorship, which was, at the time, presiding over a supposed transfer of power to elected civilian authorities. Gen. Policarpio Paz García, then-president of the dictatorship, saw in the growing unrest of the late 1970s an echo of the revolutionary movements that were gaining strength in Guatemala, El Salvador, and especially Nicaragua. In an attempt to avoid a similar descent into civil war and upheaval, which might have weakened the position of the military, depending on its outcome, Paz García moved to return power to civilian leadership by calling for a constituent assembly in 1980, which set elections for 1981.[28]

Although the 1981 elections were free of direct military intervention, there can be little doubt that the process of developing the 1982 Constitution was heavily influenced by the dictatorship that presided over it. The 1980s could hardly be described as a success for civilian rule;[29] the country was nicknamed the "USS Honduras" for its complete capitulation to the US Contra wars and was, for the first half of the decade, effectively ruled by Gen. Gustavo Alvarez Martínez and US ambassador John Negroponte, who together founded the Battalion 3-16 death squad. Meanwhile, civilian president Roberto Suazo Córdova attempted to amend the new Constitution to stay in power after 1985, offering the military another opportunity to assert its power to stop him. In so doing, it established once again that the military was by far the most powerful force in the country, bolstered by an average of approximately $50 million per year in US military assistance from 1981–1988.[30]

This context framed the signing of the 1982 Constitution and, as such, it is no surprise that it gained little support from common Hondurans. In their important primer outlining the arguments in favour of convoking a constituent assembly, Joaquín A. Mejía, Victor Fernández, and Omar Menjívar argue that the 1982 Constitution "was not a product of a genuine social pact" and sought only to "promote an image of democratic change" in order to destabilize the demands for legitimate democracy being made by more radical left movements across Central America.[31]

Many in Honduras' social movements argue that the problem with the 1982 Constitution lies not in the document itself, but in the manner in which it was written and the way it has been applied. In an interview in 2012, Honduran lawyer Jari Dixon explained to me:

> I don't think the 1982 Constitution is a bad constitution. Most of it is good. It has respect for human rights, it respects the right to work, the right to education, respect for life, health, free association, freedom of thought—it's not a bad constitution. The real question is, why is it so ineffective?... There's no peace. There's no harmony. There's no health. There's no work. There's no education. There's no security. We are at the gateway to a failed state. So why doesn't the 1982 Constitution work? A functioning rule of law is essential for the Constitution to work. But the rule of law has been broken.[32]

Dixon worked in the public prosecutor's office for fourteen years under that Constitution, believing he could improve society by pursuing cases and rigorously upholding the law. When he pursued a corruption case in Copán in 2004, he found himself at odds with his attorney general, who had previously worked for President Callejas and was determined to eliminate any connections between Callejas and the corruption cases. Dixon and some colleagues were fired for pursuing the cases, and although he would be reinstated eventually, he insists that while the Constitution itself is fine, the law is applied to the rich and the poor only selectively—that is, only when and how it suits the rich.[33]

Others insist that the document itself is fundamentally flawed. As Berta Cáceres of COPINH noted in a speech in 2009, "... not one time are women mentioned in the constitution. How is that possible? How in a society where they talk of democracy and justice could women not even be mentioned?"[34] According to Miriam Miranda, co-ordinator of the Organización Fraternal Negra Hondureña (Fraternal Organization of Black Hondurans, OFRANEH), "the poorest sectors of this country are included in the constitution only to go and vote," and Jorge Lara Fernández, a professor of sociology at the University of San Pedro Sula, added that, "poor Hondurans, women, Indigenous people, black Hondurans, people with different abilities, people with different sexual preferences are not included in our constitution."[35] Among the many things missing from the current legal apparatus in Honduras, Mejía, Fernández, and Menjívar point to the prospects, in a new Constitution, for promoting "a new economic model" that would build genuine social equality and promote respect for human dignity and social, environmental, and cultural rights.[36]

Both these positions are partially right; Dixon is entirely correct to note that the capacity to enforce the rule of law has been massively damaged, and the movement activists who condemn the 1982 Constitution's omissions and shortcomings have identified real issues. What is clear is that a process of constitutional reform—navigating the debates between the different positions on the foundations of Honduran law—could have been meaningful only if it was undertaken democratically, developed by those whom it was meant to serve. Having the oligarchy refashion their management of Honduras from the halls of Congress would have been nothing new; in fact, the mockery that Congress made of its own legal system in its attempts to block the *constituyente* only emphasized just how corrupt and self-serving was Congress' use of that system and its Constitution.

As Mejía, Fernández, and Menjívar insist, the 2009 coup itself demonstrated that the 1982 Constitution had changed nothing in Honduras, and had allowed successive governments to rule in the interests of the powerful with little regard for the well-being of the majority.[37] Honduran doctor and professor Rutilia Calderón described the importance of the project at length:

> From 1982 until now [the constitution] has never been invoked for the common good, for the good of the excluded sectors of this country.... The construction of a reform process is not to produce a formal document called "The Constitution," it is to create new forms of relating between different sectors of society—to close the gap of inequality and to attain a just distribution of the wealth that this country has.[38]

Zelaya's support for a constitutional assembly generated a rupture with many of his remaining allies in the Liberal Party and represented an important victory for social movements that were finally beginning to make major gains after years of dedicated organizing work.

SUNSET ON THE ZELAYA ERA

Zelaya's time in office, then, was complicated and contradictory. On the one hand, his own disaffection from the neoliberal project became linked—albeit uncomfortably—with the more substantial critiques of neoliberalism advanced with increasing fortitude by the social movements. On the other hand, the movements themselves were unsatisfied by the slow pace, inconsistent application, and often contradictory logic of Zelaya's reforms and, as a result, the second half of his administration was marked by both major strikes and protests against his government, as well as significant demonstrations in support of proposals that Zelaya was endorsing against the wishes of his peers, especially the project for constitutional reform.[39] By 2008 and 2009, the lines of struggle had shifted such that the executive branch—Zelaya and his closest supporters—was just as likely to side with the movement against Congress and the Supreme Court as it was to side with the established legal institutions against the movement.

Indeed, frustrations with Honduras' legal structures had boiled over dramatically in April and May 2008, when seven federal prosecutors staged a thirty-eight-day hunger strike in the Honduran Congress to protest the state's refusal to pursue corruption cases.[40] Jari Dixon was one of the prosecutors who participated in the hunger strike, as well as a three-day sit-in at Congress in January 2009, and after their efforts made little headway, he became disillusioned:

> We had hope, before, that we might be able to change the people in power, but I realized that this is not about the people in power; it is about the system. We could spend hundreds of years taking people out of the public prosecutor's office or the attorney general's office, but ultimately, it is a structural problem.[41]

Thus, while Zelaya's government was more receptive and responsive to these pressures than his predecessors, which was a significant change in the status quo, the degree to which Honduras was transformed under Zelaya should not be overstated. Analysts have rightly noted Zelaya's "contradictory embrace" of both neoliberal projects and the populist rhetoric that seemed to oppose them.[42]

The push for reform, then, came not from Zelaya but from the people; it came from ordinary Hondurans organizing around issues that were of direct and serious consequence to them. In this sense, arguments that foreground the importance of the social movement are correct. At the same time, however, the fact that Zelaya proved to be significantly more responsive to popular politics than his predecessors complicates the picture. His reforms may have been inconsistent and did not radically alter the structural realities of Honduran life, but his readiness to bend to the will of popular movements was unprecedented in recent Honduran history and opened up the prospect of real change for the first time since the great strikes of the 1950s. Canadian journalist Jesse Freeston, who produced a documentary in 2012 on the *campesino* movement in the Aguán Valley, told me that the Hondurans he has worked closest with felt that Zelaya "passed the power test," making good on campaign promises to the poor that previous presidents had consistently broken, once in office, and that he had built a different kind of relationship with Honduran activists than any previous administration.[43]

In fact, Zelaya's popularity—he is known in Honduras by the nickname "Mel"—is reflected in the mythology that is built up around his personal appeal and charisma; popular Honduran poet Roberto Sosa describes him:

> Mel has been blessed with a bombproof, coup-proof solidarity with the people, along with a gift for plain, unpretentious speech and great personal warmth. He has a huge heart, and, contrary to what his detractors say, he is open-minded and very intelligent. Moreover, he is a lover of poetry.[44]

Even if we acknowledge that these may be exaggerations, Zelaya *is* regularly described as someone who could speak to people and relate to them, in a manner uncommon among the Honduran oligarchy. Populist appeal on its own does not make Zelaya a reformer, but what is significant is that there developed a kind of dynamic between his populist character and the social policies he was enacting that was opening increasing space for reform.

Indeed, Zelaya's endorsement of the *constituyente* was arguably the most important gain for burgeoning Honduran social movements since the establishment of legitimate civilian government in the mid-1990s. Given the power that the Honduran oligarchy and foreign capitalists have been able to wield over the past three decades through the legal mechanisms of the state, under the 1982 Constitution, an opportunity to reorganize and refound the basis for that power, if conducted properly, could have made a number of much more significant reforms possible down the line. No administration for decades prior to Zelaya's had even considered such a departure from traditional Honduran politics—hence the swift and dramatic action taken against it—and, although Zelaya did not design or initiate the demand for reform, to ignore the important differences between his government and those that preceded him is to profoundly misunderstand the context of the coup and the popular resistance that followed. In short, what was significant in Zelaya's time in office was not so much the reforms he passed but the prospects for broader reforms embedded in the reopening of the Constitution, a project for which Zelaya was willing to provoke the full ire of his own social class to defend.

GOLPE DE ESTADO

Contrary to the unsubstantiated claims blithely and relentlessly repeated in the North American media since the 2009 coup, nothing in the reopening of the Constitution would have allowed Manuel Zelaya to run for re-election that year, though this useful misdirection was reinforced regularly by the oligarchy not only to convince the international community that the coup was necessary but, as Darío Euraque has argued, to convince the military to reassert its role in Honduran politics so dramatically.[45] Nonetheless, the claim that Zelaya was moving towards making himself "president for life" was constantly repeated by nearly every mainstream media outlet in North America, and notably Canada's national newspaper, the *Globe and Mail*, which offered this editorial comment a week after the coup:

> It is important that Manuel Zelaya's machinations to rewrite the Honduran constitution to allow for a *generalissimo* clause were brought firmly and finally to an end. Like his idol, Venezuelan President Hugo Chavez, who won a referendum earlier this year to eliminate term limits, Mr. Zelaya wants to revert to the days in which Latin American heads of state could extend their rule indefinitely.[46]

But this fabrication hardly stands up to even the simplest examination—least of all the invention of a so-called "*generalissimo* clause"—and it says more about the state of the Canadian mainstream media than it does about Honduras.[47]

The process was to be as follows: on June 28, 2009, Hondurans would have voted in a non-binding referendum on whether they supported the addition of the *cuarta urna* (a fourth ballot) in the general elections scheduled for November 29 of that year. Normally, Honduran elections feature three ballots, corresponding to each of the three levels of government; that is, one for the local mayor, one for a *diputado* or representative in Congress, and one for the president. If the June 28 referendum came back with a strong "yes," Zelaya would have added the fourth ballot asking the question: "Do you support the creation of a national constituent assembly to redraft the constitution?" Accordingly, the Constitution could not possibly have been changed *before* the November 29 elections, since it could only have gone ahead if approved in those elections, and so Zelaya could not have stood for re-election. In fact, the primaries for that election had already taken place and the public was fully aware of which candidates had successfully moved forward. Zelaya's name was not among them; even had he wanted to, it would have been illegal and impossible for Zelaya to be a candidate in 2009.[48]

The notion, then, that Zelaya intended to manipulate the process to stay in power is patently absurd. Rosemary A. Joyce has argued that one of Zelaya's aims in pushing for the referendum was to re-engage Hondurans in the electoral process after two decades of steady declines in voter turnout and public confidence in elected leaders.[49] After all, the Honduran social movements had demonstrated their strength in the streets, not with ballots, and it may well have been Zelaya's calculation that the *constituyente* would have kept the movements' energies tied into electoral and legal processes that would limit their radical potential. Nevertheless, the Honduran Congress, packed with members of the oligarchy, felt that the reopening of the Constitution—under conditions they could not necessarily control—could represent a real threat to their stranglehold on power and refused to accept the idea. In response, Zelaya pledged, in March 2009, to appeal directly to the people through a referendum and vowed to pursue the fourth ballot if the people asked for it. That referendum was scheduled for June 28, 2009.

Of course, that process never went ahead because the morning that this non-binding poll was supposed to happen, Zelaya was abducted by the military and flown to Costa Rica. It was clear, months earlier, that the decision to reopen the Constitution would be contested by the established power structure in Honduras. Between March and May 2009, a variety of different state officials tried to dissuade Zelaya from pursuing the referendum; the Supreme Court, the Electoral Tribunal, and Congress all claimed that the poll would be illegal and, in the days leading up to the referendum, the attorney general's office threatened to have Zelaya arrested if he continued to insist upon it.[50] These claims were based on a law hastily drafted and passed by Congress—just days before the referendum—that prohibited any referenda from taking place within six months of an election.[51] Following the new ruling, Gen.

Romeo Vásquez Velásquez, head of the armed forces and a graduate of the notorious School of the Americas, announced on June 25, 2009, three days before the referendum, that the military would refuse to facilitate the poll by withholding logistical labour, not allowing his staff to distribute ballots and boxes. Zelaya had him immediately fired. The next day, the Supreme Court ruled that he must be reinstated, but Zelaya dramatically refused, saying, "...If an army rebels against a president, then we are back to the era of the cavemen, back to the darkest chapters in Honduran history."[52] Zelaya and his supporters retrieved the ballots and boxes themselves and began distributing them across the country.

Choosing to interpret Zelaya's persistence on setting up for the poll as acting against the Constitution, the Supreme Court ordered the armed forces to arrest President Zelaya, based on the clumsily constructed law passed just days before, a pretext that does not stand up to critical scrutiny.[53] The next morning, Zelaya was abducted in his pyjamas and taken out of the country. The *constituyente* was cancelled, the military and police cracked down on the protests and displayed their authority in the streets, and the organizers of the coup hastily constructed the legal edifice upon which their rule would be based. Nine of Zelaya's ministers were detained, while countless others went into hiding, and a special session of Congress was called to hear the presentation of a fake letter of resignation, purportedly written by Zelaya, who immediately denied having written it.[54] Congress agreed to transfer the presidency to Roberto Micheletti, head of Congress, whose first act was to order a twenty-four-hour curfew for all Honduran citizens, which would actually last for three days.

Anticipating international rebuke, the oligarchy acted quickly to defend what had taken place. "I did not get here through the ignominy of a coup d'état," insisted Micheletti.[55] Added one of his advisors:

> The decision was adopted by unanimity in the Congress. That means all of the political parties. It has been endorsed by sectors that represent a wide array of Hondurans—the Episcopal Church, the Catholic Church. And well, of course, the Armed Forces. The difficult part will be for the international community to see things as the Honduran people see them.[56]

The difficult part might, rather, have been convincing the international community that the people in these well-placed institutions of authority actually represented the Honduran people in any meaningful way. Certainly, the

Honduran oligarchy was on board; on June 29, 2009, the day after the coup, the most significant organization of the Honduran business elite, the Consejo Hondureño de la Empresa Privada (Honduran Council of Private Enterprise, COHEP), issued a statement declaring that "what occurred today [sic] was not the changing of one president for another; today, [sic] framed in national unity, respect for the Constitution, national laws, and institutionalism was achieved." Amílcar Bulnes, president of COHEP, added that:

> The private sector worked hard with ex-President Zelaya, but in the end he turned his attention to other themes, away from the country's priorities, from national issues.... The transitional government should make sure that there are no empty stomachs by generating job opportunities.[57]

Notably, the statements from the *golpistas* (coup-plotters) and their supporters, which saturated the Honduran mass media, framed the discussion as though the real problem was not the coup, but the fact that the international community had condemned it and that most countries refused to recognize or do business with the *de facto* regime. "When it rains, it pours," cried *El Heraldo*. "The poor of this country will be even more impoverished if sanctions are imposed." Taking the point further, COHEP's director, Benjamín Bográn, added, "Who are they going to sanction? The politicians or the Honduran people? Because every time you impose sanctions, it is not the rulers who suffer, but the people."[58] The oligarchy had never before shown such concern for the people.

In the meantime, the Asociación Hondureña de Maquiladores (Honduran Association of Maquiladoras, AHM), an association of owners in the *maquiladora* industry, was busy organizing marches in support of the coup, though they had to provide all the materials and could only garner some attendance by forcing their employees to participate.[59] Outfitted in white T-shirts and massive Honduran flags, the pro-coup marches were a fabrication for international consumption. As Honduran scholar Darío Euraque explained:

> Never in the history of Honduras has there ever been a mobilization along the lines of the white t-shirt [march] ... they didn't have a culture of resistance, of mobilization, so a lot of their music and placards and paraphernalia ... was not even local. A lot of it was borrowed from Venezuela, Cuban Americans, lots of it was in English, peppered with English phrases and very manufactured placards and so forth.[60]

In fact, AHM and other organizations representing the oligarchy had been staging rallies such as these for months prior to Zelaya's ouster, usually against Zelaya or the proposal for constitutional reform, and many Hondurans participated in the so-called "White Marches" simply to get paid, in sharp contrast to the dangerous and certainly unpaid protests that were held in opposition to the coup.[61]

LA RESISTENCIA

What followed the military takeover has been called the largest, sustained, peaceful demonstration in Honduran history: for 161 straight days, Hondurans took to the streets of Tegucigalpa, San Pedro Sula, and cities and towns across the country. The numbers fluctuated—sometimes as high as hundreds of thousands—protesting right up to the day of the "elections" on November 29, 2009. Predictably, they were met with widespread and violent repression. From June to November 2009, between thirty and forty people were killed in political violence and hundreds more were detained, beaten, kidnapped, raped, and otherwise victimized by an increasingly militarized state apparatus.[62] On July 5, about a week after the coup, Manuel Zelaya attempted to re-enter the country but was prevented from landing at Tegucigalpa's Toncontín airport by the military, which unleashed a torrent of violence against the massive crowds that had gathered to greet Zelaya. Nineteen-year-old Isis Obed Murillo was among them, and was shot in the head and killed by the army. A few months later, members of his family showed me a shard of his skull and told me his story in a community meeting in a small kitchen in Jutiapa, near Danlí; he was the son of a long-time activist in the movement, Jose David Murillo, who was detained immediately following his son's assassination. While David Murillo was in detention, his daughter received a text message from his son's phone, which read, "I am your father HA HA HA."[63] Meanwhile, on September 21, Zelaya returned to Honduras a second time and took refuge in the Brazilian embassy, where he remained for some four months, guarded by police under orders to arrest him the moment he left Brazilian territory.

Nonetheless, the coup and its attendant violence had the unintended consequence of cementing the bonds between the very diverse organizations that had been working together under the CNRP. That body created the new FNRP soon after the coup, and it quickly became the most important popular organization in Honduras. Its members and supporters, like the CNRP before it, came primarily from the poor, working, and marginalized classes but, unlike the CNRP, the new organization also drew people in from the relatively small professional and political classes, including lawyers, doctors, left-liberal politicians, and civil servants, many of whom were—like Zelaya himself—previously the targets of CNRP actions, but suddenly found themselves aligned with the movement in response to the coup.[64] Marlon Hernández, for instance, was a journalist with *Diario Tiempo* and was well-connected in the oligarchy, but as a researcher with the Liberal Party he increasingly found himself compelled by Honduras' profound social inequality and sympathetic to the demands of the social movements. The coup marked a breaking point for Hernández, who, almost immediately, pledged his support for Zelaya and the resistance.[65] The FNRP worked closely with local human rights organizations and some foreign NGOs, but its autonomy from foreign interlocutors (whatever their intentions) was never in question. The characterization—promoted by the oligarchy and its North American allies—of the movement as a Chávez-exported ring of professional troublemakers and socialists was viewed as utterly absurd in a movement whose Honduran roots stretched back for decades.

But the *golpistas* and their beneficiaries were determined to stamp out this increasingly united movement; repression of the resistance was violent and thorough. Human rights groups like the Comité de Familiares de Detenidos Desaparecidos en Honduras (Committee of the Families of the Disappeared and Detained in Honduras, COFADEH) worked tirelessly after the coup to produce detailed documentation of the brutality. On November 28, 2009, they, as part of a coalition of the six leading human rights groups in Honduras called the Plataforma de Derechos Humanos, produced a report detailing the campaign of state terror that had been unleashed over the previous five months. That report was presented to the Tribunal Supremo Electoral (Supreme Electoral Tribunal, TSE) on the day before the coup government held elections to try to legitimize its authority in the country. In a formal declaration demanding that the elections be cancelled, on account of the impossibility of them being fair and free in the context of the coup and state terror, the human rights platform declared:

> [These elections are being conducted] in a context of grave and systematic violations of human rights. Since the day of the coup, we have documented 33 violent and politically motivated deaths, torture, cruel and inhuman and degrading treatment, sexual assault and restrictions on freedom of association, assembly, expression, opinion and more.[66]

They go on to note that holding elections under these circumstances was an absurd prospect, given that the same people who were committing this violence were those who were supposed to be responsible for running fair elections. They also drew attention to some of the highest-profile cases of repression. Carlos H. Reyes, a trade unionist, member of the social movement and, initially, an independent presidential candidate, was hospitalized after a brutal blow from police in a peaceful demonstration. Ulises Sarmiento, a well-known member of the Liberal Party who sympathized with the resistance, had his home ransacked by soldiers with automatic weapons in the department of Olancho. Eliseo Hernandez Juarez, a vice-mayoral candidate in Macuelizo, Santa Barbara, was assassinated.[67]

Not surprisingly, the violence was not limited to high-profile politicians; rather, it fell hardest on those who had the least resources to protect themselves. Victor Corrales Mejía and his son, working-class members of the FNRP, were arrested in November 2009 and beaten in their home. Police arrived in the middle of the night, hit Victor in the head and spine with batons, and threatened to kill him. "They kicked in my door, they threw me out like I was a sack of corn. They want to intimidate us," he told me, "but our desire for democracy is stronger than they are."[68] In Comayagua, where the resistance was strong, the mayor threatened to give the names and addresses of anyone who interfered with the elections to the military. In fact, the military sent a letter a month before the elections demanding such lists from all the mayors across the country.[69]

At the same time, the media were kept on a tight leash in order to contain the resistance. Immediately following the coup, journalists who were not loyal to the oligarchy were repressed by the military. Reporters from Venezuelan TV station Telesur, who attempted to provide live coverage of the coup, were consistently harassed and the few Honduran media outlets brave enough to speak out against the coup saw their journalists detained and beaten, their signals interrupted, and their equipment ransacked.[70] Radio Globo, which emerged as one of the most significant alternative media outlets after the coup, quickly resorted to broadcasting almost exclusively online from secret locations after the first months of repression. When Globo programming director David Romero chose, on June 28, 2009, to report that a coup was taking place, he found himself dragged in front of Gen. Romeo Vásquez Velásquez, who told Romero what he should be reporting:

> First [I was told] to recognize that what happened was a [presidential] succession and not a coup d'état. Second, that it was necessary because Manuel Zelaya Rosales was

violating the constitution and wanted to extend his term limit. And third, that the nation comes first, that [the coup] was to save the country from Chávez.[71]

Romero was proud of his station for standing up to the regime: "We've always believed Honduras needs profound changes," he said, "and that the oligarchy which has caused this country to be in a state of poverty … can't keep running the country."[72] He also quickly discovered that he had support, when he saw their station's market share of 7 percent before the coup jump to 28 percent after, largely in response to their critical coverage.

Radio Globo was one of a handful of media outlets—including Radio Progreso and Radio Uno, television station Canal 36 (Cholusat Sur), and newspaper *El Libertador*—that chose to defy the regime and the rest of the corporate media, and faced relentless harassment as a result. Some, like Canal 36, were shut down altogether after having equipment destroyed, signals interrupted, offices ransacked, and editors assassinated. In October 2009, Roberto Micheletti issued a Presidential Decree, which was used to take critical media off the air for twenty-two days; Reporters Without Borders highlighted this action in a press release on October 21, 2009, noting that it was a measure "targeted at those that oppose the coup."[73]

The decree went into effect on September 28, 2009, and it gave authorities the green light to "halt the coverage or discussion through any media, be it verbal or printed, of demonstrations that threaten peace and public order" or that compromised the "dignity" of government authorities or decisions; it was used primarily to justify destruction and confiscation of equipment at Radio Globo and Canal 36, the two critical media outlets with the best nation-wide coverage.[74] And always lurking behind this systematic harassment was the threat of violence against those who did not bend to the regime's pressure, like *El Libertador* photojournalist Delmer Membreño, who was kidnapped and tortured in Tegucigalpa on the same day that Decree 124-2009 took effect. He described the experience to Sandra Cuffe, with his body still marred by bruises and burns:

They put a balaclava over my head, they handcuffed me, and they burned my body. They hit me, and they uttered threats against the newspaper I work for, *El Libertador*.… They burned my body with cigarettes. Here [on my arm], my face, and my chest. They ripped my shirt and left me without shoes ... "Cry, cry! Why aren't you crying, you commie?" That's what they said.… They said that the director better be

> careful, that they were following him, and that what they had done to me was nothing in comparison to what they were going to do to him.[75]

On the other side, the pro-coup media fell upon themselves to support the regime and denounce the FNRP at every opportunity. In his detailed 2009 assessment of the media in Honduras, Manuel Torres Calderón argued that the country was a "plutocracy" in which the same families who controlled the banks, commerce, agroindustry, energy, telecommunications, tourism, the *maquiladoras,* and the service sector also controlled the overwhelming majority of the news and entertainment media.[76] Those same oligarchs are embedded in the political and judicial system, either directly or by proxy, and exert immense influence over the politics of the country by their control of the media. As of 2009, there were four major newspapers in Honduras: *El Heraldo* and *La Prensa* were both owned by Jorge Canahuati Larach and his family; *La Tribuna* was owned by former President Carlos Flores Facussé; and *Diario Tiempo* was owned by the family of Jaime Rosenthal Oliva, whose family also owned two of the major TV stations. Three additional TV stations were owned by the families of Rafael Ferrari and Manuel Villeda Toledo. Torres Calderón concluded:

> There is no precise data on the total wealth that each of these families possess. All of these businessmen also control a variety of other interests (banking, securities, exports, production, imports, telecommunications, data transmission, oil and gas, water, etc.) alongside their ownership of the major media outlets. This is one of the principal problems affecting the quality of freedom of speech in Honduras....[77]

No surprise, then, that almost the entire Honduran media was mobilized to support the coup.

In addition to selective coverage of events and transparently pro-coup reporting, the *golpista* media abandoned any semblance of liberal journalistic integrity by engaging in a variety of fraudulent and terroristic practices. In July 2009, the newspaper *La Prensa* applied an embarrassingly clumsy dose of Photoshop to an image it published of a victim of state violence, the above-mentioned Isis Obed Murillo, taking the time to erase the blood that stained his shirt and was dripping from his head.[78] On November 1, 2009, Belén Fernández reported that the main Honduran newspapers were taking photographs of protestors at FNRP demonstrations and delivering them to the police.[79] The media even began acting as an unofficial organ of the regime, disseminating its campaign of popular intimidation, as on November 8, 2009, when *El Heraldo* asserted that "calls against the election process on November 29 will not go unpunished."[80]

Meanwhile, even organizations that were not directly linked to the resistance—but which posed other challenges to the state's neoliberal agenda—were being targeted in the context of police impunity. On November 28, 2009, the Red de Comercialización Comunitaria Alternativa (Network of Alternative Community Development, COMAL), a *campesino* organization that helps small farmers to market their produce and runs educational campaigns designed to build networks between *campesinos* and social movements, had its offices attacked, computers and money stolen, and employees beaten. I arrived at the COMAL offices in Siguatepeque at around 3:30 p.m. to find the grounds crawling with military and police—notably from the Comando y Batallón de Reacción Antiterrorista (Anti-terrorist Commando Battalion, COBRA) paramilitary units—who quickly detained us near the gate to the compound. The head of the operation explained to my colleague, Adelid Vega, a lawyer working with COFADEH, that the compound was suspected of housing guerrillas, and that the police were investigating a report that weapons were stashed there. When the military/police brigade left, we were finally able to enter the grounds to survey the damage, which was considerable, and were given this update from director José Trinidad Sánchez:

> The police said it was a search-and-seizure of firearms and weapons against the safety of the people. They began searching all the offices, smashing windows to get in. Like all organizations like ours, we have done political work around the coup and our strategy towards it. There were papers on how the coup has been for us and how do we want to refound the country. It is not illegal to talk about it, but when they found this "evidence" they called it "subversive materials." They took everything … and took a lot of reports on community meetings. At the end of the reports were names, which they were very interested in.[81]

Alongside the campaign of terror, the oligarchy used its considerable resources to undermine the political legitimacy of President Zelaya and those who opposed the coup. In a pamphlet distributed by the military in the department of Intibucá on November 14, 2009, the *golpistas* described the resistance as a "boring film":

> Twenty-first century socialism is the same thing as twentieth century communism, only it is more tedious because we know that nothing is going to happen. This boring film is being promoted by criminals such as Fidel Castro, Hugo Chávez, Rafael Correa, Daniel Ortega and in Honduras by drug-dealer Manuel Zelaya Rosales, supported by Latin-American drug cartels ... Right now, the ideas of these criminals are being enforced by threats: bombs, sabotage, burning of businesses, insults, lies and murder ... These people are not civilized. What they are doing is truly criminal and similar to the actions of communists in the 80s in Central-American countries.[82]

The FNRP categorically denied the claims that they were connected to drug traffickers or engaged in bombings and sabotage; there has not been a single identifiable case of such violence being brought against the coup regime even once since the coup took place.[83]

PANTOMIME ELECTIONS

This was the context for the "elections" held by the coup regime on November 29, 2009—widespread repression, military lockdown, state terror, and tight control of the media—hardly circumstances under which democracy will flourish. On the day of the vote, the FNRP urged Hondurans to stay home and boycott the "farce elections," and that is precisely what happened. On election day—a day that is normally a boisterous street party, with people lining up for free meat from the primary political parties whose red and blue flags would be in full display—Honduras was suspiciously quiet and subdued. Most reports from human rights observers across the country suggested that the polling stations had more military and police attending them than civilians, which was certainly the case at the polling stations I visited.

That evening, the TSE itself admitted that only around 1.7 million people voted, in a country of nearly 8 million, with 4.6 million eligible to vote. That makes for a turnout of around 35 percent of eligible voters—about 20 percent of the entire population—the lowest since the return of formal democracy in the early 1980s. Of these, some 7 percent of the votes were reported as blank or spoiled, in many cases spoiled in protest, covered in anti-coup statements and images.[84] Inexplicably, the TSE nonetheless announced a "projected" turnout of 60 percent, which became the number repeated in almost every international news source.[85] The TSE never provided a breakdown of how it came to that number and the only partial explanation it offered for the inconsistent figures was an arbitrary decision to exclude the 1.2 million absentee Hondurans—those living outside the country—from the total number of "eligible voters,"[86] despite the fact that they *were* eligible to vote and many of them did.[87] For its part, the FNRP estimated a turnout of around 30 percent, and Honduran journalist Felix Molina still insists that it was likely less than 25 percent.[88]

A few days after the election, video journalist Jesse Freeston of *The Real News* was able to get into the TSE headquarters and produced a video that documented that the TSE had generated fraudulent voter totals designed to create the illusion that Hondurans had not boycotted the election; one TSE employee admitted that the official results were "pure fabrication."[89] Indeed, in a special issue of *Nueva Sociedad* dedicated to the coup in Honduras, Álvaro Cálix demonstrated that the elections were fraudulent even by the standards of minimal liberal democratic norms.[90] It should not come as any great surprise that the TSE was involved in the fraudulent consolidation of the coup; two of the TSE's three presiding judges were illegally appointed to their positions under coup leader Roberto Micheletti.[91] But most Hondurans connected to the social movements understood that even if the vote-counting process had been carried out legitimately on election day, these elections were still unquestionably a sham or, as Felix Molina put it, a pantomime of a proper democratic process.[92] As the Human Rights Platform explained in its above-mentioned November 28, 2009, document:

> Holding reliable elections does not depend solely on the implementation of sophisticated technology, international observers or the strict adherence to the formal process; it also requires knowing that there was a clean process preceding the elections, produced by a climate of full freedom, one where candidates and the electorate can express themselves openly and in a context of absolute equality, without fear of assassination, torture, detention and incarceration.[93]

Indeed, an interview I conducted with Edward Fox, a former USAID official, Republican Party campaign financier, and an elections observer sent from Washington to legitimize the process, demonstrated quite plainly that the few organizations that went to Honduras for the elections were not interested in investigating anything that was happening away from the polling stations.[94] Fox claimed to have heard nothing about human rights violations, cast suspicion on the groups documenting the violence despite not being able to name a single one of them, and justified his endorsement of the elections by telling me that he had spoken to the US ambassador who is, Fox reminded me, "there all the time."[95] Meanwhile, his organization, the Washington Senior Observer Group, reported that they:

> Witnessed the enthusiastic desire of thousands of Honduran citizens to cast their ballots. Many took time to thank us for our presence today. Without exception, they expressed confidence in the electoral system, pride in exercising their right to vote, and a profound hope that their election is a decisive step toward the restoration of the constitutional and democratic order in Honduras.[96]

They further asserted that they saw "no voter intimidation by any group, individual, or party" and that their observations "coincide with those reported by other observers and by the media throughout Honduras."[97]

Nonetheless, when I asked Edward Fox about those other observers, the groups that had been documenting the violence and terror, he admitted that he had not spoken to any of them. Avoiding them must have taken some effort because, when the Honduran Human Rights Platform presented its report to the TSE on November 28, the US observers were there; in fact, the human rights delegation had their meeting scheduled for 2:00 p.m. but had to wait until well after 4:00 p.m. because TSE officials were meeting with the unofficial US observers. We were all there together, and at one point I overheard the US observers chatting amongst themselves derisively about the human rights group and about Honduras in general. When I confronted Edward Fox on this point, he quickly changed the subject.[98]

Since all the major, international elections-observation organizations refused to validate the Honduran elections, the coup regime worked diligently to acquire the services of like-minded, far-right organizations, like the Washington Senior Observer Group. *Granma International* reported that the job of finding election observers was entrusted to the COHEP president, Amílcar Bulnes, and that he managed to find some 300 to 500 individuals from a variety of right-wing think-tanks and business groups.[99] The list included former Central American right-wing leaders like Alvaro Arzú from Guatemala and Alfredo Cristiani from El Salvador, and representatives from neo-Nazi groups like UnoAmérica, which was linked to an assassination plot against Bolivian president Evo Morales. Far-right lobby groups like the Latin American and Caribbean Network for Liberty, closely tied to the notorious National Endowment for Democracy (NED), were on the list, and I also met representatives of the International Republican Institute (IRI), the international wing of the Republican Party in the United States.[100]

These so-called observers worked very hard to avoid observing that which was patently obvious to most Hondurans. It wasn't just voters who had boycotted the elections; almost all independent candidates in the country withdrew their names, and even many candidates from the moderate wing of the Liberal Party—from which Zelaya himself was drawn—pulled themselves out of the process in public defiance of what they considered farce elections. Indeed, the process that the coup regime put in place could best be described, following the work of Edward Herman and Frank Brodhead in the 1980s, as a "demonstration election": the purpose was never to facilitate any meaningful political participation but, rather, to demonstrate enough of the superficial edifice of democracy to satisfy its international partners that it could appear legitimate enough to support.[101]

Many of the candidates who boycotted the elections were high-profile figures who would have been almost guaranteed to win a first or second term in office had they stood for election. The most obvious example, as noted above, was Carlos H. Reyes, a union leader who was set to run as an independent candidate on a reformist platform that would have likely stolen votes from the centre-left Unificación Democrática (Democratic Unification, UD) and the Partido Innovación y Unidad Social Demócrata (Party of Innovation and Social Democratic Unity, PINU), as well as the presiding Liberal Party. Significantly, President Zelaya had given his endorsement to Reyes rather than the Liberal candidate Edwin Santos. Polls across different points in 2009 had Carlos H. Reyes ranking as high as third out of six presidential candidates in popularity. Reyes was an active member of the FNRP and, on July 30, 2009, he was bludgeoned in the head by a police baton at a demonstration in Tegucigalpa.[102] On November 9, 2009, convinced that there was no chance that the regime would allow legitimate elections to take place, he officially withdrew, stating that "the observers contracted by the Supreme Electoral Tribunal are not a guarantee for the security and transparency of the electoral process because they are the same organizations that have justified the coup d'état."[103] Indeed, Edward Fox's comments are a testament to the wisdom of Reyes' concerns.

Four days after Reyes' withdrawal, he was joined in the boycott by Rodolfo Padilla Sunceri, then mayor of Honduras' second-largest city, San Pedro Sula. Padilla was a member of the moderate wing of the centre-right Liberal Party and was a popular frontrunner in San Pedro Sula, but withdrew his candidacy on November 13, 2009, citing the impossibility of a meaningful democratic process and adding that "the people don't believe in this process."

Another prominent candidate to drop off the ballot was Maria Margarita Zelaya Rivas, vice-presidential candidate for Zelaya's Liberal Party and Manuel Zelaya's cousin. "My resignation speaks," she stated, "for those that cannot express their thoughts for fear that the *de facto* government will take reprisal against them."[104] An additional 110 mayoral candidates and 55 congressional candidates, many of them leading in their respective races, pulled out of the election in recognition of the illegitimacy and unpopularity of the process, though David Matamoros, Secretary of the TSE, claimed in *La Tribuna* that only 0.1 percent of the candidates had dropped out of the election.[105] It is worth repeating here that candidates for these elections had been selected through a process of primaries before the June 2009 coup, with the official TSE convocation taking place on May 29, 2009. The scheduled date for the elections was November 29, 2009, and all of those who withdrew from them had been nominated prior to the break from democratic order.

The centre-left parties referred to above (UD and PINU) faced a difficult choice with regard to the elections, since state recognition as a legal party—and the crucial funding that comes with it—would have been revoked if they withdrew. Both parties were split on the question of whether to participate. UD, in particular, had struggled very hard over the past decade to achieve the legal status it had and throwing that away was unacceptable to many; it was a party organized out of the few activist groups that survived the 1980s and was reliant on the support it got from its official status, including paid employees for parties that gained seats and 350,000 *lempira* for campaign financing.[106] Tomás Andino, who ran for office with UD in 1997, argues that the party was fundamentally co-opted by the oligarchy in 2006 when it entered into an alliance with the National Party. By the time of the coup, UD was a marginal player in the Honduran left, and its decision to participate in the November 2009 elections was disappointing to many, but hardly surprising. César Ham, the leader of UD who had forged the alliance with the National Party in 2006, was widely discredited for supporting the coup and was "rewarded" for his decision with a cabinet appointment in the Lobo regime, which has only further delegitimized UD's role in the resistance.[107] Ham was named the director of the Instituto Nacional Agrario (National Agrarian Institute, INA), by then embroiled in the state's efforts to rollback land reforms.

The regime, predictably, denied that there was any momentum behind a boycott campaign and tried to write-off the boycott as a product of "foreign meddling." Coup leader Roberto Micheletti told the *El Tiempo* newspaper on November 16, 2009, that hundreds of foreigners had been entering the country in order to disrupt Honduran democracy. "We have knowledge of this," he claimed, "our military, supported by our allies and friends, have initiated an investigation that has secured information about people from Venezuela or Nicaragua coming here to try to cause trouble to the electoral process." Micheletti proceeded to use this alleged foreign intervention to justify a massive military presence and the threat of drastic penalties for anyone who tried to disrupt the elections.[108]

Even speaking out against the elections was made dangerous. As noted above, the *El Heraldo* newspaper promised would-be demonstrators that there would be swift punishment for campaigning against the elections, and *El Tiempo* added that calling for any interference to the electoral process could earn a person four to six years in prison.[109] The regime made certain that these were not empty threats. Renowned environmental activist and Goldman Prize-winner Padre Andres Tamayo was charged for calling for an election boycott and, after spending several weeks under house arrest in the Brazilian embassy, he was deported to El Salvador after having lived in Honduras for twenty-six years. Meanwhile, Andrés Pavón, director of prominent human rights organization CODEH, found himself charged with defamation and impeding the elections after making statements expressing fear of more military massacres and encouraging people to stay safe at home on election day.[110]

Such fear was not unfounded. As José Miguel Cruz rightly noted, "The coup was supported and enforced by police officers in the streets who, for years, had been identified as responsible for extrajudicial killings and human rights abuses."[111] In addition to the 12,000 police and 11,000 soldiers on duty on election day, the coup regime called up 5,000 reservists on November 13, 2009, and brought on an estimated 15,000 private security agents from fourteen different companies, temporarily granted military fatigues, weapons, and powers.[112] These heavily armed commandos patrolled the streets, the voting stations, and the highway checkpoints across the country. As I travelled with Honduran human rights observers through different cities and towns in the southern departments on election day, and in the days leading up to it, we were subjected to almost constant stops and searches, and as we sat in community meetings, we heard story after story of intimidation and violence. On the day that the elections took place, I ate dinner with a group of people from a small community in Danlí, who had hung a banner on the main road into town declaring themselves "Melista" (supporters of Mel Zelaya) and saying "no to the elections and yes to the *constituyente*." As we chatted, a group of ten or fifteen military vehicles rumbled past the front door, reinforcing the sense that simply stating opposition to the electoral process was enough to bring state violence to your door.

The boycott was, nevertheless, a demonstration of strength by the movement. Across the country, the decision to stay home and boycott in silence was carried out by most Hondurans; in a few cities, pockets of people chose to heed Manuel Zelaya's contradictory message (broadcast only the day before the elections) to rally in the streets, and where they did they met predictable repression, as in a series of violent clashes in San Pedro Sula.[113] The following day, the movement took to the streets in earnest to celebrate its defiance of the election process. Across the country, tens of thousands made their presence felt; in Tegucigalpa, the movement organized a caravan, which slowly snaked through the labyrinthine streets of the capital city, horns honking, FNRP flags flying, upturned and un-inked pinky fingers in the air in visible demonstration that the people had not voted.[114] The caravan was an awe-inspiring display of the strength of the movement and, above all, it made it impossible for anyone in the capital city to deny that the boycott had been a massive popular demonstration. This is a point worth emphasizing, since so much of the whitewashing of the coup would rest upon the perception that Hondurans had happily and freely participated in the electoral process.

Indeed, it is worth returning to the description I wrote the evening after the elections:

> Honduras today is like an Orwellian nightmare. A façade of calm as soldiers patrol the streets with automatic weapons; a theatrical production of democracy in a state that no longer has a functioning code of law; a discourse of peace that so completely fails to convince, it almost seems like it is intended to mock its victims. Indeed, one placard yesterday read, "2 + 2 = 5? Do not insult us, *golpistas*."[115]

It was all, really, an elaborate piece of theatre. When my flight arrived in the capital a week earlier, packed with North American journalists, the cabin announcement said, "Welcome to Honduras, a country of peace and justice." A week later, as the journalists flew home, the airport kiosks were selling white T-shirts celebrating Honduran democracy. For all the energy the regime was putting into repressing the social movement, it clearly understood that it needed to construct the edifice of legitimacy in the international community in order to bring the coup to its successful completion. This required both an effective mimicry of democratic process and liberal freedoms, and a complicit audience willing to ignore everything beyond that flimsy canvas. Fortunate, indeed, for the *golpistas*, that they were able to count on a few powerful allies to fulfill that role. Chief among them was Canada, which, from the very beginning, was the strongest international partner to the coup; the Honduran oligarchy and armed forces performed a pantomime of democracy and the Canadian state played the chorus. In fact, as the next chapter will demonstrate, Canada played a critical role in ensuring that the events described above were carried out effectively and with impunity.

3 THE VIEW FROM OTTAWA
Seeing and Unseeing the Demise of Democracy

A casual observer of Canada's public statements in the first months following the Honduran coup could be forgiven for thinking that Canadian officials were utterly naïve about the reality in Honduras. Indeed, with statements that repeatedly invoked the themes of peace, restraint, caution, and dialogue, it might have appeared that Canada was just trying to help. But naiveté does not rule Canadian diplomacy, especially not towards a country where Canada is the second largest foreign investor, with foreign direct investment (FDI) of over $600 million and climbing.[1] Rather, Canadian officials used this empty rhetoric to actively mask the brutal reality in Honduras—a reality from which Canadian businesses are benefiting—in what has become an important component of Canada's imperial project.

Indeed, the Canadian state has gone to great lengths to support the violent military dictatorship in Honduras, in spite of its rhetorical commitments to the very values and politics threatened by the coup. Repression and resistance continued throughout the period of Canada's escalating engagement with the Honduran regime, which included Canada's efforts to whitewash that very repression and deny the popularity of the resistance. Thus, the coup fits into the long trajectory of foreign intervention in Honduras which, in its current form, manifests in the collaboration between foreign states and capital, and their local counterparts in the political-military-capitalist elite.

CANADA AND THE COUP

From the outset, it was notable that Canada's response to the coup was among the slowest and softest in the western hemisphere. Consider the reactions from across the hemisphere: while Presidents Chávez and Morales of Venezuela and Bolivia predictably condemned the coup in strong language, even centre-left and liberal governments were swift in their rebuke. A statement from Argentinean president Cristina Fernández de Kirchner read, "I do not hesitate to call this a return to barbarity. All countries of the continent and the entire international community should demand the return of the democratically elected president."[2] The foreign ministry of Ecuador immediately asserted that it would recognize no government in Honduras except that of Manuel Zelaya, and the Brazilian embassy demanded the "immediate and unconditional" return of Zelaya to power. Mauricio Funes of El Salvador expressed his full solidarity with Zelaya, and Fernando Lugo of Paraguay insisted that the *golpistas* should be imprisoned.

Canada, by contrast, waited the entire day before offering a statement. Some fifteen hours after the dramatic footage first hit the airwaves, Canadian Minister of State for the Americas Peter Kent finally echoed international calls for the restitution of the rule of law in Honduras:

> Canada condemns the coup d'état that took place over the weekend in Honduras, and calls on *all parties* to show restraint and to seek a peaceful resolution to the present political crisis, which respects democratic norms and the rule of law, including the Honduran Constitution.[3]

I emphasize "all parties" to highlight Kent's misleading characterization of two sides in conflict, when, in fact, there was only one side in a position to exercise power or restraint: the military and oligarchs who had kidnapped a duly elected president, undermined a legitimate public consultation, and seized dictatorial power by force. Furthermore, Kent makes particular reference to the Honduran Constitution, an interesting choice given that the poll disrupted by the coup was gauging public appetite for redrafting that very Constitution.

If this was a disappointing first response, Canada's position only became more supportive of the *golpistas* over the following months, despite the relentless and unmistakable project of state repression. Canada's official statements over these months served both to obfuscate the truth and misdirect public attention, while its actions offered implicit support to the coup regime. A week after the coup, Peter Kent told the OAS that the international community had tilted too far in favour of Zelaya: "The coup was certainly an affront to the region, but there is a context in which these events happened … there has to be an appreciation of the events that led up to the coup."[4] Indeed, Canada's second official statement on the coup made certain not to tilt towards Zelaya, focusing instead on an insistence that he *not* return to Honduras until the time was right. Before moving into the typical patter of rhetorical calls for non-violence, Kent's statement read:

> In light of the mediation process involving representatives of President Zelaya of Honduras and the *de facto* government this weekend in Costa Rica, Canada wishes to stand with our colleagues in the region and reiterate the call for restraint in the timing of President Zelaya's return to Honduras. A return to Honduras should only occur when a peaceful solution has been found and conditions are appropriate. A return to Honduras prior to a negotiated resolution is strongly discouraged. Actions resulting in violence will not be in the best interests of the people of Honduras.[5]

Remarkable, indeed, that Kent's statement should emphasize the need for restraint from Zelaya; the statement did not even once condemn the coup regime for its ongoing campaign of violence.

From July to September, Peter Kent consistently chided Manuel Zelaya for "recklessly" attempting to re-enter the country of which he was the legal head of state, and insisted that he and his supporters negotiate a settlement in good faith with the coup regime, again misleadingly suggesting that Zelaya and the FNRP bore some responsibility for the crisis and that the coup regime was in a legitimate bargaining position. This presentation of events was repeated often, both in international statements and in the domestic media: for instance, in July, Peter Kent told the CBC that Zelaya's attempts to re-enter the country were "very unhelpful," an extraordinary statement given that Canada still recognized Zelaya as the legal president with six months left in his term.[6] All the while, Kent's statements carefully avoided any direct criticism of the coup regime, repeatedly "calling on all parties to show restraint," and implicitly blamed Zelaya and the FNRP for the violence they faced. When Zelaya returned to Honduras in September and was barricaded into the Brazilian embassy, Kent's statement expressed concern with "the violence that erupted in the aftermath of President Zelaya's *sudden* return to Honduras."[7] The use of the word "sudden" here implies that the irregularity of the situation should be attributed to Zelaya, as if the violence that was unleashed by the coup government was caused by Zelaya's "sudden" action, not the rather sudden kidnapping of a president and fabrication and forgery of his resignation letter.

All the while, Canada endorsed a Costa Rican-brokered negotiation between Zelaya and the coup regime, but it was evident from the start that the coup regime had no intention of letting go of power; the negotiation served to stall for time while the regime prepared for the November elections, which would provide a more satisfactory "resolution" to the crisis. Canada repeatedly invoked the negotiations as the best way forward, giving undeserved legitimacy to the coup regime, while quite predictably, the talks broke down not long before the scheduled elections.[8] What was perhaps most interesting about Canada's encouragement of the negotiations, though, was the fact that the emphasis on this process allowed for an important shift in Canada's language about the coup itself: by October, it was no longer being called a "coup" but, rather, a "political crisis." An October 9 statement referenced the "political crisis" six times without one mention of a "coup." Canada never again referred to a "coup" at all until several years had passed and the regime was fully integrated into the international community.[9]

The November elections provided the key opportunity for Canada to embrace the coup regime. Even before the elections, with international organizations refusing to send observers to what was so transparently an undemocratic process, Canada laid the groundwork for its support in the following statement:

> Canada is disappointed with the lack of progress on the implementation of the Tegucigalpa-San José Accord, signed by both parties on October 30. Unfortunately, this has meant that Canada could not provide support for the electoral process. Although the elections will be watched closely by the international community and members of civil society, there will be no formal observation missions from the Organization of American States or the UN. The peaceful conduct of the November 29 elections will be an important step in moving out of the current political impasse. For the sake of all Hondurans, we urge that they be run freely and fairly, in a safe and secure environment.[10]

It is an astonishing feat of doublespeak that allows Kent to simultaneously acknowledge that the international community is refusing to formally observe the elections—in clear recognition of their illegitimacy—while he *also* insists that the process will be a key step in resolving the "political crisis." How could illegitimate elections possibly be part of a process of reasserting electoral representative democracy?

As the predictably fraudulent results came in, it became clear that Porfirio "Pepe" Lobo of the National Party was to be given the presidency. In contrast to his tardy response to the coup in June, this time Peter Kent was the first foreign minister to offer his congratulations to Lobo, who lost the 2005 elections to Zelaya and had been a strong supporter of the coup. In his statement, Kent lauded the Honduran people for engaging in "relatively peaceful and orderly" elections, run "freely and fairly, with a strong turnout, and with no major violence."[11] Given the military and police lockdown, the massive, daily demonstrations, the complete silence of what was left of the critical Honduran press, and the political graffiti that covered nearly every edifice in every corner of the capital, it seemed utterly absurd to suggest that Honduras had just witnessed free, peaceful, fair elections. Indeed, the reality was quite the contrary.

But the fabrication of legitimate elections in 2009 was the basis for Canada's re-engagement with Honduras during Lobo's first year. On January 27, 2010, Lobo was inaugurated as Honduran president while over half a million people protested in the streets—the second largest public demonstration since the June 2009 coup. Most of the Honduran corporate media refused to cover the demonstration; one station that attempted to show the size of the protest was prevented by the military from using its news helicopter.[12] In the weeks prior to Lobo's inauguration, coup leader Roberto Micheletti was declared a member of Congress for the rest of his life, an unprecedented appointment for a nominally democratic body, and immediately after Lobo took office he successfully proposed and passed legal immunity for all of the military leaders of the coup.[13]

Peter Kent quickly offered Canada's congratulations, thanked Lobo for "generously" providing former president Zelaya safe passage to exile in the Dominican Republic, and repeated the now-typical distortions, calling the military coup a "political crisis" and calling Lobo's regime a "unity government."[14] Meanwhile, Kent's statement was silent on the assassination of Walter Trochez, a twenty-seven-year-old LGBT activist who had been documenting human rights abuses by the coup regime, just weeks prior to Lobo's inauguration. Even the US state department had issued a statement, three days earlier, demanding an investigation into Trochez's death. Meanwhile, Peter Kent's statement congratulating Pepe Lobo was published on the same day that he published a seperate public statement regarding Venezuela. Kent criticized the Chávez government in Venezuela for shutting down six media outlets, describing this as "evidence of shrinking democratic space," and added that "freedom of expression and access to information from a wide range of sources are fundamental elements of healthy democracy."[15] Stirring words, but even if we accept Kent's report on Venezuela as accurate, we must note the hypocrisy in his position: that which was labelled "shrinking democratic space" in Venezuela was called "a process of renewal" in Honduras.[16]

Indeed, Peter Kent's trip to Venezuela in January 2010 saw him meet with a variety of groups in the right-wing opposition to the Chávez government, though he was unable to find time to meet with a single representative of the official government.[17] In a remarkable reversal, his time in Honduras less than a month later had him meet with not just Pepe Lobo but also three of his Cabinet ministers, including Arturo Corrales (former spokesperson of coup leader Roberto Micheletti) and Mario Canahuati (son of *maquiladora* magnate Juan Canahuati and former president of the Consejo Hondureño de la Empresa Privada (Honduran Council of Private Enterprise, COHEP). Nonetheless, Kent did not meet with any of the myriad community and civil society organizations documenting—and often experiencing—the violence and terrorization being perpetrated by the state.[18] Justifying his aggressive statements on Venezuela, Kent told the press, "In the past, our obsession with consensus and resolving differences within the [OAS] has sometimes meant that countries don't speak out against those who are less diligent in defending the principles of democracy [for] which we all officially pledged to defend." Again, this reflects a profoundly hypocritical position in light of Canada's relationship to a regime in Honduras that took power by military force.[19]

There was a further perverse irony in Kent's sanctimony with regard to the alleged repression of the press in Caracas. The veteran journalist-turned-minister never once bothered to speak of the complete crackdown on the Honduran press after the coup, which saw all news outlets, TV, radio, and print, forced to choose between supporting the coup or being shutdown, sometimes violently. Radio Globo, as noted in the previous chapter, was under constant harassment since the coup and during Pepe Lobo's administration; its offices were ransacked in September 2009, its signal was disrupted on numerous occasions in 2009 and 2010, and its reporters were consistently attacked.[20] For instance, *Tras la Verdad* (Seeking the Truth) was one of Globo's most popular shows and was very critical of the coup regime; its host, Luis Galdámez, was shot on September 4, 2010, by gunmen outside his home in Tegucigalpa. He survived the attack, but as he said on the air shortly after, "the threats are constant, the persecution is constant."[21] Felix Molina, one of Honduras' most popular radio journalists and a firm supporter of the FNRP, told me that he has to be careful not to be photographed so that the authorities cannot link his face to his name.[22] Though he managed to escape direct violence in the immediate aftermath of the coup, Molina found himself a target of assassins in 2012 and again in 2016; in fact, he survived two separate attempts on his life on May 2, 2016.[23]

But Canada's support for the regime that was violently clamping down on the media was steadfast. On February 20, 2010, Peter Kent concluded a series of meetings with Pepe Lobo, describing his time in Honduras as a "fruitful visit," and praising Lobo's efforts towards "national reconciliation."[24] The day after Kent's statement was published, Claudia Larisa Brizuela, daughter of a critical Honduran radio journalist and union organizer, was assassinated on the front steps of her house in San Pedro Sula, killed in retribution for her father's involvement in the peaceful resistance to the coup.[25] Canada issued no statements on Brizuela's murder, and the pro-coup Honduran newspaper *La Tribuna* insisted that the police were "hot on the trail" of gang members suspected of the killing, though it was obvious to her father, Pedro Brizuela, that she was targeted in order to silence him.

Indeed, the weeks leading up to Kent's "fruitful visit" were particularly bloody. On February 3, the body of Vanessa Zepeda Alonzo, anti-coup activist in the Sindicato de Trabajadores del Instituto Hondureño de Seguridad Social (Social Security Institute Workers Union, SITRAIHSS) was thrown out of a car in Tegucigalpa. On February 15, gunmen on motorcycles shot and killed Julio Fúnez Benítez, an active member of the Sindicato de Trabajadores del Servicio Autónomo Nacional de Acueductos y Alcantarillados (Aqueducts and Sewer System Workers Union, SITRASANAA), outside his home in Brisas de Olancho, Tegucigalpa. On February 17, critical journalist Enrique Gudiel from Danlí found his seventeen-year-old daughter Dara dead. He had already been given a warning to end his critical broadcasts; his daughter had been kidnapped once before. When Gudiel found her the second time, she had been hanged. Strange fruit, indeed, that Canada's representative was endorsing in Honduras.[26]

Violent retribution for anti-coup journalism became an expected risk after June 2009, and it was particularly pronounced in the early part of Pepe Lobo's regime. Despite reporting his regular death threats to the Inter-American Commission on Human Rights (IACHR) while covering the ongoing agrarian conflicts in the Aguán Valley, Nahún Palacios was shot repeatedly in his car on March 14, 2010, by gunmen with AK-47s. Nine months earlier, on June 30, 2009—just two days after the coup—Honduran soldiers had broken into his home and held his children at gunpoint while destroying his video equipment. No proper investigation was conducted into his death, and his body was exhumed in August 2010 with the case left "unsolved." Palacios was news director at Aguán Television Canal 5, and had covered FNRP events and the repression of poor farmers by prominent *golpista* Miguel Facussé.[27]

BREAKING THE SOCIAL MOVEMENT

All of this had to be selectively and wilfully ignored in order for Canada to maintain its position in support of the Lobo government, and the above description is but a small piece of the overall picture of repression that has characterized Honduras under the coup regime. Indeed, direct targeting of movement activists is not the only form that the violence took; the rupture of the rule of law at the highest level accelerated the breakdown of all civil society institutions that worked to limit the aggression of local and foreign oligarchs, such that the capitalist classes and armed forces were able to crack down on any person or group that threatened their interests—whether directly linked to the FNRP or not—with impunity.

An illustrative example could be found in the ongoing conflict between *campesino* communities in the Aguán Valley and the estate of Miguel Facussé, a member of one of Honduras' most powerful families and one of the central figures behind the coup. Members of the peasant community of Guadalupe Carney were asserting their access to land to which they believed they had a legal right but that had been forcibly taken over by Facussé. In fact, according to a FIAN-Honduras document of November 16, 2010, the land was bought in 1977—illegally according to the Constitution at the time—by a US citizen who was forced to turn the land over to the Honduran government in 1983 for the construction of a joint US–Honduran military base. When the base—which had been used to train the Honduran military in torture techniques[28]—was dismantled, the land was sold to wealthy cattle ranchers, despite protestations in the community that the land was owned by the state and legally ought to be turned over to landless peasants through the Instituto Nacional Agrario (National Agrarian Institute, INA). In 1993, after much struggle, the state formally agreed to distribute this land among landless *campesinos* in the region, but the cattle ranchers who had moved in did not cede the land and the state refused to confront them, leaving *campesino* groups to defend their land on their own against the powerful and wealthy oligarchs who routinely used private security companies to attack and harass *campesinos*.[29]

Not surprisingly, this already dangerous conflict for Honduran *campesinos* was made far worse by the June 2009 coup, as its architects were members of the same oligarchy that dominates the Aguán Valley. Miguel Facussé—one of Pepe Lobo's closest associates—occupied several hundred acres in the region and his hired guns showed little restraint in efforts to evict the *campesinos*; in November 2010, four activists in the Movimiento Unificado Campesino del Aguán (Unified Campesino Movement of the Aguán, MUCA) were killed by private security guards—some of them ex-paramilitaries from Colombia—working for Facussé.[30] The attack, which also left four people wounded and two "disappeared," was carried out as part of an eviction of members of MUCA claiming their legal right to the land. Yet, Honduran police did not arrive until the violent eviction was in its eighth hour, and they did nothing to assist the MUCA activists; the end result of the arrival of the police was the completion of the eviction and the maintenance of Facussé's occupation.[31]

MUCA had spent nearly a decade building its legal case around the land, but it consistently found that whenever its cases came close to bearing fruit, the prosecutors in question would be bribed or threatened and the cases would be thrown out. Nevertheless, MUCA grew in strength and continued to file lawsuits and stage demonstrations—including a dramatic thirty-six-hour occupation by some 500 *campesinos* of a key stretch of highway in February 2006—just a few days after Manuel Zelaya took office.[32] MUCA was able to reach an agreement with the Zelaya government to have the situation properly investigated and, unlike his predecessors, Zelaya appeared to be making good on his promises.[33] MUCA maintained its pressure—occupying one of Facussé's African palm processing plants on June 8, 2009—and as of June 12, 2009, MUCA had a second agreement with Zelaya to have a detailed legal report on MUCA's claim to the land within thirty days. When I spoke to Joni Rivas, one of MUCA's co-directors, in May 2012, he was quick to note that although MUCA had been vocally and publicly demanding action from the Zelaya government, they had to acknowledge that his administration had been somewhat receptive to those demands. On June 19, 2009, Zelaya visited the Aguán personally, to guarantee that the land would be returned to the *campesinos*, and the oligarchy responded by attempting to assassinate Fabio Ochoa, a lawyer working on MUCA's case, on June 23, 2009.[34]

Five days later, Zelaya was overthrown and the coup regime subsequently reversed all of the progress made under Zelaya by the introduction of overwhelming physical force, including, in one case, the complete destruction of an entire community. On July 13, 2011, Amnesty International's Canadian office issued an urgent call for support for the victims of military/police attacks against the community of Rigores, which had left over 500 people homeless and displaced:

> The eviction order was issued on May 23, but the community was not informed. The police arrived in Rigores at 10:00 am on June 24 and told community members that they had two hours to pack up and leave. At around 2:00 pm, the police began

> to destroy communal buildings, people's homes and their belongings. Nobody was offered alternative housing, resettlement or access to productive land, or compensation, either in advance of or since the eviction. Nor was anyone guaranteed safe access to tend their crops, many of which were destroyed during the eviction.
>
> Around 80 people, mainly women and children, have taken shelter in the Rigores Community Centre, about 3 km away. The centre is not designed for people to live in. The building is overcrowded, and lets in rainwater, leaving half the building constantly wet. The centre has very few toilets and washing facilities. The community members, particularly young children, are at risk of disease. The community depends on the land from which they were evicted in Rigores for their survival.[35]

Just days after the Amnesty International report, on July 17, 2011, two more *campesinos* from MUCA were killed. The following week, on July 23, 2011, one of MUCA's leaders, Julian Alvarenga, was killed in a marketplace where he was buying food with a friend, who was also wounded in the attack.[36] As of my May 2012 interview with Joni Rivas, MUCA reported that hundreds of its members had been detained and charged with crimes—often theft—and fifty-six *campesinos* had been assassinated by paramilitaries, police, and military in the service of large landowners like Facussé.[37]

The coup also provided an opening for the state to crack down on Honduran teachers, whose union of over 65,000 members, the Federación de Organizaciones Magisteriales de Honduras (Federation of Teachers Organizations, FOMH), has been among Honduras' strongest and most defiant civil society sectors over the past decade. Between 1997 and 2009, teachers managed to pressure four consecutive governments into writing, signing, and actually implementing the Teachers' Statute, which institutionalized regular pay increases and benefits.[38] The teachers' unions were instrumental in pushing Manuel Zelaya to adopt a number of reform-minded positions, and they were an important component in the building of the CNRP and, later, the FNRP. Between June 2009 and June 2011, teachers engaged in a variety of job actions, including a hunger strike in June 2010 to protest firings of school officials connected to the FNRP,[39] and two major strikes in August and October of that same year in response to the Lobo government's refusal to pay millions of dollars in back pay and an estimated $159 million in "missing" pension money.[40]

Predictably, the teachers experienced severe state violence. Popular high school teacher Blas López was discovered dead from gunshot wounds on January 30, 2010, just three days after Pepe Lobo was inaugurated. In March 2010, well-known teacher and activist José Manuel Flores was shot to death in front of his students at the high school where he taught.[41] A year later, on March 18, 2011, Ilse Ivania Velázquez Rodriguez was killed during a police attack on the offices of the Instituto Nacional de Previsión del Magisterio (National Institute for Teachers, INPREMA), which the teachers had occupied to demand the millions of dollars owed to their pension fund.[42]

Alongside the campaign of violence, Lobo and his associates used their domination of the Honduran media to paint a masterful smear campaign against the teachers, calling their strikes "human rights violations" and suggesting that the teachers were akin to terrorists.[43] The public campaign against the teachers helped spur on the creation of largely pro-coup parents' organizations that helped bring momentum to the regime's clamp down by delegitimizing the teachers' demands;[44] that is, teachers were criticized in the context of their particular material struggles—around the underfunded, understaffed, and overstretched education system—and this made it easier for the regime to delegitimize the broader coup resistance, in which they played a crucial role. The mobilization of public anger towards the teachers was manifested in direct and sometimes violent actions by parents against teachers' strikes, and made it easier for the state to justify its own crackdown on teachers in the resistance.[45]

Meanwhile, far from reining in the violence, the Lobo government increasingly facilitated and encouraged it through a series of new laws that emboldened the already deeply repressive apparatus. In November 2010, the regime passed new "anti-terrorist" laws, which criminalized a variety of movement organizations and severely restricted rights of free association. In the months that followed, Congress amended the Constitution to allow police to forcibly enter people's homes without a warrant and to detain people without charge for up to forty-eight hours.[46] With help from its North American partners, the Honduran regime drafted and passed a related law that empowered the police and armed forces to intercept peoples' private communications for surveillance.[47] What is more, extensions to the definition of the crime of "sedition" allowed the Honduran police, according to the United Nations High Commissioner for Human Rights (UNHCHR), to arrest anyone "engaged in actions with a political dimension, such as painting graffiti with a political message or the simple act of participating in a political demonstration."[48] Lobo also proposed the creation of a new tax on businesses but, rather than use it to moderately redistribute wealth, he intended to earmark the money for increased security costs. The tax was meant to cover Lobo's commitment to the police of an additional 1.5 billion *lempira* in each of the next five years and, as Felix Molina puts it, reinforce the relationship wherein "the oligarchy pays for the police force it wants."[49]

Far from ushering in a new era of unity, as the Canadian government claimed, the consolidation of the coup government made matters significantly worse for groups and individuals either connected to the social movement or engaged in any activity that could undermine the interests of the oligarchy, the narco gangs, the state, or the armed forces. On February 25, 2011, José Trinidad Sánchez, executive director of the Red de Comercialización Comunitaria Alternativa (Network for Alternative Community Trade, COMAL), received a text message that read:

> Trinidad WE KNOW WHERE YOU ARE YOU LIVE IN EL PORVENIR your days are limited so enjoy what you have robbed from Comal as of today count down your days you are being watched you dog.[50]

Less than a year earlier, Trinidad's twenty-five-year-old son had his head slammed into a wall by police accusing him of being a Cuban spy. I spoke with him in 2009 when the COMAL offices were first ransacked by the military and, as we surveyed the damage, he told me, "We represent the poorest people here. We help them to sell their product, but we also teach them why they are poor. For this, we are a threat."[51]

To be interpreted as a threat, then, is to be targeted for violence. Cases like that of Trinidad Sánchez are common, and the patterns are repeated in every sector that seems to present a challenge to the current order. Labour unions continued to be aggressively harassed by state violence, as on March 1, 2011, when Eduardo Argueta Santos, an active member of the Sindicato de Trabajadores de la Industria de la Bebida (Beverage Industry Workers Union, STIBYS) who had recently denounced the systematic targeting of trade unionists, was shot in the face on his way to work.[52] In the same month, Miriam Miranda, renowned Garífuna activist and a leader in OFRANEH, was arrested, beaten, and detained for hours without access to medical attention. In the litany of racially charged insults that she received from police, it was clear that the assault was politically motivated.[53] In February 2011, Annarela Velez was targeted because she was the vice-president of C-Libre, a civil liberties watchdog organization. Students who demanded free education were routinely attacked: in 2011, hundreds of students were incarcerated or charged with criminal offenses and many faced extreme violence, like seventeen-year-old Nahun Alexander Guerra, who was killed on August 22, 2011.

Human rights observers themselves, not surprisingly, are directly targeted. In December 2011, COFADEH released a report that detailed the myriad ways that its work, and that of other human rights organizations, was being undermined, ranging from direct violence against human rights observers and advocates to attempts by the state to criminalize their organizations using the new anti-terrorist laws.[54] COFADEH's own staff, for instance, were regularly threatened and intimidated with text messages or phone calls, threatening violence against individuals and their loved ones, often containing personal information designed to make the victim paranoid. Targeted individuals were followed in the streets, by men on motorcycles or by vehicles with dark, tinted windows. Sometimes the vehicles would park outside people's homes for days. Other times the same vehicle would pass its target multiple times daily, over a sustained period of time. Warning shots might be fired, menacing notes could be left on doorsteps and doors, armed men would sometimes actually force themselves into people's homes. The regularity with which these threats were followed by actual physical attacks made them genuinely and profoundly terrifying for the victims.[55]

Meanwhile, by the end of 2011, over 650 human rights workers—individuals working feverishly to document this campaign of terror—were facing criminal charges as a result of their work.[56] Feminist and women's groups consistently reported that their attempts to document and defend human rights abuses against women were met with open hostility from state authorities. Gladys Lanza, veteran activist in the women's movement in Honduras and president of the Movimiento de Mujeres por la Paz "Visitación Padilla" (Visitación Padilla Women's Peace Movement), described an example of the routine violence she and her colleagues face:

> We live in fear. We can't go out at night. One woman who works here [documenting violence against women] was assaulted right in front of our building. We took a video of the assault to the police and they did nothing. She was badly beaten, her clothes were ripped, she had bruises on her arms, her things were taken. But the police did nothing.[57]

This is not an exceptional situation but, rather, the norm. Organizers and workers in the women's organization Centro de Estudio de la Mujer–Honduras (Centre for the Study of Women in Honduras, CEM–H) were, for instance, constantly harassed and intimidated by armed men who followed them on motorcycles, entered their homes without warrants, and sent threatening messages while they tried to organize demonstrations around the Day

Against Violence Against Women in 2010. The demonstrations, too, were subjected to repressive violence from local and national authorities.[58]

What is more, the extreme violence meted out by the state since 2009 exacerbated already existing patterns of violence in Honduras. Gladys Lanza reported that after the coup, violence against women rose by 50 percent. In 2009, there were 108 women murdered before the coup, but over 300 women were murdered in its aftermath, between July and December. These figures only represent those women who were killed; they do not include the tens of thousands of women who were beaten, raped, tortured, or subjected to other forms of violence.[59] Lanza added that going to the police was hardly an option for most women: "Many times it is in the very police stations where they are attacked and raped."[60]

The grafting of direct political violence onto a pre-existing matrix of social violence is crucial for understanding this moment in Honduras, and is perhaps best exemplified in the acceleration of the extrajudicial killings of youths, described earlier. Though the killings received a fair bit of attention in the late 1990s, this violence actually persisted throughout the 2000s; *Casa Alianza* reported that between 1998 and 2009 there were nearly 5,000 violent deaths of youths under twenty-three years of age. After the coup, the number of youth killings shot up even higher: in 2008, over 2,100 youths were killed but, in 2009, the total exceeded 2,500.[61] As in the case of violence against women, the coup served to invigorate and empower the forces of reaction: an existing culture of impunity for killing urban poor youth was buttressed by an example of impunity at the highest level. Meanwhile, the endorsement of violence and the entrenchment of the Honduran right made it easy for the definition of the "dangerous youth" to be expanded to encompass political activists, so that violence against *both* politicized and non-politicized youth increased.[62] Indeed, while observers from the Global North often demand to see specific, verifiable cases and figures for "political killings" or "coup-related violence," the reality is that the coup served to exacerbate existing and ongoing violence and further blur the distinction between "political" and "common" criminality, such that a neat separation of these categories is neither possible nor meaningful.

TRUTH AND RECONCILIATION?

In light of the ongoing repressive campaign pursued by the Lobo regime, one can only reflect on its creation of a so-called Truth and Reconciliation Commission with mirthless irony. The commission was passed into Honduran law on April 13, 2010, and held its investigations between May 4, 2010 and July 7, 2011, concurrent to the repression documented above. It was widely and immediately discredited as another sham for the whitewashing of the regime. On the day it was inaugurated, Berta Oliva of COFADEH noted that the presidential decree that established the commission did not even admit that what happened in June 2009 was, in fact, a coup d'état. She added that any meaningful attempt to bring reconciliation of any kind would require that all sides of a dispute be included in the process; naturally, Lobo hand-picked the commissioners to ensure that the results came out favourably for the *golpistas*.[63] That COFADEH—and countless other groups that opposed the coup—continued to face violence while the commission conducted its inquiry made the legitimacy of its findings a doubtful proposition.

Undaunted by these critiques, Canada enthusiastically supported the Truth and Reconciliation Commission and was eager to send a representative to sit on the commission. Peter Kent described the commission as "essential to advancing the process of national reconciliation," and Canada provided both political endorsement of the commission and logistical support by sending Canadian corporate law consultant Michael Kergin to sit as a commissioner. Peter Kent's office announced its congratulations to Kergin, claiming without irony that "Canada was deeply involved in all efforts to reach a peaceful, negotiated solution to the political impasse in Honduras, and has committed to assisting the country with its reconciliation process."[64] Kergin, Kent noted, was a "distinguished Canadian diplomat" with "extensive experience in the Americas."[65]

As it happens, "distinguished" is precisely how corporate law firm Bennett-Jones described Michael Kergin when it hired him earlier in 2009 to be a senior consultant. "Mr. Kergin has had a distinguished career in public service," said CEO Hugh McKinnon,[66] whose firm specializes in matters related to energy and resource-extraction companies and describes itself as having a "sterling profile as the leading energy and natural resources firm in the country."[67] However, what distinguishes Michael Kergin most—with respect to his role on the Honduran Truth Commission—must be his connection to another infamous Latin American coup d'état: the 1973 overthrow of Chilean president Salvador Allende. Kergin joined Canada's foreign service in 1967 and in the 1970s he was posted to New York, Cameroon, and, most notably, Chile.

It is worth pausing briefly to reflect on Canada's foreign policy behaviour towards Chile during Kergin's era. When democratic elections came out in favour of socialist candidate Salvador Allende in 1970, Canada immediately suspended all foreign aid and petitioned the IMF to withdraw support from Chile. When Allende invited Prime Minister Pierre Trudeau to Santiago, he refused. This remarkably hostile attitude towards a democratically elected government stood in stark contrast to Canada's position in 1973, when Allende was overthrown by a violent, CIA–orchestrated military coup. Within three weeks of the September 11 coup, as Augusto Pinochet consolidated power through fear and violence, Canadian Ambassador Andrew Ross wrote to Ottawa that there was "no useful purpose to withholding recognition unduly" of Pinochet's regime, and that to do so might "delay Chile's eventual return to the democratic process."[68]

That refusing to recognize a military regime on the basis of the illegality of its accession and the violence of its rule could be called "withholding recognition unduly" is remarkable in itself, as is the half-hearted hope for Chile's "eventual" return to democracy. Pinochet's dictatorship was one of the most notorious in recent Latin American history, and Canada's support for it certainly did not hasten the return to democracy; Pinochet held power for some seventeen years and he died as a process had been set in motion to have him indicted by an international tribunal for crimes against humanity. But in 1973, Canada happily extended its arms to his regime, reopening trade relations and foreign aid, which amounted to over $1 billion in aid and loans—including money loaned for the purpose of purchasing Canadian military technology for the state and its secret police agency (DINA)—and the same amount in direct foreign investment.[69]

While Kergin himself was likely only marginally involved in establishing Canadian policy towards Chile in this period, it is instructive to witness the similarities between Canada's position on Chile in the 1970s and its position in Honduras in the 2000s. Moreover, Kergin's institutional location and experience in Chile in the 1970s speaks volumes about the perspective he would bring to bear on the Honduran coup. Following his time in Chile, Kergin was named Canada's ambassador to Cuba, a post he held from 1986 to 1989,[70] a period in which Canada largely served as the eyes and ears of the United States; US state department officials acknowledged that Canada provided the best military intelligence it had on Cuba, as Canada's Communications Security Establishment (CSE) used the Canadian embassy in Havana as an interception point for the private communications of high-ranking Cuban officials.[71] After his time spying on Cuba, Kergin filled a variety of diplomatic posts in Washington, primarily that of ambassador (2000–2005), after which he entered into semi-retirement with the corporate law firm Bennett-Jones.

Bennett-Jones claims to be "a leading business law firm founded and focused on principles of professional excellence, integrity, respect, and independent thought."[72] Those lofty claims, however, stand in stark contradiction to their actions and the clients they represent. In 2012, their website boasted of their work on behalf of much-maligned Canadian mining company Barrick Gold, advocacy for Compass Petroleum Ltd., purchases by Canadian subsidiaries of British Petroleum, and other work with a variety of similar corporations.[73] Bennett-Jones had experience in Honduras directly, in its work on behalf of Canadian investors who were defrauded by the Canadian owners of the Merendon mining project in Honduras.[74] It is clear that Michael Kergin had a great deal of expertise with respect to international trade and corporate law. It is unclear how that should qualify him to sit on a human rights commission following a coup whose leaders were cosy with the firms that Kergin represents in his day job.

Nevertheless, in the context of Canada's broader interests in Honduras, which will be sketched out in the next chapter, Kergin was a perfect fit for the role. His diplomatic postings in other Latin American countries provided some legitimacy for his inclusion in the panel while his strong connection to the Canadian corporate sector ensured that he would not oppose the new regime. In addition to Kergin, the commission was headed by former Guatemalan vice-president Eduardo Stein, and the other commissioners were former Peruvian justice minister María Amadilia, and Julieta Castellanos and Jorge Omar Casco, president and former president respectively of the Universidad Nacional Autónoma de Honduras (National Autonomous University of Honduras, UNAH), both of whom supported the coup.[75] This was, in effect, a coalition composed of Pepe Lobo's arms-length allies, proposing to investigate claims of human rights violations while they continued to take place. As Annie Bird succinctly put it, "While the US and Canadian governments ... assist the Honduran government in creating the illusion of 'reconciliation,' death squads assassinate journalists, teachers and unionists."[76]

Indeed, it is worth underlining the fact that Canada's participation in the commission flew in the face of a number of international organizations that vehemently rejected the legitimacy of the project. The Center for Justice and International Law (CEJIL), drawing on reports from the Inter-American Commission on Human Rights (a subcommittee of the OAS), detailed the circumstances that made the Honduran Truth Commission irredeemably flawed and concluded that "far from providing support for a serious process of reconciliation, they may generate new sources of indignation."[77]

Among other things, CEJIL noted that the commissioners were handpicked supporters of the regime, that it was not empowered to investigate human rights abuses, that the perpetrators of the coup had already been granted legal amnesty for their actions, and that Pepe Lobo had specifically expressed that the commission was "not for judging anybody, but rather for finding reconciliation for the Honduran people,"[78] to which the CEJIL report responded by insisting that "avoiding the assessing of responsibility is a guarantee that impunity will be perpetuated."[79]

The commission released its findings just over a year later, on July 7, 2011, timed to coincide with the signing of the Cartagena Accord and the reintegration of Honduras into the OAS. Predictably, the commission offered little more than bland recommendations for minor reform to Honduran governance structures, expending much energy on detailed speculation around the possibility of corruption in the Zelaya government, but refusing to place any direct responsibility for the violence and repression of the coup and its fallout on any of the individuals involved in actually perpetrating it. While the commission acknowledged that what happened on June 28, 2009, was, indeed, a coup d'état, it worked hard to bury the coup in a context of constitutional violations by the Zelaya government.

Canada's representative, Michael Kergin, reflected on his experiences on the commission in September 2012 in a short article that is an excellent articulation of the commission's position and, especially, Canada's angle within it. As background to the coup, Kergin's piece details, rather extensively, speculation that Zelaya's government was implicated in corruption. After exhausting every possible accusation of corruption and illegality, Kergin briefly acknowledges that it is all hearsay and none of it could be proven, before reaching the conclusion that all of the primary figures in the coup d'état were implicated in actions that broke with the 1982 Constitution.[80] Cleverly, then, Kergin leaves the impression that, while no one quite followed the letter of the law, the crisis was fomented by Zelaya, who had increasingly become a puppet of Hugo Chávez, and who, in pursuing the constituent assembly in the first place, had "borrowed a leaf from the Chávez playbook."[81] Indeed, the mild critique of the *golpistas* comes at the tail end of many pages of speculative denouncements of Zelaya's behaviour, ranging from "rampant rumours" of Venezuelan development money "funnelled" to labour and peasant organizations and "slush funds," to the "abrupt" raising of the minimum wage without congressional approval, to "peaked anxiety over President Zelaya's closeness to Chavez." Meanwhile, Kergin consistently presents the Honduran

Armed Forces, Congress, and Supreme Court as acting with restraint in the face of irrational and dangerous provocations by Zelaya.[82]

Kergin reiterates Canada's early claims that the November 2009 elections were legitimate, free, and fair, and that the Lobo government is therefore legitimate. Meanwhile, he expends just one paragraph describing the "clumsy" reaction of the armed forces to the rising of Zelaya's "partisans," noting that a dozen people were killed by "disproportionate use of force," and that eight other people appeared to have been assassinated. Following Peter Kent's portrayal of Zelaya's attempts to re-enter Honduras in 2009 as "reckless," Kergin describes Zelaya's efforts as "melodramatic" and implicitly connects the increased repression in that period to Zelaya's behaviour. In describing the process of the commission itself, Kergin acknowledges that Zelaya and the resistance—again labelled "Zelaya's partisans"—refused to participate and created a rival truth commission which, despite the efforts of the official commission, would not co-operate with his.[83]

Kergin rather ironically relates the commission's finding that the Honduran Constitution needs reform, offers a number of other banal observations about the need for more transparent governance and rule of law, and presents recommendations for reparations for "verifiable" cases of human rights abuses. Despite acknowledging that it was a coup d'état, Kergin describes Honduras' "former president testing its borders," conveniently forgetting that Zelaya was still legally the president when he "tested" those borders.[84] He also offered a partial explanation of the post-coup violence as being based on a "traditional culture of violence in Honduras," a statement that smacks of a kind of colonial victim-blaming; since Hondurans are "traditionally" violent, according to Kergin, we shouldn't be too critical of one group of Hondurans for being violent to another.[85] Instead, presumably, a more "civilized" state should intervene to make them less violent, even though that same "civilized" state is, inevitably, implicated in inflicting violence of one sort or another upon the subjects of its teaching.[86]

Kergin's colonial arrogance stretched as far as to claim—in spite of a nation-wide social movement that was demanding a reopening of the Honduran Constitution to popular amendment—that Hondurans did not like Zelaya's version of participatory democracy, preferring instead "the Honduran norm" of representative democracy and the two-party system.[87] Kergin seems to imply that Hondurans just didn't want to have too much say in how their lives were governed and preferred for someone to tell them what to do, an absurd claim to anyone paying any attention to the actual organizing and actions of Hondurans over the past two decades.[88] In light of Kergin's reflections, then, it is hardly surprising that Canada gushed with enthusiasm at the commission's findings and its tepid criticism of the regime; newly appointed Minister of State for the Americas Diane Ablonczy expressed hope "that Hondurans will never again experience such an ordeal," ignoring the rather obvious fact that the ordeal was ongoing.[89] Further emphasizing Canada's complicity in the project to whitewash the Honduran coup was the fact that 10 percent of the commission's report was placed in a Canadian library, to be kept classified for ten years.[90]

THE CARTAGENA ACCORD

Coinciding with the release of the Truth Commission's findings, and against the backdrop of the steady, continuing cycle of resistance and repression, on May 22, 2011, Pepe Lobo's government signed the Cartagena Accord, along with representatives of Colombia and Venezuela, which significantly altered the terrain upon which state violence was taking place. The accord negotiated the return of former president Manuel Zelaya and other political exiles to Honduras with a promise to have charges against them annulled, and it included other guarantees with regard to upholding rule of law, ensuring protection of human rights, and carrying out public referenda on matters of significance. It also specifically asserted the legal right of the FNRP and associated organizations to form a political party to contest the 2013 elections.[91]

Many of the terms of the agreement smack of a kind of absurdity. The passage that guarantees that the government should keep tabs on the protection of human rights "in a special way" seems rather comical in a context where, surely, the protection of human rights ought to be taken for granted. Its assertion of the responsibility of the government to allow public referenda is another ironic piece, given that Zelaya was ostensibly overthrown because he was pursuing just such a referendum. As Dana Frank wryly noted, only the repatriation of Zelaya was not already a legal responsibility of the government of Honduras, though perhaps the coup regime did not consider itself beholden to those laws since it did not take power legally.[92] Jari Dixon, a member of the public ministry fired by the *golpistas* when he began attending FNRP rallies in his time off, explained in 2009 that the coup itself broke the Constitution and, as a result, nothing from that moment can be considered properly legal or illegal, as "the entire system of the rule of law became a falsehood."[93] It is worth adding, as well, that the so-called "Compliance Commission," headed by the foreign ministers of Venezuela and Colombia to ensure that all parties adhere to the accord, was designed to have no more than rhetorical power.

Nevertheless, the accord led to Zelaya's return on May 28, 2011. His return, which came at a moment of particular difficulty and discouragement for the FNRP, produced an immediate surge of hope and excitement in Honduras. According to Jesse Freeston, the crowd that gathered to meet Zelaya at the airport was the largest single congregation of Hondurans in one place in the country's history.[94] Nonetheless, Zelaya's re-entry into the dynamics of the resistance produced mixed reactions: while some applauded the amnesty granted to the exiles and believed that the accord would open up space for democratic dissent, others viewed it with suspicion and openly wondered whether it would lead to any real changes in the climate of repression in Honduras.[95] Indeed, one of the primary consequences of the accord—and this was no doubt understood by all of the parties involved in creating it—was to thrust Manuel Zelaya back into the centre of the storm. His reintroduction to the resistance not only changed the dynamics within it, it also changed the way it was perceived outside of Honduras. If the resistance was perecieved to amount to Zelaya himself, then the return of Zelaya would seem to end the crisis and Honduras would, according to this logic, go back to normal.

On the strength of this claim about Zelaya's return and the successful spinning of the Truth Commission, Honduras was granted re-entry into the OAS. In a context where gross human rights violations were continuing to take place, the accord simply provided another piece of the democratic veneer for the coup regime, effectively endorsed by the perceived victim of the coup, Manuel Zelaya. Naturally, this led many in the resistance to question the logic of Zelaya's decision. Before the coup, President Zelaya was often the target of political actions, strikes, and demonstrations, and he was considered not so different from the oligarchs who had ruled the country for decades. Indeed, even the *golpistas* themselves recognized that Zelaya was once one of their own. As Adolfo Facussé put it, "Mel Zelaya is one of us and—well—it just got out of his control. But the people think that he is an instrument of Chávez and that the fight is with Chávez."[96] The bargain Zelaya struck with the coup regime in May 2011 secured his own re-entry to Honduras and, given the status he gained as president-in-exile, he carried much sway in the resistance; after all, its current form had coalesced around the demand to have him reinstated. Upon his return to Honduras, he quickly—and somewhat controversially—mobilized the FNRP around the creation of a new political party which would contest the 2013 elections.

This did not sit well with many of the committed activists for whom resisting the coup was simply one part of a larger struggle for social justice in Honduras, for the creation of an Espacio Refundacional, or a refoundation of the country. One such Espacio activist is Carlos Amador, the son of Honduran writer Ramón Amaya Amador, whose *Prisión Verde* is one of Honduras' most important and enduring pieces of literature. According to Carlos Amador, the move towards electoral politics—ushered along by the repatriation of Zelaya—served only the interests of the regime, who sought to water down the resistance or, as he put it, "to stamp out the construction of popular power and direct democracy outside of parliamentary institutions."[97]

Even organizations that try to tow a careful line between the divisions in the resistance have acknowledged that the Cartagena Accord threatens to undermine, rather than strengthen, the capacity and security of the movement. COFADEH initially offered a cautious response to the accord, asserting its trust that former president Zelaya signed the agreement in good faith, but insisting that the coup regime could not be trusted to carry out even the minimal steps it pledged in it. COFADEH noted that the text used in the document reflected "doubts, ironies, intentions and evasions" on the part of the regime.[98] They also likened the discourse of the accord to that used by presidents Callejas, Maduro, and Flores in the 1990s—some of whom helped edit the text of the Cartagena Accord—in attempting to bury the memory of, and escape responsibility for, the violence and state terror of the 1980s. Indeed, the text itself is evidence enough of the accord's superficiality, a sample from which reads:

> While admitting that during the political crisis there have been people who consider that their human rights were violated, the Government of Honduras, through the Ministry of Justice and Human Rights, commits to attend these denunciations in order to contribute to the reconciliation of Honduran society within a framework of verifiable guarantees ... and awaits support from the Office of the United Nations High Commissioner for Human Rights.[99]

It should be apparent that the language used—"there have been people who consider that their human rights were violated"—is both a slap in the face to the many victims of the regime and an almost unbelievable denial of responsibility for those crimes. It is, moreover, remarkably similar to the language that Canadian officials have used.

A month after COFADEH's statement on the accord, director Berta Oliva added to her earlier doubts, calling Cartagena "a trap,"[100] in which even some of Zelaya's closest associates found themselves caught. Enrique Flores was President Zelaya's chief of staff and was exiled with Zelaya in the Dominican Republic, following the inauguration of Pepe Lobo. Upon the signing of the Cartagena Accord, which guaranteed "the return, safety and freedom of the former officials of the government," Flores boarded the same plane as Manuel Zelaya and returned, together with his former president, to Honduras. On their arrival, Flores was put under house arrest and charged under trumped-up accusations of corruption. As Todd Gordon and Jeffrey Webber observed, "That the Honduran state would detain such a high-profile figure is a warning that no one who crosses the dictatorship will be protected from its punitive actions." They added that the arrest of Flores "reveals the utter confidence with which the state is willing to carry out its agenda even with the ink of Cartagena barely dry."[101]

There were plenty of reasons, then, to be suspicious of the motivations behind the Cartagena Accord and Canada's support for it. However, it was clear that the majority of Hondurans would support the new party, the Partido de Libertad y Refundación (Liberty and Refoundation Party, LIBRE), and it gave an embattled movement a shot in the arm at a time that it desperately needed one. Given the historic size of the crowd that greeted the returning Zelaya at the airport, organizers in the FNRP had to take seriously the fact that, while he did not emerge from the social movement itself, the coup had made Zelaya, by far, the country's most popular figure. The movement had been fully mobilized for eighteen months and its organizers and supporters were exhausted and demoralized; if Zelaya could rejuvenate the movement, it would make a world of difference.

THE MOVEMENT AND THE PARTY

The severity of the crisis in Honduras and the total collapse of legitimate civilian government, however, led those in the Espacio Refundacional to ask how engaging in an electoral process could possibly lead to a change of the system itself. It was the central question debated in the movement after the signing of the Cartagena Accord.[102] Over the course of 2012, predictably, the context for the debate became ever more complicated. Manuel Zelaya's wife, Xiomara Castro de Zelaya, was quickly named LIBRE's presidential candidate, but there soon emerged five separate currents within the party, one of which was subsequently disbanded. I spoke with leaders and activists in most of the five currents. Four of the five came out of the traditional Liberal Party apparatus and drew not-unfounded criticism and scepticism from the social movement side of the FNRP. These currents almost certainly represented the best hope for the *golpistas* and their imperial allies of co-opting the movement into more easily manipulated reformist politics, a point that was particularly evident as I met the leaders of these currents in mid-2012.

One of these currents was the Movimiento Resistencia Progresista (Progessive Resistance Movement, MRP), led by a successful and wealthy public notary, Rasel Tomé. Tomé insisted that MRP was the backbone of the movement and spoke at length about the tortures and indignities he faced for having supported Zelaya during the coup.[103] Tomé deserves credit for supporting President Zelaya, but his political experience was based primarily in the Liberal Party and his distance from the social movement was reflected in an ideology that broke sharply from the demands in the streets. "Other countries have globalization," he explained, "and we want to participate in globalization ... we are not into extreme positions like socialism, which failed, or capitalism, which also failed."[104] Leaving aside the obvious question of what social formation he thought Hondurans wanted—if neither socialism nor capitalism—what is truly significant is Tomé's suggestion that Hondurans wanted globalization. The Honduran social movement had historically positioned itself against those manifestations of imperialism and neoliberalism that are most often identified with "globalization." As such, it was apparent that Rasel Tomé and the MRP did not represent the will of the movement.[105]

The other three Liberal Party-based currents were similar to the MRP. The fifth current, however, represented something quite different. This fifth group was called the Fuerza de Refundación Popular (Popular Refoundation Force, FRP), and it represented those elements most closely connected to the social movements within the political party. The FRP's presence in the LIBRE party is what most distinguished LIBRE from the traditional Liberal party, and the question was whether FRP and other candidates drawn from the social movement would be able to influence significantly the direction that the new party took, which was put to the test in November 2012 when the party held its internal primaries. FRP members were typically long-standing activists within the movement, who were convinced that the electoral process was the only viable option for the movement at that point. Juan Barahona was one of the most recognizable faces in the movement for two decades, beginning as a leader of the Bloque Popular, and he was also one of the most prominent figures in the FRP. Drawing inspiration from the experience of Venezuela, Bolivia, and other left-leaning Latin American governments, Barahona asserted, "In the 1980s, the left could take power by force. But today, we take power through popular democracy."[106]

He and other members of the FRP were committed to projects for radical change. When I asked if a LIBRE victory would usher in a period of social democracy, Barahona replied by pounding his desk, "No more social democracy, no! We want socialism!" He went on to add that he understood why people were wary of the electoral process and the LIBRE party, but that it would do no good "to sit with our arms crossed, refusing to participate" when the party had gained so much momentum and looked to be the primary alternative to the oligarchy in this moment.[107]

Another prominent member of FRP, Gilberto Rios, acknowledged that LIBRE was not a revolutionary party, but insisted that it was democratic and progressive, and that this made it a critically important space for the left to build upon the more radical politics that emanated from the social movement.[108] If there was hope, it lay in the prospect of LIBRE nominating candidates drawn largely from the FRP and the social movement, who would stand a very good chance of winning in the national elections in 2013. However, this strategy relied on the assumption that the elections would be conducted fairly, which, in retrospect to many Hondurans, looks rather niave. Already in May 2012, journalist and LGBT activist Erick Martinez was disappeared and assassinated, not long after being named as a potential LIBRE *diputado* candidate. He was one of many popular figures in LIBRE, and especially in the FRP, who had been threatened and harassed. I was in Tegucigalpa when he was assassinated, casting the first significant shadow over the decision to pursue the electoral route. It was to be the first of many.

Not only was the climate of fear and intimidation ramped up in the months leading up to the elections, the process itself was, by most accounts, another sham election in which the ruling National Party installed its favoured representative in the presidency. Juan Orlando Hernández, who emerged as the president after the 2013 elections, had been laying the groundwork for his rise to power for years. He was appointed by Pepe Lobo to be president of Congress in 2010 and held the powerful position for the length of Lobo's term, most notably carrying out the "technical coup" in 2012, during which four supreme court judges were illegally deposed in the middle of the night and their replacements appointed the next day. Not long after, he was able to similarly replace the attorney general and, indeed, by the time he ran for the presidency in 2013, he had already stacked the key posts in the Honduran state apparatus with loyalists.[109] He had even created a new wing of the armed forces, a special unit called Policia-Militar (Military Police, PM) which would emerge after his election as essentially his personal paramilitary force.

The electoral process that brought him into office was, not surprisingly, widely discredited in Honduras. The Tribunal Supremo Electoral (Supreme Electoral Tribunal, TSE) was stacked with Juan Orlando's supporters and he was declared the victor despite widespread allegations of fraud, vote-buying, and other irregularities, and despite the fact that the largest opposition party salvaged its own tally sheets that suggested an entirely different outcome.[110] The electoral process was so sketchy that it was denounced by an Austrian member of the EU observation delegation:

> I can attest to countless inconsistencies in the electoral process. There were people who could not vote because they showed up as being dead, and there were dead people who voted … the hidden alliance between the small parties and the National Party led to the buying and selling of votes and [electoral worker] credentials.… During the transmission of the results there was no possibility to find out where the tallies were being sent and we received reliable information that at least 20 percent of the original tally sheets were being diverted to an illegal server.[111]

Indeed, LIBRE led the polls for almost the entire campaign period[112]—from May to October 2013—and only in the final poll before the vote did Juan Orlando appear to have caught up, to the delight of foreign capital.[113] In the meantime, Juan Orlando's campaign received $11 million in financing from Washington and, as it later turned out, millions of dollars stolen from Honduran public institutions.[114]

Following the elections, duly elected *diputados* from the LIBRE party were marginalized and attacked, even in Congress itself. On May 13, 2014, the president of Congress ordered LIBRE members to be ejected from the building, after they had opened the doors of Congress to protestors fleeing police violence. Over 200 members of Juan Orlando's military police descended on the legislative building and violently ejected both the protestors and the LIBRE *diputados*. In the ensuing melee, several people were injured, and two LIBRE *diputados* were hospitalized.[115]

In the meantime, Juan Orlando established the institutional infrastructure to potentially maintain long-term dictatorial power in Honduras. Using state institutions stacked with his supporters, he successfully pushed through a reform to the Constitution which allows him to run for re-election after his term ends: precisely what the military claimed Manuel Zelaya was doing in order to justify the 2009 coup.[116] He also prepared for any possible resistance to his rule, from disaffected members of the oligarchy or military, by building his own paramilitary force. His new Policia-Militar unit answers directly to the President, and was created under the guise of "cleaning up" the armed forces. The military has around 10,000 soldiers, but by 2014 the Policia-Militar was already up to 5,000 Juan Orlando loyalists and was better funded and equipped than the traditional forces.[117] Leticia Salomón has argued that "the armed forces believe they are the defenders of the constitution, so a coup against Juan Orlando is entirely possible."[118] Nevertheless, Juan Orlando came out of the National Party, traditionally connected to the military, and still has family and friends in the military.

Still, the military has clearly indicated a preference for a dictatorship within which it has a prominent role; Juan Orlando did not rise through the ranks to become a general of the armed forces, and disrespecting this hierarchy does not sit well with the top brass. If he can use the military police as a paramilitary force responding directly to him, he would be effectively weakening the power of the traditional military and police. Foreign capital will work with him insofar as it appears that he can create stability and security for business, but if his actions provoke a crisis that interferes with the profits coming out of the mines and factories, he may lose favour. It is impossible to know just how well-connected he is to organized crime, but it stands to reason that he has an arrangement with some—but not all—factions. Recent developments suggest that the terrain is shifting within the narco-trafficking networks, and wars between rival organizations are heating up.[119] These may well be a reflection of the tension that is brewing within the rest of the ruling class.

THE FNRP PERSISTS

It is worth concluding this chapter by noting that in spite of the tremendous weight of forces stacked against it, the Honduran social movement remained strong. In 2015, Honduras was rocked by the "torch marches," wherein demonstrations of as many as 60,000 people filled the streets of the cities at night carrying torches, demanding the immediate resignation of Juan Orlando in the wake of a massive scandal in which the ruling government stole money from the national pension fund to finance the electoral fraud of 2013.[120] The defiance displayed by these protests forced the international media to talk about Honduras, and to report on the "widespread calls of electoral fraud" and corruption in the present government.[121] In 2016, when four men tied to both the military and a hydroelectric company assassinated community activist Berta Cáceres, the social movement again responded with massive protests, refusing to be defeated, claiming "Berta did not die, she multiplied."[122]

Fortunately, the crimes of the coup regime were still being regularly and thoroughly documented and reported. Human rights organizations like COFADEH and FIAN continued to risk their own members' lives in keeping track of the relentless attacks, and in conducting proper investigations into major crimes like murder, work that the police often refused to do. The state claimed most political assassinations to be the result of routine gang violence. For instance, on May 3, 2010, Lobo's Minister of Security Oscar Alvarez "guaranteed" La Tribuna that there was "no connection" between journalists' work and their assassinations.[123] Six years later, the same claims were made when a leader from COPINH, Nelson García, was assassinated just weeks after the high-profile murder of Berta Cáceres. It is clear that in post-coup Honduras it is up to human rights organizations, community groups, and independent journalists to determine which attacks are related to gang and narco conflicts, which are politically motivated, and which are a combination of both.[124]

Indeed, the latter point is key, since that work is complicated by the fact that the regime regularly uses its discreet connections to the gangs to distance itself from political attacks. Though the rank-and-file of Honduran gangs tend to be young working-class men and boys, many gangs are connected to—and populated by—former police and paramilitaries who in many cases still maintain close ties to the official organs of the state. In fact, members of the resistance have regularly asserted that Romeo Vásquez Velásquez—general of the armed forces during and after the coup and head of the Empresa Hondureña de Telecomunicaciones (Honduran Telecommunications Company, HONDUTEL) under Pepe Lobo's government—had links to the Mara Salvatrucha gang.[125] In addition, the large network of "legal vigilantes," who operated as extrajudicial executioners in the 1990s and early 2000s, continue to occupy a space somewhere between police and death squads. In 2007, a former security minister acknowledged that some 30 to 50 percent of Honduran police were involved in organized crime and narco gangs.[126] By 2012, police corruption was so rampant that the state was forced to make much ado about a police reform commission to be headed by widely respected Honduran historian Victor Meza, who nevertheless expressed grave doubts about the prospects for reforming an institution that was "infiltrated at every level by criminal organizations."[127] These networks and connections, built up between the official and unofficial wings of the repressive apparatus, make it easy to understand how state violence could be plausibly dressed up to look like gang violence, if its targets weren't so obviously and consistently opponents of the coup regime.[128]

Nonetheless, the work of documenting the violence continues to be done. Alongside grassroots human rights and community organizing is a network of courageous Honduran journalists, supported by a variety of international independent news media in getting their message to a wider audience, who have made it all but impossible for anyone to claim ignorance of the ongoing repression in Honduras under the coup regime. The availability of this documentation—in Spanish and English, from sources Honduran and international, from local organizations like FIAN to international NGOs like Amnesty International—casts a particular pall over Canada's decision to put its full diplomatic, political, and economic weight behind the coup regime.

In June 2009, Canada was slow and soft in condemning the first military coup in Honduras since the 1970s. In November 2009, it was only by intentionally ignoring a well-organized campaign by human rights organizations—and working very hard to do so—that Canada could claim Honduras had seen free and fair elections. In 2010, it was only by pretending not to notice the daily reports of ongoing state violence that Canada could contribute to a so-called Truth Commission that would inevitably produce only the truths its sponsors wanted to spin. Over the past five years, the news from Honduras has gone from bad to worse, as even mainstream liberal organizations like Amnesty International have published hundreds of pages of reports detailing the human rights catastrophes. And yet, Canada spearheaded the campaign to reintegrate Honduras into the OAS, and Stephen Harper was the first head of state to visit the country thereafter, directly supporting its police and military infrastructure.

Many Canadians wanted to believe that the problem was the Conservative government. But upon his election in 2015, Liberal prime minister Justin Trudeau appointed Chrystia Freeland to the role of international trade minister; a generous reward for Freeland, who wholeheartedly supported Harper's FTA with the military regime in Honduras. "Not every country in the world is perfect," Freeland told Parliament in 2014, "and we have to trade in the global economy. We believe that having a strong trading relationship can and must be a way to be a positive force in those economies."[129] In making this claim, Freeland defied experts from Canada and Honduras who testified again and again, in parliamentary hearings, that the FTA was a "grossly flawed" mechanism for effecting positive social change and that the only beneficiaries would be a small group of Canadian businesses, "while [local] communities [would] pay with their lives and lands."[130]

Indeed, the silence from Canada's new prime minister after the 2016 assassination of Berta Cáceres, arguably the most visible and internationally recognized activist in Honduras, made it clear that the Trudeau government is as close a friend to the Honduran coup as was the Harper government before. Berta had received dozens of death threats in her life, but the most recent one had come from a Canadian company, Blue Energy, which was seeking to build a hydroelectric dam on a river that belonged to Berta and the Lenca community from which she came.[131] While Canadian statements project the rhetoric of peace, security, and prosperity, it is evident that Canada's government has little interest in creating true peace or security for Honduras' poor majority. Rather, its goal appears to be the prosperity of Canadian businesses, as we'll see in the next chapter.

4 A FRUITFUL PARTNERSHIP
Canadian Investments in the Banana Republic

What is most telling about Canada's relationship to Honduras is the extent to which Canadian capital has taken advantage of Honduras' circumstances to extract profits from its people and resources, and the extent to which the Canadian state has worked to secure those circumstances. Canada has emerged as Honduras' second largest investor,[1] with over $600 million in foreign direct investment (FDI),[2] and the social movements—whose growing power was represented by the possible reopening of the Constitution in 2009—were increasingly posing a threat to the flow of profits. Significantly, since the 2009 coup, the forces that were threatening Canadian profits have been hammered down, and the conditions for long-term profitable Canadian investment in Honduras have been substantially improved. This chapter is devoted to documenting Canada's direct investments in Honduras—with particular attention to the mining, garment, and tourist industries—and, perhaps more importantly, Canada's broader project for the construction of a Honduras that will be "right" for Canadian capital in any number of possible industries.

EXTRACTING PROFITS

The intersection of Canadian capital and Honduran people is nowhere more acrimonious than in the mines, long woven into the legacies of both parties. Canada's ill-reputed mining companies have left a well-documented trail of crimes against the communities they affect—crimes against human security and health, against the environment upon which those societies are built, and against those communities' very social fabric itself—that stretches from the diamond mines of Canada's north to the gold mines of Central America to the copper and cobalt mines of the Congo.[3] For Hondurans, the experience of struggling against rapacious mining companies stretches at least as far back as the Spanish conquest, during which thousands of Indigenous people were enslaved and forced to work in mines around Tegucigalpa, San Juancito, and elsewhere.

The encounter between Canadian mining companies and Hondurans has followed predictable patterns. The first thrust came in the aftermath of Hurricane Mitch, as Canada extended an aid and reconstruction package to Honduras worth $100 million over four years, provided that Canadian companies be permitted to move in and assess Honduras' investment potential.[4] As Honduran social institutions were being disarticulated by the wrenching introduction of neoliberalism, Canadian mining firms quickly determined that they could establish a profitable presence, and established a national association, the Asociación Nacional de Mineros (National Mining Association, ANAMINH), to negotiate a new mining code with the Honduran government. The 1998 mining code that came out of those negotiations embodied the very laws that the Coordinadora Nacional de Resistencia Popular (Co-ordinated National Popular Resistance, CNRP) and the social movement struggled against throughout the first decade of the 2000s and included provisions for lifelong concessions to foreign companies, minimal taxation, and subsurface land rights for "rational resource exploitation."[5]

Indeed, that mining code was challenged by community movement activists, largely from the Siria Valley, as unconstitutional, a challenge that was upheld by the Honduran Supreme Court in 2005 in the context of massive popular mobilization. The ruling upheld the importance of community consultation and acknowledged that mining was "highly contaminating and damaging to life." As a result of the ruling and pressure from anti-mining activism, the moratorium on new mining concessions was upheld throughout Manuel Zelaya's term in office, while a new mining code was developed in dialogue with the social movement.[6]

Nevertheless, between 1998 and 2005, Canada emerged as Honduras' leading foreign investor in mining, taking advantage of the very laws deemed unconstitutional in 2005. Indeed, just a few months before the 2009 coup, Canadian companies were actively and aggressively pressuring the Zelaya government to roll back the ruling. A comprehensive report by the Americas Policy Group (APG) of the Canadian Council for International Co-operation (CCIC) described these companies' behaviour, noting that Canadian companies had organized together to pressure the state; one Canadian company was part of a consortium that dangled the prospect of $1.75 billion in investment if the moratorium was lifted.[7]

Much of my analysis of the Honduran mining sector is developed out of a series of interviews with Pedro Landa, a long-time activist in the alternative development organization Centro Hondureño para la Promoción del Desarrollo Comunitario (Honduran Centre for the Promotion of Community Development, CEHPRODEC), who came to Canada in March 2011 to testify before the Parliamentary Standing Committee on Foreign Affairs and International Trade (SCFAIT) in Ottawa, in an attempt to convince Canadian officials that a free-trade agreement (FTA) with the coup government would only deepen the disastrous consequences of the coup.[8] His testimony was ignored, and he returned to Ottawa in January 2012 to speak against Canada's participation in the rewriting of the Honduran mining code. Before the coup, Zelaya's government had been working with the social movements to develop a mining code that would be more just; a complicated struggle that was, by no means, going exactly the way movement activists might have wanted. Nevertheless, there was dialogue, there was progress, and there was an expectation that further progress could be made with continued pressure from the social movement. At the time of the coup, a draft proposal for a new mining code had been prepared; it would have strengthened environmental and labour regulations and introduced a comprehensive community consultation process.[9]

Ironically, after the coup, the regime used the lack of an existing mining code to justify writing its own—radically different from Zelaya's—heavily influenced by the interests of foreign, especially Canadian and Chilean, mining companies and trade and diplomatic officials. When Pedro Landa came to Canada to speak against the new mining code, he described the many ways it was designed to benefit the companies instead of the communities: it failed to ban the cyanide-leaching open-pit method; it failed to protect Honduran water systems; it offered further tax breaks to companies; it made concessions easier to grant and harder to repeal; it made community consultations a rare exception; and it limited public access to information about mining operations. Pedro Landa and the Honduran communities affected by these companies' actions were ignored; the new General Mining Law was passed in 2013. Meanwhile, CEHPRODEC was among several Honduran organizations which filed a constitutional challenge against the new mining laws, in 2014, to no avail.[10]

There were 154 mining and energy concessions already granted before the moratorium, almost all falling on or around Indigenous territories and communities, of which nearly 100 have been owned by Canadian companies at one time or another during their operation.[11] In 2011, 200 additional concessions were requested; of those, 150 were requested by Santos Gabino Carvajal—a former manager at the El Mochito mine and the President of ANAMINH—on behalf of the Canadian company Breakwater Resources Ltd. Breakwater, which operated two mines in addition to El Mochito, was subsequently bought out for $663 million by a company called Nyrstar, headquartered in Belgium, which now operates the El Mochito mine.[12] Other notable Canadian mining companies in Honduras include: the Maya Gold Company, which owns a 120,000 acre concession in Choluteca; First Point Minerals, which mines gold and silver in Choluteca and zinc and copper in the Siria Valley; and Standard Mining, which controls eleven concessions in Santa Bárbara.[13]

It is worth describing a handful of these projects in some detail. One of the earliest cases of Canadian mining in Honduras was the San Andrés mine in the Department of Copán, on a site first explored by the infamous Rosario Mining Company. A subsidiary of the Quebec-based Noranda ran the mine between 1974 and 1976, but dropped the concession on account of what it considered excessive taxation. When the Honduran Constitution was redrafted under the military dictatorship in the early 1980s, the tax codes for mining concessions were changed, and the mine was reopened. It was bought by Greenstone Resources in 1995, then operated by Yamana Gold, and it now belongs to Aura Minerals. All of these were Canadian firms. Greenstone Resources, for its part, went bankrupt in 2000, after having razed the village of San Andrés amidst promises of rebuilding the community elsewhere. When it went bankrupt, it owed La Union (the municipality where San Andrés is located) some $100,000 and had not fulfilled most of its promises to the communities it had destroyed; over 90 percent of the people it displaced did not have legal title to the land they were promised by the company.[14]

San Andrés was the first open-pit mine in Honduras, making extensive use of cyanide, a toxic chemical best known in the North for its ubiquitous use in murder mystery novels.[15] It is no mystery that cyanide is a killer; the San Andrés mine uses cyanide to leach some four million tons of ore each year.[16] It has also managed to spill tons of the poisonous chemical into the Rio Lara—the primary river in the region's water system upon which four major communities are reliant—with predictably murderous results. A variety of health crises ranging from skin disease to respiratory collapse have plagued the communities of San Miguel, Azacualpa, Campo Plantonares, and San Andrés; the latter was forcibly relocated to make way for the mine in the first place. In 2003, the Rio Lara served up 18,000 dead fish, as clear an indication as any that the water supply had become completely toxic; similar incidents in 2006 and 2009 only reinforced communities' awareness that the mine was slowly poisoning their land and bodies.[17]

In addition to the cyanide leaching, the company used explosives to open the mine in the first place, which, combined with the deforestation of nearly 5,000 trees, led to a crisis of soil erosion and a collapse of the fertility of agricultural land in the region. The lack of fertile soil for cultivation meant that communities that once survived on small-scale agricultural production were no longer able to sustain themselves, and many of the community members have had to take on the dangerous and poorly paid work in the mine itself.[18] Aura Minerals is actively pursuing four more adjacent sites—for which concessions were applied in 2002[19]—that have not yet been granted, but they will now be considered under the new Honduran mining code. In the meantime, the company is currently trying to dig up and "relocate" a local cemetery near La Unión, claiming that it is "unused" land, even while community members are still being buried there. In April 2016, the company went as far as to send 180 armed men to block a civil society delegation of Canadians and Hondurans who were trying to visit the community and bring attention to Aura Minerals' behaviour.[20]

CONDEMNED TO DEATH

Perhaps the most notorious case of Canadian mining in Honduras is that of the San Martín mine in the Siria Valley, owned by Vancouver-based Goldcorp. The San Martín mine was actually shut down in 2008, but its legacy remains profoundly present in Honduras; in fact, the Honduran owners of its local subsidiary are currently facing criminal charges in Honduras for failing to act on knowledge of the dangerously high levels of acidity and heavy metals—lead, arsenic, and mercury—the mining operation deposited in the regional water supply.[21] Juan Almendares, former director of the Universidad Nacional Autónoma de Honduras (National Autonomous University of Honduras, UNAH) in Tegucigalpa and long-time activist in Honduran social movements, led countless medical brigades to the Siria Valley during and after its eight-year operation, and he reported that when the mine opened in 2000, 8 percent of people living in the region had suffered skin diseases. By 2010, the rate had increased to 80 percent.[22]

When I interviewed movement activist Carlos Amador in May 2012, he described the Siria Valley as having been "condemned to death" by Goldcorp's mine.[23] Amador, who had just returned from a medical brigade with Dr. Almendares and has testified at Goldcorp shareholder meetings in Canada, described health disasters that had resulted from lead and arsenic poisoning: skin disease, diseased hair follicles such that women in their thirties were losing their hair, high levels of lead in people's blood, even a recent case where a woman had lost twin babies as a result of arsenic poisoning.[24] The company, however, denied that there were any problems in the Siria Valley. In fact, Goldcorp was quick to note that the Honduran state had confirmed that *if* there were any health problems in the region, they were *not* the responsibility of the company, which insisted that any problems must have predated the mine. Indeed, said Amador, when "the executive director of Goldcorp was here in Honduras in December, he claimed that he was in the mine, that he bathed, and ate, and that he was fine. I'd like to know what he was eating."[25]

In 2007, responding to pressure from the social movements associated with the CNRP, the Honduran public health ministry took a series of blood samples from some sixty people in the Siria Valley and discovered that their blood was laced with dangerously high levels of arsenic, lead, mercury, cadmium, magnesium, chromium, and nickel. The results of the study, however, were not released until 2011, at which point two executives from Goldcorp were taken to the Honduran court to defend themselves against charges that they had contaminated the environment and caused serious medical crises. The judge ruled in favour of the company, despite the fact that one of the people tested in 2007—five-year-old Lesly Yaritza—died in 2010 after suffering from a degenerative muscle condition in her legs that left her barely able to walk at the time of her tragic and premature death.[26]

Meanwhile, Goldcorp faced no sanction from the Canadian state and is hailed by the Canadian media as an exemplar of corporate social responsibility. The company has been named one of the best 100 Canadian companies to work for, by *The Globe and Mail*, and even one of the top ten companies, by the *National Post*.[27] In 2011, Goldcorp spent a quick $25,000 to whisk five Canadian members of Parliament down to Guatemala to be wined-and-dined around its mining operations there,[28] at the same time that momentum was gathering around a social movement-led health tribunal investigating Goldcorp's activities in Central America, which, not surprisingly, reported major violations of public health and safety:

> We find Goldcorp guilty for its activities in Honduras, Guatemala and Mexico, which we find to be seriously damaging to the health and the quality of life, the quality of

> environment, and the right to self-determination of the affected Indigenous and campesino communities. We also find the States where the accusations come from guilty of being complicit and irresponsible for not protecting the rights of those affected by mining. We also find the Government of Canada guilty for supporting and promoting in various ways the irresponsible mining investments in Mesoamerica.[29]

The Health Tribunal was organized by a coalition of over forty organizations from across the Americas and used liberal international guidelines as its benchmarks, including the United Nations Declaration on the Rights of Indigenous Peoples (UNDRIP), the International Labor Organization's convention number 169 (ILO-169), the World Health Organization's (WHO) Ottawa Charter for Health Promotion, and the Inter-American Commission on Human Rights' (IACHR) Declaration on the Rights and Duties of Man.[30] The twelve judges were drawn from civil society organizations in seven different countries, including Canada, and they were primarily doctors, academics, public health officials, and human rights defenders.[31] Goldcorp executives, for their part, continue to boast about the supposedly responsible way in which they have shut down the San Martín mine, despite the ongoing health crises it is causing and its condemnation by the Health Tribunal. Indeed, Goldcorp is actively pursuing other operations in Honduras. On the same day that I spoke with Carlos Amador, he was warned that he could face criminal charges for his activism against a massive deforestation project on a 1,866 hectare concession to Goldcorp just a few miles away from San Martín.

Goldcorp has extracted a great deal of wealth from Honduras and around the world; the Canadian media proudly reported in 2012 that Goldcorp was making record profits, which reached as high as $5.4 billion in 2011.[32] Aura Minerals, for its part, has been recording an average of $280 million in annual revenues, though, notably, its profits have been less than projected and no doubt its managers are anxious to increase productivity to prevent a sell-off.[33] The point is not whether one company or another is successful in its operations; rather, the point is that Canadian companies are heavily committed to *making* their Honduran operations successful and that, in the context of the coup and the behaviour of the military government, it has been in the interests of these companies that the Canadian government support the military government so that these companies would enjoy the best possible conditions for making profits.[34]

What is crucial here is that none of the profits that Canadian companies have been extracting from the mining industry in Honduras would be possible without a compliant Honduran state committed to allowing these companies to behave in the ways that they do. The growing strength of the social movements in the 2000s posed a threat to Canadian mining profits insofar as the movement was insisting on a major increase in the level of Honduran state intervention. Whether by creating stronger labour, health, or environmental regulations, enforcing existing ones, forcing companies to pay higher taxes, forcing companies to carry out legitimate community consultations before breaking dirt on new operations, or by any number of other means, Hondurans were expressing a clear and vocal message that the status quo—megaprofits for Canadian firms at the expense of Hondurans—was not acceptable.[35] To the extent that Zelaya was listening, and that the *constituyente* might have actually made some of those changes real, Canadian firms had much to lose from that reform project and much to gain by a resurgent Honduran right wing in power.

This dynamic is as visible in the mining sector as anywhere, since it was no secret that Zelaya's moratorium on new concessions was blocking the further development of potentially profitable investment in mining and since Canada was so active in writing the new mining code. In 2010, Canadian ambassador Neil Reeder and CIDA representative Daniel Arsenault were in Honduras for meetings with Breakwater Resources about how to influence the direction of the new mining code.[36] Sure enough, over the following months, high-level discussions between Canadian and Honduran state officials and mining companies were held regularly, and a DFAIT mission in 2011 reported that "Honduras is in the process of transformation from the anti-mining Zelaya administration to the pro-sustainable mining and pro-CSR Lobo government,"[37] a rather farcical misrepresentation for those familiar with the situation. By 2012, Canada's role in developing the new mining codes was public knowledge; the Honduran newspaper *El Heraldo* proudly asserted that ministers from the two countries had agreed that Honduras would "contract consultants using Canadian funds to analyze the law in order to ensure that it includes minimum international standards and such that the experience of Canada is also reflected in the law."[38]

Though both countries cloak their statements in the discourse of corporate social responsibility, the proposed legislation itself put the lie to this rhetoric. On January 23, 2013, the new mining code was passed, despite contravening several of the basic rights guaranteed to Hondurans under the 1982 Constitution, and despite the fact that 91 percent of Hondurans reported that they did not support the status quo for mining operations, as reflected in the new code.[39] The new laws gave mining companies almost unlimited access to water for use in their operations, leaving only 10 percent of the country's water protected for Honduran communities. Concessions were reopened to being granted and the new laws allow for concessions with no limits; theoretically, companies could be granted parcels of land in perpetuity. They place no restrictions on the use of acid drainage, and therefore leave no protection for communities against long-term groundwater contamination.[40] At the same time, they assert that no authority can declare any territory permanently prohibited from mining, generating a legal loophole that companies will likely be able to use if they seek concessions on territory otherwise protected by the Honduran state. Calling mining an activity of "public interest," the new laws provide no safeguards for communities that fall within conceded territory, which will make it easier for mining companies to displace Indigenous communities.[41] The new laws deepen the shroud of secrecy around mining operations, allowing companies to withhold technical and financial information from the public.[42]

Finally, the "security tax" that the Lobo government approved in 2012 was added to the new mining code, such that companies would pay a 2 percent tax to the state that would be earmarked specifically for security costs. This only deepened the relationship between the security apparatus and the mining companies, which were now paying a direct fee in exchange for the state's protection.[43] The new mining code, developed with the direct input of Canadian state officials, served to open Honduran people and resources to ever greater exploitation at the hands of Canadian enterprise, offering a rather stark demonstration of the collusion between the Canadian state, the Honduran coup regime, and Canadian mining companies.

WORKSHOPS OF CANADIAN CAPITAL

Quebec-based Gildan Activewear announced record profits in the final quarter of 2012—some $89 million in just three months—and boasted of a strong positive outlook for 2013.[44] They were right: Gildan's revenues hit $2.2 billion in 2013,[45] and the company was posting quarterly profits in 2014 that were regularly above $100 million.[46] Gildan is also one of the most infamous sweatshop employers in the world, with a laundry list of labour violations so well-documented that they make up a major portion of the company's "Wikipedia" entry. Employing over 18,000 Hondurans in its factories, it is the largest private-sector employer in Honduras.[47] Like its counterparts in the mining industry, Gildan is heralded by the Canadian mainstream media as a leader in responsible corporate practices, named by *The Globe and Mail* and

Maclean's as being among Canada's top fifty "corporate citizens."[48] Nevertheless, the company has been publicly shamed for its practices on a consistent basis since it began shifting its manufacturing from North America to the Global South in the late 1990s, with its Honduran operations among its most notorious.

Details of Gildan's activities are difficult to obtain, especially as its host government in Honduras is increasingly protecting companies from public scrutiny. This is evidenced in the new mining code described above, and the *maquiladora* industry has long been notorious in this regard. When Honduras made international headlines in the 1990s following an expose of Kathie Lee Gifford's celebrity-branded clothing line, it was a result of an exhaustive series of investigations through garbage dumps and rubbish bins in Honduras and the Dominican Republic by Charles Kernaghan and the National Labour Committee (NLC). As Joel Bakan describes in his important work on the modern corporation:

> Following garbage trucks to dumps and then sifting through what they leave behind is helpful, Kernaghan has found, for discovering the locations of factories in the new global economy and for finding out what goes on inside them.... "They hide these factories and sweatshops around the world," says Kernaghan, and refuse requests for the factories' names and addresses "because they know it's easier to exploit teenagers behind locked metal gates, with armed guards, behind barbed wire."[49]

Kernaghan's interventions with the NLC in Honduras were somewhat effective in exposing the outrageous conditions in Honduran sweatshops to North American audiences and were an important part of the momentum building around anti-sweatshop activism in North America at that moment. The legacy of that work is contested in Honduras. The Honduran media—controlled by the same parties as the *maquiladoras*—framed Kernaghan as a "puppet" of the imperial powers and treated the Honduran sweatshop workers who collaborated with Kernaghan as if they, too, were traitors to the country. Even the *maquila* workers were divided on whether it made sense to rely on Northerners' support in the struggles in their own workplaces.[50]

Nevertheless, Kernaghan and the activists he worked with in the late 1990s did important work in a moment when the Honduran social movement was just beginning to recover from the trauma and dislocation of the 1980s. By the late 2000s, using reports from movement activists and Gildan's own records, it became possible to construct a fairly clear picture of the company's operations in Honduras. According to Gildan's annual report for 2011, it operated three major textile facilities in Honduras, in addition to two smaller sock factories and a network of smaller sewing operations. Indeed, the company called Honduras its "largest manufacturing hub" and has been actively constructing new facilities and acquiring existing workshops in Honduras since the June 2009 coup; in 2012 Gildan bought out Anvil Knitwear, which ran its own textile factories in Honduras, including the Star S.A. factory in El Progreso, a case we'll return to later in this chapter. It is notable that one of Gildan's other major manufacturing hubs is in Haiti, arguably the poorest country in the Caribbean basin and another country where Canada's political interference is well-documented.[51]

Gildan's complete record of exploitative behaviour in Honduras would require a book in itself, so we will examine just a few cases where the Canadian state has supported the company directly, with full knowledge of its actions. As far back as 2002, Gildan's factory in El Progreso was a source of some embarrassment, as its miserable treatment of workers was brought into the Canadian mainstream by a CBC television special. Health and safety violations, less-than-living wages, sexual harassment and gender-based discrimination against its primarily female workforce, and a litany of other exploitative measures made international headlines and led to the workers at the El Progreso factory organizing to form a union and fight back.[52] In 2003–04, nearly 100 workers were fired for being involved in the unionization effort, but the Canadian government, under the Liberal leadership of Jean Chrétien, brazenly ignored the mounting evidence of Gildan's labour violations and awarded it, through CIDA, an "Excellence in Corporate Social and Ethical Responsibility Award," to bolster its legitimacy as it denied that it was mistreating its workers.[53] Honduran and Canadian labour organizations continued to file official complaints, and when the pressure became too great, Gildan simply closed the factory, laid off its 1,800 workers, and shifted more production to its other plants.[54] The case of the El Progreso plant is important insofar as it demonstrates that the Canadian state was, as far back as the early 2000s, directly implicated in Gildan's behaviour.

This dynamic has followed Gildan wherever it has gone in Honduras. Between 2008 and 2011, the US-based, labour NGO Workers Rights Consortium (WRC) documented systematic persecution of workers who were trying to organize unions at Gildan and Anvil factories. Workers would be fired or threatened with being blacklisted across the sector, so that they would not find any work, would suffer verbal, physical, and sexual harassment from managers and from other workers, and they received death threats, which are to be taken very seriously in the Honduran context.[55] At the one factory where workers successfully formed a union, Star S.A., union leaders have faced constant harassment; one reported being approached by another worker and told "it would be cheap to get you all killed, they will charge me 5,000 Lempiras to kill all six of you [the union's leaders]."[56]

WRC's most recent report on the Star S.A. factory makes it very clear that not only was management aware of the threats, they were often in collusion with the perpetrators. A useful demonstration of that collusion can be found in the story of Rafael Magana, a particularly aggressive anti-union worker who has been accused of threatening unionists since the mid-2000s. During a 2009 job action, Magana told a union leader "the time you have left to live is the time I give you. I have you in my hands." In 2012, he said he would "destroy" the union and told another activist that "the cemetery [was] full of brave people." WRC reports on his relationship to Gildan/Anvil management:

> Multiple workers provided evidence that Human Resources staff at Star not only tolerated Magana's behavior, but colluded with certain workers in promoting anti-union messages in the plant. According to credible, mutually corroborated worker testimony, Magana enjoyed a privileged relationship with Human Resources Manager Wendy Aguirre and met with her regularly in her office.[57]

WRC was in communication with Gildan while carrying out the report, but Gildan denied any knowledge of the anti-union activities, stating that it was "not aware of any evidence that these complaints of harassment were in fact reported to management" despite the fact that the victims testified to the WRC that they had indeed filed such reports.[58]

Even under "normal" conditions, Gildan's treatment of its employees is deplorable. The best source of credible information on the conditions in Honduran sweatshops today are the workers themselves; the most important organization of *maquiladora* workers in Honduras is the women's collective, Colectiva de Mujeres Hondureñas (Honduran Women's Collective, CODEMUH). Maria Luisa Regalado, one of its general co-ordinators, reports that the women employed by Gildan often work up to eleven-hour shifts and avoid getting up to go to the bathroom for fear of not meeting their quotas. The quotas themselves are reinforced by dividing the women into "teams," with each team responsible for a certain level of production and punished collectively if that level isn't met; for instance, company supervisors will sometimes withhold workers' lunch tickets if their team fails to meet its quotas.[59]

The result is that the workers are encouraged to discipline one another to work harder, and as many of them develop serious health problems, they are injected with painkillers by company doctors in order to prolong their ability to work. As their bodies collapse and their productivity falls, they are dropped into lower-wage categories. The workers are routinely assessed for what percentage of fitness they are at and paid accordingly; that is, if the doctor claims that a worker is operating at 50 percent physical capacity, she will be paid at 50 percent of the full wage. When the painkillers are no longer enough and workers are no longer able to keep up, they are often fired without warning or compensation.[60] This was how Gildan treated Lilian Castillo, who was fired in 2013 when she developed tendonitis in her left shoulder and couldn't meet her quotas.[61]

Castillo's situation is common. In 2008, Adrienne Pine described a conversation she had with a doctor who had once worked for one of the *maquiladoras*, who explained that workers who needed treatment had to work while they waited to see the doctor, lest productivity drop, meaning that their bodies were being pushed even as they were trying to get help for existing problems.[62] CODEMUH has filed hundreds of reports of health violations at Gildan's factories—mostly muscular-skeletal issues in shoulders and backs as a result of conducting some forty to fifty repetitive actions per minute—and despite consistent efforts to dialogue with the company on these matters, they have found that, rather than supporting workers with health problems, Gildan punishes them.[63]

What is more, among the package of neoliberal shocks that the Lobo government passed after the coup was a new set of regulations around temporary work, which gave employers like Gildan an ideal loophole to get around the relatively minor social securities that do exist in Honduran law. Under the new laws, Gildan hires temporary workers for periods of up to two months and then lets them go completely; during that time, they have no access to any social security, no leaves or support for pregnancy, and no vacation time. In addition, Gildan is often able to cloak its activities by using subcontracted companies; for instance, Gildan forces potential employees to submit to humiliating physical examinations, which are now typically conducted by a private Honduran firm. Regalado describes the examinations:

> The exams are physical and psychological. It is very invasive; the women have to take their clothes off, down to their underwear. Doctors touch every part of their body, and if they let on that they feel any pain at all, they may not get the job ... the women

> have to get down on their knees and they are touched on the legs, their arms, their shoulders, everywhere.[64]

These allegations are supported by nearly every investigation into factory conditions with the exception of those undertaken by the company itself.[65] Gildan even tries to manipulate third-party investigations of its factories. In 2015, a Montreal newspaper sent a reporter to Honduras to visit Gildan's facilities and write about the company. The reporter was paraded through an absurdly false production of a "normal day" at the factory: the facilities were clean; workers were selected to give glowing reviews of their treatment; and supervisors were running regular breaks to allow the employees to do yoga and stretching. However, when the reporter went off-script and asked workers direct questions in Spanish, they laughed at the performance, explaining that they had never had these exercise breaks and that this was the first day in weeks that the bathrooms had been cleaned. The Gildan representative who had been co-ordinating the tours was forced to apologize to the furious reporter, and no story ever emerged from the experience.[66]

Moreover, the physical and structural violence inflicted on the women in Gildan's factories has a direct relationship with the broader dynamics of violence in Honduran streets and homes, especially since 2009. To cite just one example, as Gildan requires more and more hours of work from its employees, and as those hours go later into the night and are not up for negotiation, women find themselves forced to travel home from work well after dark, where they often face harassment and physical violence from men in the streets, especially police. "In one meeting, we had twelve women from the factories and we asked if any of them faced violence to and from work," Regalado reported. "Every single one of them said that they had been assaulted between one and three times."[67]

It is hard to imagine the Canadian state openly declaring itself in favour of the dynamics described here. Nevertheless, it is precisely these conditions that Honduran social movements have been struggling against over the past decade, and Canada's endorsement of the military regime since 2009 has placed it firmly on the side of *maquiladora* owners like Gildan. Canada's position cannot be explained by ignorance; CODEMUH sent an open letter to Prime Minister Harper in 2011 in anticipation of the Canada-Honduras FTA, insisting that the Canadian government take Gildan's mistreatment of workers seriously:

> The Honduran Women's Collective, CODEMUH, has continually and systematically produced information about the vulnerable position faced by workers in the *maquila* industry in Honduras, about the violation of human and labour rights, and the damages done to the health of workers by their work activities, especially in the company Gildan Activewear, a transnational company owned by Canadians ... We demand that you ask promptly for a report on labour and human rights conditions for the women and men who work at Gildan Activewear installations in Honduras; and that the Canadian government monitors working conditions for workers with Canadian transnationals. The Canadian government must force companies to comply with national laws, international conventions and international treaties to do with human and labour rights and corporate social responsibility.[68]

The Canadian government has not pursued CODEMUH's requests to force Gildan to comply with international labour treaties.

Instead, Gildan continues to receive accolades for its commitment to corporate social responsibility in the Canadian media, and when Prime Minister Harper signed an FTA in Honduras, he praised Gildan as a leader in responsible corporate behaviour in Honduras. After a visit to one of its Honduran factories, Harper endorsed the company and asserted that "[Canada is] always concerned about the image and record of Canadian companies when they are involved in business anywhere in the world."[69] His comments buttressed the statements made the previous year by Peter Kent, who claimed that "Canadians should be proud" of Gildan Activewear and its peers in Honduras.[70] Such pride would be misplaced; in the aftermath of the 2009 coup, when even US sweatshop employers Nike and Adidas issued statements against the interruption of democracy and the violent repression, Gildan proceeded with business as usual, and welcomed the coup as good news for Gildan, since it would likely bring a more business-friendly government.[71]

THE BANANA COAST

The third significant sector for Canadian investors in Honduras is the growing tourist trade on the country's North Coast and the Bay Islands. In the months following the 2009 coup, letters poured into Ottawa and Washington from the North American residents in the region, pressuring their governments to support the coup regime and its commitments to developing the tourist industry. Tom Stollery, a Canadian investor in Villas Paraiso Escondido, a forty-acre resort on the North Coast, wrote to Prime Minister Harper on behalf of the company in July 2009 to express concern over its "support" for

President Zelaya. Although Canada could hardly be said to have supported Zelaya, the letter from Canadian investors is instructive:

> If Zelaya is allowed to return to power in Honduras and with outside influence from the ALBA group of countries it will result in the loss of democracy, freedom of speech and human rights for all Hondurans. The removal of democracy in Honduras will stop foreign investment and will result in financial losses to foreign and Canadian investments in that country. This loss of investment will ultimately cause economic hardship for Honduras and its people which is already one of the poorest countries in the western hemisphere.[72]

Notwithstanding the dubious claim that Zelaya—and not the coup government—posed a threat to Honduran democracy and human rights, it is worth noting how quickly and clearly the terrain of the letter's discourse shifts to the protection of Canadian investment. Stollery may well have been right that the direction Zelaya was taking could have resulted in financial losses to Canadian investors, given this project of social democratic reform, but his insistence that Canadian investment in Honduras was protecting people from economic hardship is rather unconvincing.

Another letter writer from a North American resort complained that tourism was suffering as a result of the "lies" being told about bloodshed in Honduras and insisted that the island of Roatán was only "technically a part of Honduras" and that it remained "peaceful, tranquil and beautiful," having had "no incidents of any kind."[73] The author of this letter was not entirely incorrect; the tourist enclave in Honduras' north is indeed a world apart from the rest of the country. Its main function is to serve as a tropical playground for North American adventurers and retirees, protected from the realities of Honduran life by an infrastructure and security apparatus designed to render invisible the stark inequality and exploitation that makes Honduras such a prime location for these resorts and villas in the first place.

Indeed, the attraction for Canadian investors is the price; with some property being sold for as little as $85 per square foot, the emerging North Coast retirement communities are becoming increasingly popular among Canadian seniors looking for a cheaper place to set up in the sun.[74] Tourism from Canada represents the largest source of income in the industry in Honduras, and as property developers gradually expand their scope in the country's north, the result is increased conflict between land developers and local communities. In particular, North Coast developers are snapping up land—buying it cheaply, through a variety of often-sketchy means—that is claimed as protected land by Honduras' Garífuna people.

The ancestors of the Afro-Indigenous Garífuna people arrived in the Caribbean on a slave ship that wrecked near St. Vincent. When the English invaded St. Vincent in 1796, the Garífuna were displaced, and primarily settled along the north coasts of Honduras, Belize, and Nicaragua, as a culturally distinct network of communities organized economically around practices of redistribution and reciprocity, in what has been described as a communitarian and "matrifocal" or matriarchal economy.[75] The United Nations Educational, Scientific, and Cultural Organization (UNESCO) has declared the communal Garífuna culture one of nineteen "Masterpieces of the Oral and Intangible Heritage of Humanity." But the survival of the Garífuna people and culture is being directly threatened by the seizure of the territory and resources upon which that cultural life depends.

As far back as 1992, the Marbella Tourist Corporation began seizing land near Triunfo de la Cruz, prompting conflict between the company and the newly formed Comité de Defensa de Tierras Triunfeñas (Defense Committee for Triunfo Land, CODETT) which culminated, in 1997, in the murder of three community leaders and incarceration on trumped up charges of a fourth.[76] As the tourist industry grew, it often took the form of ecotourist developments like marine parks and biological reserves that were promoted in the language of sustainability and environmental protection but actually served to facilitate the grabbing of Garífuna land for ultimately destructive and unsustainable practices. One 1993 decree, for instance, banned any extraction of marine life from the North Coast waters, effectively criminalizing local fishing and lobster catching, essential aspects of Garífuna cultural and economic life. Garífuna practices were, in fact, environmentally sustainable and woven into the fabric of community life; Garífuna fishing posed no threat to fish stocks, but banning fishing facilitated the establishment of scuba diving resorts and marine reserves for tourists.[77] Similar restrictions were applied to practices like logging; while foreign mining companies were deforesting massive swaths of land on their concessions, small Garífuna communities were being blocked from minor, sustainable, subsistence practices like using local palm trees to repair their homes.

Meanwhile, the tourist projects that have moved in have not, themselves, adhered to any meaningful standards of sustainable development; new roads are built poorly and promote erosion and siltation, while construction along the shoreline has destroyed mangroves and corals.[78] Overdevelopment of scuba projects and other tourist activities weakened the North Coast ecology—and the Garífuna communities that had traditionally protected it—and left the region especially vulnerable to disasters like Hurricane Mitch. Tourist businesses gradually bought up land by taking advantage of ambiguities in the nature of land titling—i.e., buying land from individual Garífuna "landowners" rather than negotiating with the communities at large—usually beginning with forested or coastal territory, so that the developments came to more or less surround the actual villages and settlements. This slowly cut the communities off from their resource bases and weakened them, such that it became easier to buy out individual residential plots, hastening the full encroachment of companies in traditional territory.[79]

This breaking of traditional Garífuna practices has not gone unchallenged. In the case of Club Marbella, for instance, the Organización Fraternal Negra Hondureña (Fraternal Organization of Black Hondurans, OFRANEH) presented stiff resistance. As a result, the company trying to build the resort, Inversiones y Desarrollo El Triunfo SA (Investment and Development Triunfo, IDETRISA), exploited the fissures between official state leadership and Garífuna community leadership structures, and even went as far as to establish an alternative Garífuna leadership group to challenge the current leaders. Since Garífuna territory is held communally, the company could not simply buy the land from one owner but, rather, negotiate any sale of land with the local *patronato*, a group of community representatives chosen internally. Since they refused to give permission for Club Marbella, the company funded and supported an alternate group—with links to organized crime—to try to present itself as the legitimate *patronato*. The company then used its influence in the official Honduran government to register the fake *patronato* as the official community leadership, which promptly sold the land to the developers. OFRANEH took direct action against the company, dismantling the walls it had begun building while denouncing the fake *patronato*:

> Our anxiety has only increased with the illegal sale of land which, being authorised by the parallel council created within the community by the municipality – a council currently led by the intimidating brothers, Martínez y Braulio Martínez – means that the authorities have failed to take action against the parties reported to them. The Club Marbella development (by IDETRISA) is one such case, where a concrete wall is being built around land which is community property, with total disregard for the project and crops of the women's group.[80]

In this case, OFRANEH was able to force the Tela office to withhold recognition of the fake *patronato*, but the tactics used here are common along the North Coast.

What is more, the supposed benefits of the increased tourist trade have yet to "trickle down" to the Hondurans who claim the land as their own.[81] Tanya Kerssen describes Garífuna communities as being "boxed in on all sides," referring to the palm oil and banana plantations, the enclosure of coastal land and waters, and the criminalization of subsistence activities.[82] Meanwhile, Honduran journalist Felix Molina describes it as a "new Apartheid," as walls are being built—quite literally—to keep the Garífuna separated from the growing community of Canadian retirees.[83] Indeed, it appears that Garífuna culture holds less appeal to the northerners who bring down their dollars to experience a sterilized version of local custom than that of the Maya: the resorts typically offer tokenized presentations of "traditional Mayan culture" even while they are actively undermining the traditional existence of the Garífuna.[84]

The emblematic case of Canadian investment in Honduran tourism is that of Life Vision Properties, owned by Canadian pornography magnate Randy Jorgensen. Building on two decades of success and notoriety with his Adults Only Video retail chain, Jorgensen now buys and sells property in Honduras through Life Vision and constructs the infrastructure on those sites through his Jaguar Construction company.[85] Jorgensen is positioning himself as one of the key figures in the development of the North Coast tourist industry; his "Banana Coast" cruise port development—aptly named, given its continuation of the legacy of colonialism—is now Honduras' largest. The collusion between Jorgensen and the Honduran state is public knowledge: Life Vision Properties' website features a promotional video in which Pepe Lobo himself speaks directly to potential investors, assuring them that Honduras is an attractive place for their money: "We have a new legal and regulatory framework for investment promotion and protection making us one of the most attractive places to invest in Latin America."[86]

With direct support from the Honduran state and armed forces, it is hardly a surprise that Jorgensen is not worried about local opposition. When Canadian journalist Dawn Paley asked him about Garífuna claims that his properties were being built on land that belongs to them collectively, his response was telling:

> For Canadians, the easiest way to compare it is to compare it to our own native Indians [sic] in Canada ... Depending on what's going on, they may or may not decide that they have a land claim going on ... As soon as there is any development going on generally, the Garífuna start checking around and seeing if there isn't some way that they can extort some funds or something out of whoever is doing that development.[87]

It seems quite clear from Jorgensen's dismissive response to the idea of Indigenous land claims—in Honduras or Canada—that he does not take seriously even the possibility that the Garífuna could have a legitimate grievance.

But Garífuna communities have been organizing against Jorgensen and the emerging tourist trade since the mid-2000s. Evaristo Perez Ambular, a Garífuna organizer based in Trujillo, has been struggling for nearly a decade against Canadian companies: "There are many Canadians in our communities on the coast, and we haven't seen a positive presence from them," he said. "They use our bridges and our roads, and they don't leave us a thing."[88] Much of the property held by Jorgensen was bought for cheap from one individual falsely claiming to represent the Garífuna communities in the region in 2007. Community leaders denied that the individual ever had the right to sell the land, but the Honduran state upheld Jorgensen's right to the land and Jorgensen went ahead with building a $15 million port at Trujillo to receive cruise ships, with an attendant set of resorts and shopping malls.[89] The first ship arrived in 2014, and promotion of the resort made reference to the fact that it was located at the site of Christopher Columbus' landfall in Honduras, either unaware or indifferent to the irony.[90]

Tourist enclaves like the "Banana Coast" have displaced communities and upset customary practices—fishing, shipping, agriculture, and the complex dynamics and networks of traditional Garífuna culture—and have replaced those practices with an industry that adds very little new value to the Honduran economy. The money that does trickle into the pockets of Hondurans comes predominantly in the form of the low wages paid to resort service staff and in the growing market for cheap Honduran prostitution.[91] International reporting on the HIV crisis in Honduras' north regularly refers to the rapidly increasing rate of prostitution, but it typically fails to connect it to the concurrent rise in North American tourist development, as if a "natural" Garífuna "promiscuity" were the real cause of the problem.[92]

Indeed, Jorgensen's advertising campaigns for his tropical resorts typically feature attractive young women in bikinis on the beach, and he was accused in 2001 of making pornographic films with underage Honduran women as actors.[93] Meanwhile, the sex industry has exploded since the resorts—and foreigners—started arriving *en masse*. Dawn Paley reports on a chilling interview with a disgraced Ontario Provincial Police officer who now lives in Trujillo:

> [Former OPP officer Rick Mowers] rattles off how much cheaper things are in Honduras, from rent and food to crack cocaine and sex. "Here sex is, in the whole country, sex is $10. So if you go downtown, and you stop and the girl gets in your car, it's $10, 200 lempiras, for you to go have intercourse," he says. Mowers didn't mention the AIDS epidemic in the north-coast region, where over 60,000 people have HIV/AIDS, the highest infection rate in Central America. [94]

As in the mining and garment manufacturing industries, it is clear that Canada's position on the military coup is in line with the interests of its entrepreneurs on the North Coast. Where Zelaya's reformist project increasingly opened the door to dialogue with—and even state support for—Garífuna communities struggling against these Canadian enterprises, the coup government has opened its arms to the tourist trade and demonstrated a violent disregard for Garífuna activism. When, for instance, some 200 Garífuna people established a temporary camp near Vallecito to demand that the state demarcate clearly the boundary for Garífuna land title, the Instituto Nacional Agrario (National Agrarian Institute, INA) representatives sent by the Lobo government did little to protect the Garífuna activists from heavily armed security personnel. The private security forces, in the employ of local oligarchs connected to the tourist trade as well as other North Coast industries, used violence and intimidation to try to break up the Garífuna camp.[95] The camp was largely organized by OFRANEH, which concluded that the state's refusal to intervene to protect the camp from violence demonstrated that it "supports and endorses the theft of land by the groups who have taken control of the territory in the Vallecito area."[96] That conclusion seems eminently convincing, especially given the violence that individual organizers in OFRANEH have faced since the coup, and given the rapidly expanding militarization of the region, largely in support and protection of private interests.

MAKING HONDURAS "RIGHT" FOR OTTAWA

Tracing the direct investment of Canadian capital in Honduras demonstrates that there are immediate interests the Canadian state is serving in its support for the coup government. However, Canada's interest in Honduras is broader than just these industries; just as Smedley Butler was hired to make Honduras "right" for the banana magnates a century ago, Canada is today looking to secure a Honduras that will be "right" for Canadian investments across a variety of sectors. Honduras fits into an overall pattern where, as Greg Albo has described, Canada's "diplomatic offices and overseas funding [are used] to support destabilization efforts of governments identified as insufficiently 'market oriented.'"[97]

Indeed, it would be an oversimplification to imagine that Canada's actions in Honduras could be explained by a simple, straight line between the interests of individual companies and state behaviour. While Canada's foreign policy in Honduras is partly shaped by the immediate needs of companies like Goldcorp, Gildan, and Life Vision, what is really at stake in Honduras, from the perspective of the Canadian state, is the broader promotion and protection of the conditions necessary for further profitable investment. The Zelaya government not only threatened to undermine the profits of existing Canadian businesses in Honduras, it was making moves that might have made Honduras a less profitable place to do business *in general.* There have been a number of developments, before and since the coup, that point to this broader agenda. Central to the Canadian project in Honduras has been the destabilization of the reform projects that, as Albo noted, would have threatened its "market orientation." The agenda that Canada has pursued in Honduras since the coup speaks directly to this emphasis on prying Honduras open to ever-deeper degrees of foreign investment and exploitation.

There is no better example of this than the proposal—developed out of a right-wing think-tank called the McDonald-Laurier Institute—for the creation of so-called "charter cities" in Honduras. The idea was to establish in Honduran law the right of the state to grant territorial concessions to businesses within which they would possess virtual city-statehood, with their own laws, police, and foreign relations. *The Globe and Mail* celebrated the idea in April 2012:

> If you took a stretch of unused land in a troubled, developing nation like Honduras, set it up as a largely independent jurisdiction with the kind of rules-based governance that Canadians are used to, could that new system take hold? Could it rub off on other parts of the country and, over time, transform entire regions? ... The answer to all three questions is, most likely, yes.[98]

The author of the article, Jeremy Torobin, adds that Canadians could and should help govern the charter cities, and he argues that, while some people might call this a form of imperialism, it would have material benefits for everyone and, thus, it shouldn't matter what we call it.

Torobin even points to the example of British control of Hong Kong as an example of how "successful" such colonization can be. He concludes:

> There is a strong argument in the "enlightened self-interest" category, aside from [charter city advocate] Professor Romer's projections about the impact on global output, or the potential windfall for Canadian companies that might build some of the infrastructure for the new cities or, eventually, have billions more overseas customers who can afford to buy their products. Namely, Canada and all advanced economies have a stake in ensuring the massive urbanization occurring this century actually makes lives better instead of creating giant new filthy, chaotic, overcrowded slums ... Canadians are proud of their internationalist credentials, and [charter cities] could be a template for doing good work abroad that has lasting effect, and that gets the most bang for our buck.[99]

There is much to unpack in Torobin's article, and in the charter city proposal itself, which was passed into Honduran law in 2012. Torobin describes the charter cities as being placed on "unused land," a claim which must immediately be questioned. It can hardly be claimed that there is any "unused" land in Honduras, even when it is not being directly applied to the creation of profits. Land is, instead, used for a variety of other purposes, from hunting and fishing, to ceremonial space, or as a corridor to connect communities. Indeed, the existing proposals for charter cities in Honduras have mostly fallen on territory that is claimed by Indigenous and especially Garífuna communities, where the notion of "use" is far broader than that of the capitalist ideologues who seek to turn it into a corporate concession. As OFRANEH argues:

> Paul Romer's propaganda talks about building "Charter Cities" in uninhabited places. Unfortunately, in Honduras they are trying to dispossess the Garífuna people of half of our territory in order to create the RED (Special Development Region). The level of disinformation and violence that exists in this country reveals that multiple human rights violations will be caused by the establishment of a neocolonial project in the 21st century.[100]

If OFRANEH, the primary organization representing the people whose "unused" land would be used for a charter city, considers it a neocolonial project, then this is surely a critique that needs to be taken seriously.

Indeed, Torobin's further claim that Canada should participate in establishing, through the charter cities, a "rules-based" society like its own, brims with colonial arrogance and fails to grapple with the fact that Canada has been actively encouraging the impunity and lawlessness that presently govern Honduras.[101] In the meantime, he notably makes little effort to conceal the colonial nature of the charter city proposal, instead opting to defend the virtuous effects of previous colonial efforts. In the original McDonald-Laurier paper promoting the idea, Brandon Fuller and Paul Romer make the extraordinary claim that "many [Chinese people] will acknowledge that, if they had a chance to replay history, they would gladly and voluntarily offer Hong Kong to the British."[102] This is a remarkable—and unsubstantiated—statement that suggests that colonized people would ultimately *choose* their colonization for all the supposed benefits it brings. It is worth pausing on this argument here, central to the rhetorical justification of the charter city proposal to which Canada has given its full support; consciously or not, this is an almost perfect contemporary replication of the *mission civilisatrice* justification of colonization that underpinned the tremendous expansion of direct colonialism in the late nineteenth century, not to mention the justifications at the heart of the colonial project that brought Spain to Honduras in the first place.[103] As such, it is instructive to note that a central justification for one of Canada's great projects in Honduras echoes perfectly those of imperialisms of the past.

By the end of the piece, Torobin finally comes around to the really compelling motivation for the charter cities—the potential profits they could create. Given the exploitative and damaging record of Canadian companies in Honduras, there is every reason to think that the charter cities would operate in largely the same way. After all, the charter cities would not attract foreign investment if they were *less* profitable than investing in Honduras proper, and if the charter cities protected the rights of workers, communities, or the environment, the costs of doing business there would be driven up. Indeed, what seems much more likely is that the charter cities would be even more exploitative and would be even further insulated from the prospect of intervention by a social-democratic, reform-minded Honduran government. That is, enshrining a kind of hyper-neoliberalism in the legal architecture of a charter city and establishing its autonomy from the Honduran state could potentially serve to forestall the prospect of a resurgent social movement forcing a future Honduran government to move towards reform.

The Globe and Mail's rhetoric around "doing good work" is rather unconvincing. What is clear is that Canada has supported the charter city idea wholeheartedly. In 2011, Canadian senator Gerry St. Germain was in Honduras promoting the idea, calling it "an historic moment" for the country.[104] In 2012, Ambassador Cameron Mackay followed up with a major effort to promote the FTA and the charter cities, telling the Honduran media that there was some $25 million in new Canadian investment waiting to flow into Honduras when the conditions were right for it. Notably, he repeated often that Honduras needed to do a better job of maintaining peace and security; "without security, there can be no investment," he told *La Tribuna*.[105] Given the violence that Canada condoned against activists in the social movement, it seems clear that the security Mackay referred to is that of private capital. Indeed, Canada's increased involvement in the security apparatus in Honduras is a point to which we will return below.

Security in the charter cities, of course, would be provided by the business interests that owned the concession and would, no doubt, look similar to the mercenary forces currently employed by local oligarchs and transnational companies, only with even less legal recourse for the Honduran state to temper their violence. This was a point that Jari Dixon, a former public prosecutor in Honduras, returned to repeatedly when we talked in 2012, shortly after the charter city laws were passed by the Honduran Congress. "This is a tragedy; even the narco-traffickers could start a charter city," he explained, referring to the fact that narco gangs and the oligarchy are intricately linked, and both are linked to foreign capital. His comments are instructive:

> The charter city laws remind me of William Walker in the nineteenth century; he landed at Trujillo with an army, declared himself president of Nicaragua, on behalf of the gringos, inviting in the Americans and the Canadians. It's a modern form of the same thing. But people haven't realized yet that this is what it means. It's already been passed into law. We're just waiting for the time that we won't be allowed to go to the beach, to use our own rivers, because we're not citizens of the charter city and it will be too late to struggle, because these people will be so protected. Look at how hard it has been for Argentina to take back the Maldives. Once those foreigners are installed here, it will be so hard to get rid of them, because their countries will protect them. The US state, the Canadian state, they will protect the foreigners that arrive.[106]

Towards the end of our interview, Dixon offered a compelling picture of Honduras' ongoing colonization. Dixon insisted that there was a thread that connected William Walker's colonial adventure to the banana companies, the mining companies, the occupation in the 1980s, and the coup and its aftermath; that thread, he insisted, was imperialism. His analysis, which is shared by many in the social movement in Honduras, reflects the central argument of this book:

> This is a new colonization. There are so many people who see that we are being colonized. Foreigners are coming here to take advantage of our poverty and misery, and our country is perfect for them to exploit. People are told that this foreign investment will be good for us, that people can go work in the charter city, that they will make money, that their lives will change, but it's a lie. We've heard it before. We had people who worked in the mines, who worked on the banana plantations, just to earn enough to eat. And the people never got pulled out of poverty. The banana companies—Standard, Cuyamel—they came in and bought up the presidents, the congress, the mayors. They ran this country in the 1930s, 40s, 50s. By the 1980s, the 90s, it was the *maquilas*, they were supposed to employ millions of Hondurans and bring people out of poverty, but now look at the women working there, they make less than the minimum wage.[107]

The charter city legislation was passed in the Honduran Congress in 2012, after just ten days of discussion. Jari Dixon is part of a group of lawyers who have filed an injunction against the legislation, which they deem unconstitutional, but Congress has threatened to overrule any injunction brought against the charter city laws. As they presently stand, the laws allow for the creation of territorial concessions within Honduras that have the autonomy to create their own laws and police, sign independent international agreements, run their own immigration systems, and raise their own taxes.[108]

THE INSECURITY STATE IN HONDURAS

Given Canadian statements about the need for security for its investments in Honduras, it should be no surprise that Canada has cultivated close relationships with the coup regime's key people regarding security. Luis Alberto Rubí, for instance, was invited to Ottawa to speak on a panel in 2011 organized by the Department of Foreign Affairs and International Trade (DFAIT) and the International Development Research Centre (IDRC) on "Confronting Crime and Impunity in Central America."[109] Ironic, indeed, that Rubí should speak on crime and impunity, given that he was Pepe Lobo's attorney general and was a central figure in establishing the shifty legal architecture behind the coup. Cables unearthed by WikiLeaks demonstrated that Rubí "was directly involved in the decision to remove Zelaya and used the legal apparatus under his control to stifle dissent and intimidate/persecute members of Zelaya's team."[110]

The security apparatus that Canada is buttressing in Honduras—which carried out the coup and related repression—is so anti-democratic and corrupt that it cannot even be described as acting consistently on behalf of the *golpistas*. Honduran social scientist Leticia Salomón insists that rule of law and democratic functioning in Honduras are fundamentally broken.[111] Lawyer Nectali Rodezno described police corruption thus:

> It's incredible—a police officer who makes $2000 a month can have a house worth two or three million—where do they get this money from? I realize from being around the courts and the legal system in my work that they gain this money through extortion, through war taxes, and through protecting the criminals who charge such taxes.[112]

Over several interviews, Rodezno discussed dozens of different cases and contexts that detailed the level of corruption, not least of which was the fact that the police themselves are charged with the process of investigating complaints of police corruption and violence. According to Rodezno, that corruption ranges from relatively minor, daily offenses right up to the very top-level connections between police, the state, and the narco gangs.[113]

Maria Luisa Borjas, who was embedded in the Honduran National Police for twenty-five years, and at one point held the second highest rank in the Ministry of Security, concurs with Rodezno's analysis. She is now a city councillor in Tegucigalpa, after being fired from her post for pursuing corruption cases. She is one of many who believe they have been systematically removed from the police for trying to do honest work: "[the government says] it wants to deal with criminality, but they punish those police who do."[114] She points to the example of former head of the national police Ramón Antonio Sabillón Pineda. Sabillón Pineda was removed from his post in November 2014, after having developed a reputation as a police director who was willing to take on corruption inside the system. He had been named to the position in the wake of a scandal that gripped Honduras in late 2011; police murdered the son of Julieta Castellanos, rector of UNAH. Castellanos was a high-profile figure who had supported the coup, and her outcry made the case a major national spectacle. Supporting her public denunciation of the Honduran National

Police was Alfredo Landaverde, who had served as both a *diputado* and as the police commissioner, and described the system as "rotten to its core"; he was promptly assassinated by men on motorcycles at a traffic light in Tegucigalpa.[115]

Borjas insists that individual police officers who try to defy the corruption and violence of the institution are, themselves, systematically rooted out by that corrupt system. Alejandro Fernández explains this further in the Nicaraguan journal *Envío*:

> Will the current police purge do any good? Are there any good cops in our precincts? Dr. Ricardo says that several of his patients are police officers. He says their life is hell, because they're pressured by a chain of command that has made the institution into a public calamity. Those who don't want to stain their hands inevitably end up tainted by their peers' misdeeds or six feet under with their mouth sealed forever. At one time we watched the law of silence in mafia movies and now we see it multiplied tenfold in this small country where nobody is safe, not even the strongest or the richest.[116]

Julieta Castellanos was outspoken in her anger at the police for the assassination of her son and the outcry prompted the Lobo government to announce a Police Reform Commission—the "current purge" which Fernández refers to above—that would be charged with the task of determining how to reform the institution, which even Lobo acknowledged was riddled with corruption. The commission would feature five members and would be chaired by Honduran historian Victor Meza. I interviewed Meza at the offices of the Centro de Documentación de Honduras (Honduras Documentation Centre, CEDOH) and he expressed hope that the reform commission could turn things around. Nevertheless, even he could not deny that the deck was stacked against it: "Once, I believed the police could help solve the problem. Soon, I realized they were part of the problem. Now I see that they are the problem."[117] Indeed, while Meza was careful in our interview to be measured in his comments—no doubt aware of the potential ramifications for him should he veer too far from the accepted line of the coup government—he had to acknowledge that the commission was likely to receive all manner of intimidation and violence should it seek to significantly alter the dynamics in the Honduran police: "I recognize the difficulty. A journalist was recently kidnapped twenty metres from this office."[118]

The prospects, then, for the commission to "clean up" the Honduran police seemed dim. A more likely scenario, however, would see the commission propose measures to "professionalize" the police and orient them more effectively towards the protection and security of private property. After all, of the five people selected for the commission, one was to be Chilean and one Canadian, in a context where Canada and Chile are the number one and two foreign investors in Honduran mining.[119] Even as chair of the commission, Victor Meza had to admit:

> The Canadians surely support their own interests here, especially in natural resources. One of our CEDOH studies showed that 52 percent of violent conflicts in Honduras are associated with natural resource extraction.[120]

Sure enough, in May 2012, Canada named Adam Blackwell to the police commission; Blackwell had been a Canadian representative at the OAS while Canada had pushed to have Honduras reinstated after the coup, and was a former ambassador to the Dominican Republic, where he was outspoken in his support for mining legislation that favoured Canadian companies.[121] In fact, Blackwell's public statements in the Dominican Republic in the early 2000s are eerily reminiscent of Canada's statements in Honduras. In 2003, Blackwell pressured the Dominican government to accept new proposals for mining legislation; the Dominican newspaper *El Caribe* reported that Blackwell was insisting that "certain changes in the mining laws [were] required to entice serious investments in this area."[122] Blackwell also noted that Placer Dome, a massive Vancouver-based mining consortium, was holding back on $300 million in investment until the new mining laws were passed. A few months later, Canadian Prime Minister Jean Chrétien visited the country and celebrated the passing of the new mining code. A year later, Canadian private capital controlled some 90 percent of Dominican mining, much of which had previously been state-run.[123] Canada's interest in the Honduran police reform commission was clearly to orient its direction in favour of a police force that would serve the interests of Canadian capital.

When I met Victor Meza again in 2015, he acknowledged that the commission had been utterly unable to change the dynamics in Honduras. Meza concluded that, "to truly change this situation, the police need to be converted into a community network,"[124] but he acknowledged that this was unimaginable in Honduras and he intimated that other members of the commission did not necessarily share his vision. Though they brought twelve recommendations to the Honduran Congress in order to clean up the police, none were implemented and, instead, the government of Juan Orlando Hernández subsequently used the commission's findings to justify the creation of his special military-police unit, which has only made matters worse.

And the military and military-police are every bit as corrupt; Fernando Anduray, a lawyer and prominent member of the National Party (the closest to the military), admitted recently that the zones in Honduras where drugs are most heavily and freely trafficked are those under military control.[125] In a high-profile case in early 2015, four officers in the military-police were busted for kidnapping a small business owner, Luis Portillo, on behalf of one of the criminal gangs. They were busted by the police.[126] A few months earlier, eight members of the military-police raped a woman who worked at a garment factory in San Pedro Sula.[127] The military-police have also been responsible for shooting up a public bus, raiding the homes of several members of the LIBRE party, beating and arresting a human rights defender, and turning a blind eye to a shipment of drugs crossing into Guatemala.[128] As Berta Oliva describes it, "they are all corrupt, they are doing battle on behalf of rival gangs or political factions, and the citizens are sandwiched in between." She added that, after meeting with the head of the armed forces in January to talk about the need to protect human rights, she saw "not a single crack where the light can come in."[129]

GRAND STRATEGIES

It is emblematic of the shift in Canadian state priorities that it has found an ideal partner, in business and politics, in one of the most violent and corrupt regimes in the western hemisphere, and in one of its poorest countries. Evidently, it has also found a military partner in that regime; in August 2011, the Honduran Congress approved a proposal for joint exercises in Honduras with the Canadian Armed Forces.[130] The Harper government denied that Canada was planning to send troops to Honduras but, later that month, an Edmonton magazine reported that troops in Alberta were being given Spanish-language training as part of their preparation for deployments in Latin America. Indeed, the training program hired film industry professionals to create "realistic villages and towns to help soldiers get a feel for what it will be like."[131]

Rumours swirled through the Honduran social movements in late 2011 that Canadian troops were already on the ground there. Sure enough, though it is unclear when they arrived, by mid-2012 Canadian soldiers had their boots on the ground as part of an international military medical force. Reports from "Operation Beyond the Horizon" suggested that it was a humanitarian aid project, but it is, nevertheless, noteworthy in the contemporary Honduran context that Canadian soldiers are establishing their more permanent presence, especially given that Canadian troops have already been running training exercises and participating in counter-narcotics operations.[132] Significantly, Lieutenant-Commander Debbie Pestell told the media that delivering medical support was actually only the *secondary* goal of "Beyond the Horizon," the first being:

> To work together as nations so that if we ever have to quickly deploy together we've already had that experience with interoperability and logistics and tactics and time and getting everybody spooled up and working together.[133]

That Canadian troops have a primary goal of preparing for quick joint deployment with the Honduran military that overthrew a democratically elected president in 2009—and has more or less ruled Honduras ever since—is indicative of the extent to which the promotion of democracy is not a Canadian priority.

These links are not entirely new; Canada has been training military personnel in Honduras and elsewhere throughout the 2000s.[134] Many of the perpetrators of the 2009 coup are graduates of US and Canadian training programs, and in 2011 Canada was organizing comprehensive workshops on military-police co-operation through the ironically named Pearson Peacekeeping Centre.[135] Nevertheless, active participation in military operations in Honduras represents an escalation of its prior engagements. The Canadian military participated in a major counter-narcotics campaign called "Operation Martillo" in mid-2012, organized by the US and carried out across Central America and especially in Guatemala and Honduras; it was deemed a "complete success" despite the fact that a US helicopter was implicated in the murder of four Honduran civilians in La Moskitia.[136] What is more, while Stephen Harper was in Honduras to sign the FTA in 2011, he pledged $9.2 million in undisclosed support for security plans in the country.[137] Canada is now actively collaborating with *and* financing the architecture of repression; the significance of this cannot be overstated, as it suggests that Canada's support for the coup regime is actually expanding from tacit political support and diplomatic work to direct technical and material assistance.

Of course, Canada is not alone in this project. Canadian imperialism—in Honduras and elsewhere—is distinct from US imperialism but deeply linked up with it. (This is further explored in Chapter 5.) It is worth noting that the increasing presence of Canadian troops in Honduras is taking place alongside a growing US military presence as well.[138] That the United States conspired with the *golpistas* in facilitating the 2009 coup is beyond any doubt; documents released by WikiLeaks have demonstrated that the American embassy knew about the plans for the coup and considered itself the most significant "power broker" in the conflict between the oligarchy and Zelaya.[139] What is more, Hillary Clinton, then Secretary of State, bragged in her 2015 memoir *Hard Choices* that while everyone in Washington knew that it was an illegal coup, they stalled for time so that the oligarchy could consolidate its position and "render the question of Zelaya moot."[140] US complicity in the coup was apparent right from the start, and my emphasis on Canada's role does not imply otherwise.

In May 2012, the US deployment in Honduras was directly involved in a massacre of four Indigenous people in the jungle region of La Moskitia. Many months of tireless investigations by community organizations in Honduras—and North American allies—were able to piece together a relatively clear picture of events. A definitive report by Greg McCain described it thus:

> On May 11th on the Rio Patuca near Ahuas, a small municipality in the Moskitia, a helicopter titled to the US State Department sprayed bullets into a *pipante*, a long, narrow dugout canoe, which carried sixteen locals. Four people were killed: 28-year-old Juana Jackson (six months pregnant), 48-year-old Candelaria Pratt Nelson (five months pregnant), 14-year-old Hasked Brooks Wood, and 21-year-old Emerson Martínez Henríquez. At least four more were seriously injured. The DEA confirms that its Foreign-deployed Advisory Support Team (FAST) participated in the operation supporting a Honduran National Police Tactical Response Team.[141]

That the US Drug Enforcement Agency (DEA) should be directly involved in a civilian massacre is a rather predictable consequence of its ongoing partnership with the Honduran military that has been committing such offences with regularity since 2009, and it is a further reminder of the alliances Canada is actively building as it enters into joint military projects with the US and Honduras.

The incident took place under the auspices of "counter-narcotics" operations, which, ironically, had been celebrated in a series of major articles in *The New York Times* and *Washington Post*, just a few weeks before the massacre. Thom Shanker's piece in *The New York Times* noted that the US had established three new operating bases in Honduras and described what he called "the nation's new way of war," with "small-footprint" missions that are designed out of the counter-insurgency tactics used in Iraq and Afghanistan.[142] Shanker added that "American troops [in Honduras] cannot fire except in self-defense, and they are barred from responding with force even if Honduran or DEA agents are in danger," a regulation that was evidently broken just a few weeks later.[143] This incident is worth highlighting because it further demonstrates that the impunity with which Honduran military and police operate extends to the foreign militaries working with them. US and Canadian troops, then, cannot be counted upon to follow even the limited degree of restraint imposed by the terms of their agreements with the Honduran military. This is a rather worrying fact, given the legacy of US military occupation in the 1980s. And, since no one from the DEA faced any reprisal for the massacre in La Moskitia, it is rather difficult to deny that foreign forces in Honduras act with impunity, which does not bode well for the social movements who are seeking to defend themselves against the further parceling out and selling off of their land and resources.

The increased North American military presence—and the impunity that continues to reign in Honduras—is just one piece of the project to impose a hyper-neoliberalism on that country to facilitate further profitable investment or, put differently, to secure more easily exploitable Honduran resources and labour. While the claim is that the emerging regional security apparatus is being built for the war against drug trafficking, the reality is that its strongest partners are not "failed" states but those run by drug trafficking networks, where the people in power are almost indistinguishable from the narco gangs.[144] Indeed, as Annie Bird has argued, Honduras' increasing militarization is taking place in the context of the deeper remilitarization of the entire region, particularly as part of the regional security partnership, Sistema de la Integración Centroamericana (System of Central American Integration, SICA).[145] SICA is widely considered to be driven by the interests of powers outside of the actual alliance, primarily the United States, Canada, and Colombia, which increasingly co-operate with the Honduran regime. "Nicaragua is not considered a partner in the drug war," Bird argues, "despite having recorded the highest number of actual drug hits. So, in fact, the real war here is against those who are resisting global capital and its neoliberal projects."[146] This broader regional security apparatus, as it is being applied in Honduras, is modelled after the Colombian example, which draws upon networks of neighbourhood "informants" who help the military produce lists of people who are connected to the social movements, and, therefore, are the real targets of the so-called "drug war."[147]

Bird's analysis is compelling because it links the Honduran case into the broader regional dynamics. Drawing her analysis from the well-documented "Plan Puebla Panama" preparations, Bird argues that transnational capital and its state-level representatives had, broadly speaking, a three-pronged strategy for the deep imposition of neoliberalism in Central America, following the end of the regional wars of the 1980s. The first of these three prongs was the legal architecture for the re-entry of capital after the wars, as manifested in the restructuring of the respective states, the signing of the Central America Free Trade Agreement (CAFTA) and bilateral FTAs, and the gradual rewriting of legal codes around natural resources, public services, and other potentially profitable industries. Second was the construction of the physical infrastructure—from a series of new highways, railroads, and seaports to hydro dams, electrical integration, and transmission lines—for the effective development of new production, shipping, and distribution centres.[148] Third was the establishment of a reliable security apparatus to protect businesses looking to take advantage of the new conditions and profitably exploit their concessions.[149] This final element of the broad strategy is, according to Bird, only now beginning to fall into place, and the coup and the project to establish and support a compliant—and necessarily repressive—security apparatus in Honduras is a key element of that regional plan.[150]

At an even broader level, it needs to be noted that the coup in Honduras may yet prove to be a key event in the effort—by the Anglo-American countries—to roll back the so-called "Pink Tide" in Latin America. The inequality and poverty associated with the imposition of neoliberalism south of the Rio Grande led, in the late 1990s and 2000s, to a resurgence of the organized left that manifested in a wave of electoral victories by left-liberal and socialist parties. While the most notable example was the rise of Hugo Chávez in Venezuela, the governments of several countries—Bolivia, Ecuador, Argentina, Brazil, Nicaragua, Uruguay, Paraguay, and Chile—shifted to the left over the course of the 2000s. While many of these governments represented a tentative compromise between the ruling classes and frustrated masses and, therefore, contained many of the inconsistencies that were manifest in the Manuel Zelaya government, it was a significant development that might have led to even greater popular mobilizations across the continent.

However, the overthrow of Zelaya in Honduras—and the support it received from Canada and the US—suggested that the imperialist powers were no longer going to accept the "Pink Tide." Since 2009, outside pressure has mounted on those governments. Nicolás Maduro, successor of Hugo

Chávez, has been subjected to concerted efforts from Washington to have him overthrown; Fernando Lugo of Paraguay was deposed in 2012 in a sketchy impeachment process, deemed a coup by many Latin American leaders; Cristina Fernández de Kirchner of Argentina was defeated by the right wing in 2015; and a parliamentary coup unseated Dilma Roussef in Brazil in 2016. In every case, North American involvement has been evident. As the "Pink Tide" has been rolled back, often replaced by far-right governments, the prospects for social justice in each country have declined, while opportunities for profits for US and Canadian firms have opened up.[151] Viewed in this light, the coup in Honduras may be a watershed moment in the history of Latin America.

Given all of this, it is profoundly significant that Canadian investment in Honduras, and Canadian co-operation with the Honduran government, have dramatically *increased* since the military coup in 2009. That is, there is a direct correlation between state violence and the intensification of neoliberalism on the one side, and Canadian participation in Honduras on the other. The coup was not incidental to Canadian investment in Honduras; rather, it spurred it forward. Bilateral trade between the two countries increased by 9.3 percent from 2009–10, in the first years of the coup. It jumped over 22 percent in 2011.[152] In 2015, after the signing of the FTA, that number had nearly doubled from the 2011 total.[153] This very clearly suggests that Canada's support for the coup regime is connected to its direct economic interests in Honduras and its broader political-economic interests in the Central American isthmus. Indeed, the assertion that Canada is behaving as an imperial power in Honduras comes first and foremost from Hondurans themselves. Jari Dixon's compelling sketch of a Honduras being recolonized by Canadian capital should be as clear an indication as any that Canada can no longer hide behind the mythology of its peacekeeping past. The peaceful, democratic social movement in Honduras, like so many in the Global South today, names Canada directly as its enemy; there is perhaps nothing that could validate the central argument of this book more than this simple and stubborn fact.[154]

5 MIDDLE POWER OR EMPIRE'S ALLY? Canada's Place in the World Today

How can we make sense of Canada's behaviour in Honduras in light of everything we have been taught that Canada represents? It would be tempting to think that the history compiled here is an isolated case; an outcome of poor policy, or Conservative Party machinations, or the power of big business. Those factors are certainly all part of the story in Canada's support for the Honduran coup, but they cannot account for the fact that this case fits the new archetype of Canadian foreign policy. To explain that, we need to go deeper than the whims of one political party or another and seek to answer the question: "What is Canada?"

Canada was born a settler colony, founded upon the conquest of Indigenous people and their forced insertion into the French and English mercantile systems. By the latter half of the nineteenth century, Canada had developed the basic structures of a capitalist state and, especially following Confederation in 1867, that project depended upon the complete colonization and genocide of Indigenous nations and their subjugation under the Canadian state.[1] Subsequently, Canada emerged as a significant capitalist power in the world and, especially since the end of the Cold War, it has applied that colonial logic first expressed in the consolidation of Canada directly to its foreign policy. Since at least the 1990s, Canada has played the role of a *bona fide* imperial power—a secondary component in a capitalist world order dominated by US military and political hegemony.

The argument here is not that Canada is dependent on the US and therefore unable to carve out an independent and benevolent foreign policy, as many progressive-minded Canadians wish to believe. Rather, we must confront the fact that Canada is an imperial power with policy autonomy in its own right, albeit one that chooses to align itself closely with projects of US imperialism. Indeed, to the extent that the objectives of Canadian capital are linked into the broader project of imposing a global neoliberal order, the Canadian state does have an interest in deepening its connection to the apparatus of US global power. Nevertheless, as we will see, Canadian capital has its own unique interests and finds itself in competition with other blocs of capital, US or otherwise, for access to the profits made possible by that neoliberal order. As such, the Canadian state, as the primary agent of this specifically Canadian capitalist class, pursues projects of imperialism not because it is beholden to the United States, but because they are necessary for the continued expansion of Canadian capital.

Documenting the full extent of the new Canadian imperialism will require multiple volumes and a wide variety of voices. Thankfully, this project is being taken up. Notable among recent attempts to theorize Canadian imperialism is Jerome Klassen's *Joining Empire* (2014), which offers a methodical theorization of this phenomena. Other significant contributions include Sherene Razack's *Dark Threats and White Knights* (2004), Todd Gordon's *Imperialist Canada* (2010), the edited volume *Empire's Ally* (2013), and Paul Kellogg's *Escape from the Staples Trap* (2015). Nevertheless, the study of Canadian imperialism is still in its infancy. This book adds a crucial piece to this growing literature but, since the purpose of this book is to trace these dynamics through the very particular case study of Honduras, I will not attempt to cover every aspect of contemporary Canadian imperialism here. Rather, this chapter will distill the crucial aspects of this dynamic, in order to situate the Honduran case in the broader trajectory of Canadian politics, and to demonstrate why this case study is so significant.

CAPITALISM AND IMPERIALISM

A snapshot of the world today reflects a persistent and growing reality of radically unequal levels of wealth, power, and privilege, both within individual states and across the international community. These profound inequalities are empirically indisputable, and are reflected in statistics that truly boggle the mind: in 2014, Oxfam reported that the world's richest 85 people controlled as much wealth as the poorest 50 percent of the world's population.[2] Regional breakdowns indicate that nearly 70 percent of the world's wealth in 2014 was held in Europe and North America (despite their accounting for less than 20 percent of the world's population).[3] Even within the wealthiest regions of the world, wealth is profoundly stratified: in Canada, the richest 86 individuals have a net worth equivalent to the poorest 11.4 million Canadians and possess more wealth than the entire province of New Brunswick.[4] I often explain this to my students by noting that at my current level of income as a college professor, it would take me more than 10,000 years to reach the level of wealth possessed by the Thomson family (Canada's richest at over $26 billion).

While much mainstream discourse about international politics ignores or obscures this massive inequality, the critical left tradition has long recognized that the roots of that inequality lay in the dynamics of capitalism and the projects of imperialism that are compelled by it. Pre-eminent Marxist geographer David Harvey has argued that contemporary capitalism cannot function without recourse to imperial projects that satisfy capital's constant, harrowing need for dynamic growth.[5] Building from this recognition, David McNally offers a compelling definition of imperialism that captures its broad historical dynamics:

> Imperialism is a system of global inequalities and domination – embodied in regimes of property, military power and global institutions – through which wealth is drained from the labour and resources of people in the Global South to the systematic advantage of capital in the North.[6]

More than a decade into the twenty-first century, it has become widely accepted that the willingness of the United States to exercise its overwhelming political, military, and economic power in the world is an expression of global and hegemonic aspirations. Even in mainstream social science, this is increasingly, if grudgingly, understood as a new form of imperialism, which is no longer defined solely by the direct occupation of territory. Mainstream observers like Niall Ferguson and Michael Ignatieff, for instance, celebrate the re-emergence of openly imperial politics. Ignatieff, as noted in the introduction to this book, actually championed Canadian imperialism as a kind of "empire lite" and was a candidate for prime minister in 2011.[7] It is notable that a prominent member of Canada's elite political class should produce one of the most important intellectual justifications of contemporary imperialism, given Canada's emergence as a significant imperial power.

Nevertheless, mainstream discussion of imperialism is typically superficial in its understanding of the phenomena and/or celebratory of its supposedly progressive project. The critical—and especially Marxist—tradition, by contrast, has produced robust debates around the fundamental nature of imperialism as well as normative critiques of its harmful and destructive logic and consequences.[8] Identifying those consequences is a central project of this book, as the experience of Honduras provides a window into many different forms of imperialism, ranging from the direct colonial occupation by the Spanish in the sixteenth century to the neo-colonial control exercised by Britain and the United States in the nineteenth century, to the regional domination of the Cold War American "sphere of influence" in the twentieth century. In each case, political and especially economic power was held by the foreign metropole, assisted by a small section of local elite, and the levers of state power were twisted to the benefit of metropolitan conquerors and businesses seeking to exploit Honduran land and people in order to extract profits.

It is with this latter form of imperialism that Canada has increasingly aligned itself. Dubbed "the new imperialism" in its twenty-first century variety by David Harvey, it is best exemplified by the vigorous—and often violent—imposition of neoliberal governance on post-Soviet and Global South states, by their metropolitan counterparts, in an effort to create new spaces of potential profits for over-accumulated capital. That is, as capital repeatedly finds itself unable to feed its desperate desire for dynamic growth—and is thus at risk of slipping into stagnation and slump—it must find "new" sources of profits. The political agents of capital, then, will create these new spaces by dispossessing states and communities—especially in the Global South—of whatever wealth they can, such that it can be snapped up and turned into profits for metropolitan capital.[9] For instance, the privatization of a state telecommunications company in Latin America, hitherto inaccessible to private accumulation, becomes a source of profitable investment for over-accumulated capital in the North. If enough of these sorts of "fixes" can be created to keep capital growing, then recession and depression—which always carry the prospect of a truly dramatic collapse—can be staved off a little longer.[10]

Indeed, it is worth emphasizing that the dynamics of capitalism are such that each capitalist or block of capitalists must always be expanding, otherwise they will be outpaced by their competitors and run the risk of going bust. As such, if profits cannot be produced within the borders of the state, capital will naturally look for potential profits outside those borders. When Lenin described imperialism as the "highest stage" of capitalism, he hit upon the crucial insight that imperialism is a tendency motivated by *desperation* to find new sources of profits.[11] Fuelled by fear that the machine of growth might slow, imperialism is an expression of the manic logic of accumulation: it is desperate, rapacious, calculated, and ruthless all at the same time, and it leads to the prioritizing of profits over every other normative concern. Marx and Engels poignantly describe the insecurity and mania—the spiritual illness—of trying to *be* imperial capital, in the *Communist Manifesto*:

> The need of a constantly expanding market for its products chases the bourgeoisie over the entire surface of the globe. It must nestle everywhere, settle everywhere, establish connexions everywhere.[12]

It is, notably, *need of capital* that is doing the chasing; the would-be capitalists are the chased. I draw this out not to elicit sympathy for exploitative capitalists, but to highlight the structural dynamics that all but guarantee that capital will pursue the imperialist road. Canadian capitalists, for their part, clearly feel themselves "chased" by the need to expand; as Thomas D'Aquino, long-time president of the Canadian Council of Chief Executives (CCCE), noted, "Canada's leading players are all engaged actively in expansion abroad for the simple reason that Canada does not have enough room for them to achieve global scale."[13]

Naturally, this imperial project is usually undertaken with the co-operation of local agents, typically from some combination of the local oligarchy and/or the established political and military apparatus, which are willing to further the imperial project in order to, themselves, cash in on the benefits of working within what Ellen Wood calls the "empire of capital."[14] Indeed, the idea that capital itself is an imperial overlord rightly points to the fact that, in the context of increasingly worrisome crises, capital finds itself compelled towards ever more co-ordinated forms of class struggle.[15] Neoliberalism, then, can be understood as a class project undertaken by global capital against the global working class, and its architecture (as manifested in the apparatus of international trade laws, the dictates of the WTO, IMF, and World Bank, or in bilateral and multilateral free trade agreements) is designed to promote the interests of capital, whatever its nationality. That said, the dynamism of capitalism is propelled forward only by competition *between* capitals, even while global capital co-operates to manage its crises.[16] Canada finds itself collaborating with US imperialism even while it pursues its own imperialist agenda to give an advantage to Canadian capital over its rivals.

A HELPFUL FIXER?

While some Canadian scholarship has been willing to accept the idea of US imperialism, few have applied such a critical lens to Canada. In fact, the predominant characterization of Canada has been that of a "helpful fixer" in global affairs, trying to maintain peace and stability in a troubled world.[17] Though the study of Canadian foreign policy is filtered through several traditions with slight differences—most notably the so-called realist and liberal schools—the thread that connects most mainstream and academic understandings of Canadian foreign policy is the assumption that Canada has been primarily engaged in the world as a well-intentioned force for "good" and that what we need to assess is whether its methods have been effective. That is, they present no doubt that Canada means well; the only question is whether, and when, its efforts have been successful.

Not only is this the standard language used by the Canadian political class, it is also easily observed in any high school or undergraduate-level textbook on Canadian history, politics, or foreign policy. Take *Democracy, Diversity and Good Government*, an introductory text co-authored by three Canadian academics in 2011, which arguably represents a relatively progressive version of mainstream discourse on Canadian politics. While the chapter on foreign policy offers a few tentative critiques of Canada's retreat from peacekeeping and notes the decline in Canadian development assistance programs,[18] it nevertheless ascribes to Canada a long-term, almost innate, desire to do good and, furthermore, assumes that the rest of the world agrees with that assessment:

> Throughout much of the world, Canada enjoys a reputation as a country that promotes international harmony, peace, and global order.... Canada as a "middle power" tries to constrain the great powers by encouraging (particularly in cooperation with other middle powers) the development of international law and multilateral organizations such as the United Nations. Through such organizations, the great powers can be encouraged to respect rules and laws that less powerful countries like Canada have a hand in shaping. Canada, particularly during the time [Lester] Pearson served as External Affairs minister, became known as the "helpful fixer" of international problems through the use of quiet diplomacy.[19]

While the text mentions that peacekeeping has been marginalized in Canadian policy for nearly twenty years, it nevertheless introduces the chapter with a special feature on Lester Pearson, his 1957 Nobel Peace Prize, and Canada's peacekeeping legacy. The assumption that Canada means well in the world is woven into every debate that the authors present, and they conclude that Canada is a "model for other countries" striving to achieve democracy and good government.[20]

Like Michael Ignatieff's remarks cited in the Introduction, the voices that set the tone for mainstream understandings of Canadian foreign policy assume that Canada has successfully solved the problems of democracy and good governance and should now turn to the task of "teaching" everyone else how to do it. Even as Canada has explicitly transitioned away from peacekeeping towards aggressive military engagement—a transition discussed in more detail below—mainstream analyses tend to explain this transition in terms of new, external threats to "global security" posed by "international terrorism" since 9/11. Typically, the only debate to be found is over what ought to be the appropriate response to this external threat. The realist tradition (reflected in the approach of the Conservative Party) tends to endorse increased military and defence spending and deployment to root out potential "terrorist threats," while liberals (often taken up by the Liberal Party and the NDP) respond with a policy framework that mixes military force with international mechanisms for conflict resolution and poverty relief in order to forestall the emergence of "terrorist threats" in the first place.[21] Nevertheless, both of these responses rest upon an analysis that sees Canadian foreign policy as being driven by the desire to make Canada and the world better and safer. Canada's benevolence is never questioned; rather, it is imagined that shifts in Canadian policy simply reflect changing trends in electoral politics, which then lead to variations in the extent and manner in which Canada's benevolence is manifest.

Leading examples of these mainstream understandings of the genesis of Canadian policy are often uninspiring. Storied Canadian historians Norman Hillmer and Jack Granatstein's *Empire to Umpire,* now in its second edition, is an emblematic account of the history of Canadian foreign policy and relations with the United States that consistently fails to assess policy at a level that goes deeper than the competing quirks and personalities of top level politicians. From those wealthy male representatives of the ruling class, the authors divine generalizations about "Canadian attitudes" and reify a variety of theoretically dubious claims about Canada, Canadians, morality, and "common sense." It is worth considering this passage:

> Jaded Canadians also forget that, troubled as their country might be by division and economic problems, it is one of the world's few success stories. Domestic prosperity aside, Canada has a reputation for trying to solve global problems, for contributing to world betterment, and for attempting to improve the lot of people in the Third World. We are not the world arbiter we sometimes pretend to be, unfortunately, but if

> the superpowers and mad-dog nation states had exercised anything like the good sense that Canadians have shown in the last century then possibly, just possibly, the world might be a better place.[22]

This type of analysis sets the tone for much discussion of Canadian foreign policy. One gets no sense of the distinctions within Canada society: the hierarchies of class, race, and gender that determine whose interests are defined as "Canadian." Nor are we given a framework for what constitutes "good sense" in the world. Since Hillmer and Granatstein praise Canada's "domestic prosperity," should we assume that they consider the profoundly unequal development engendered by industrial capitalism to be a good thing? It would then follow that imposing that system on the rest of the world would be an example of "good sense." This version of "good sense" surely does not have universal applicability. The process of Canada's colonization of hundreds of Indigenous nations was precisely the violent assertion of these "Canadian" moral codes over those of their victims. The assumption that "Canadian values" should be universal is a rather troubling manifestation of a colonial attitude.[23]

And yet, the work produced by Hillmer and Granatstein is a cornerstone for most popular writing on Canadian foreign policy, which has grown increasingly assertive of "Canadian values" in the past two decades. Andrew Cohen's *While Canada Slept* (2003) was a finalist for a Governor General's Literary Award, despite being analytically and theoretically shallow, and lacking rigor in its research.[24] Cohen treats "Canada" as though it were a wayward child, navigating its relationship with its "best friend" the United States and "maturing" into greater "self-confidence":

> Modesty is no virtue for a country in search of influence, and excellence is no vice. We have to try harder and speak louder, even if it is only to ourselves about ourselves ... at the end of the day, we can have the world's best small army, its most efficient, generous aid program, and its most imaginative foreign service. We can reject mediocrity ... what we do abroad will enrich us at home.[25]

On the last point Cohen stumbles into a rather profound truth: Canadian capital *has* made riches abroad. But his analysis neither explains how or why that is the case and, as such, is profoundly ill-equipped to assess it normatively. Instead, Cohen offers much empty speculation on a kind of essential Canadian "character," again erasing the divisions within Canadian society, as though all Canadians had an equal hand in shaping Canadian policy. Cohen's emphasis on Canadian "character" is, unfortunately, not uncommon, even in critical traditions. Writing in a 2007 collection of essays, Stephen Clarkson and Maria Banda describe Canada as "reverting to its instinctive helpful fixer role" in its diplomatic efforts after 9/11.[26] If Canada is understood as "instinctively" benevolent, explaining its deeply destructive behaviour over the past two decades would require some intellectual somersaults. Regrettably, much Canadian scholarship has excelled in this gymnastic art.

HOLDING THE BULLY'S COAT?

The stumbling block, even for progressive Canadians, has been the pervasive doubt over whether Canada *could* be an imperialist power. If Canada is an economic dependency of the United States, then the logic follows that Canada could not chart its own foreign policy even if it wanted to. This position is sometimes described as "left nationalism" and it insists that Canada needs first to assert its independence from the United States in order to regain control of its own policies, which it could presumably then turn to better ends. For those committed to the idea of a "good" Canada, this position is tempting, insofar as it seems to address Canada's bad behaviour, but retains a fundamental Canadian "innocence." The consequences of this analysis, and its critiques, are significant for how we interpret Canada's present engagement in the world. We will look at the crucial points here before turning to the problems of the present.

Two central figures in the left nationalist tradition are Kari Levitt and Mel Watkins, whose work in the 1970s built on the small but significant early Canadian political economy pioneered by Harold Innis. Levitt and Watkins developed and adapted Innis' early description of Canada as being caught in a "staples trap" in which it produced only raw materials. These staples were exported at low prices to be converted into more valuable commodities in Britain or the United States and sold back to Canadians at higher prices. Levitt and Watkins asserted that Canada had become a full-fledged dependency of the United States and that its burgeoning industrial sector had been, by the 1970s, "hollowed out" by a systematic sell-off to US capital. In *Silent Surrender*, the book that defined the left nationalist position, Kari Levitt argued:

> In Canada economic resources are allocated primarily to suit the requirements of large private corporations, and the majority of these are under United States control.... The Canadian entrepreneurs of yesterday are the coupon clippers and hired vice-presidents of branch plants of today.... Meaningful exercise of political democracy requires the

> freedom to fully shape Canadian institutions without fear of reprisal by vested corporate interest.[27]

In other words, Canadian industries were predominantly owned by US firms, which, for Levitt and Watkins, implied that the Canadian economy was profoundly dependent on US capital and, as such, could potentially be subject to the kinds of imperial discipline often imposed on Global South states.

This led them to the conclusion that Canada was a "rich dependency," caught in the dynamics that made Global South states beholden to the whims of US policy, but uniquely privileged with pre-existing wealth that persisted in the commercial and financial sectors. Though they offered little explanation for where that pre-existing wealth came from, they believed the Canadian elite was maintaining its wealth by providing commercial and financial services to US manufacturing firms, which had seized control of Canadian industry and pushed the rest of the Canadian capitalist class into the resource sector. As a result, they concluded that Canada could not possibly chart its own policy programs independent of the United States, since the Canadian economy relied so heavily on US investment, which could be punitively withdrawn.

Though Levitt was conscious of the pitfalls of "retrogressive flag-waving nationalism,"[28] her arguments invariably led to an assertion that Canada should "reclaim" its industries. But could Canada really claim to be part of the surge in anti-colonial nationalism that gripped the Global South in the 1960s and 1970s? That movement was responding to more than just foreign ownership of local industry; it was an answer to a whole range of colonial practices and attitudes designed to assert the dominance of the colonizer over the colonized, politically, socially, economically, and culturally.[29] For a Canadian nationalist response to make sense, one had to accept the idea that Canada was a colonized dependency of the United States.

But, even in the 1970s, many observers thought the comparison between Canada and Global South states was misguided. In 1975, Steve Moore and Debi Wells published an early critique of the left nationalist position, asserting that Canada was, in fact, still significantly more powerful than most Global South countries and was part of a network of imperialist powers that were collectively dominating the rest. To Moore and Wells, the important question was whether Canada was being incorporated into the multinational network of imperial powers, centred around (but not necessarily subservient to) the United States, that were increasingly co-operating to turn the mechanisms of international organizations like the IMF and World Bank to collectively dominate smaller, peripheral states.

Moore and Wells insisted that the dynamics between Canada and the United States did not look so different from those between the US and the European imperial powers, noting that dependence on the US was "a general trend" as imperialist powers in North America and Europe were consolidated through "the nexus of world trade" and "interpenetration of capital among imperial countries."[30] That is, while they did not deny that Canadian capital did, to some extent, depend on its relationships and connections to the US economy, they insisted that it be understood as part of the broader dynamics taking place among imperial powers. Moore and Wells document a variety of measures taken collectively by imperial powers to maintain the radically unequal character of global capitalism, highlighting the fact that Canada consistently participated on the side of the imperial powers. Examples included the direct combining of capitals to dominate industries in the Global South, the administration of international financial organizations like the World Bank that worked to maintain the architecture of global capitalism, and participation in military and diplomatic alliances with the imperial powers, as in the cases of NATO and NORAD. They concluded:

> The key question is not whether Canada is a junior or senior partner (it is obviously a junior partner), but whether Canada is becoming an increasingly important component part of the imperialist system or whether Canada is being rejected by imperialism i.e., whether Canada is being forced into the status of a neo-colony. The above examples indicate that Canada is a part of the world imperialist system.[31]

Canada, then, was not uniquely or colonially subservient to the United States. Rather, it was one of a number of smaller imperial powers experiencing the assertion of US power *within* the imperialist camp.[32] This work was quick to gain support; in a special 1981 issue of *Studies in Political Economy*, both Leo Panitch and David McNally critiqued the left nationalist position[33] and, over the next two decades, work published by William Carroll, Jorge Niosi, and Bill Burgess bolstered the critique of the left nationalist thesis by more carefully examining the Canadian capitalist class itself. That work consistently demonstrated that, by at least the mid-1980s, a Canadian national capitalist class controlled the majority of assets in the Canadian economy and was beginning to expand into foreign markets, a point which grew increasingly clear as time passed.[34] The significance of this work was to concretely demonstrate that a uniquely Canadian capitalist class could exert its own pressure on the Canadian state. Both domestic and foreign policy could be pursued for the purposes of Canadian capital, rather than simply being an extra arm for the United States.

Nevertheless, the late 2000s saw a significant re-emergence of the left nationalist analysis, in the work of Mel Hurtig, Mario Seccarachia, Andrew Jackson, and, especially, Linda McQuaig, whose 2007 *Holding the Bully's Coat* is still one of the most popular left analyses of Canada's foreign policy today. Fearing that Canada was slipping into a peripheral or colonial status, they argued that Canada had been sold out by a conservative comprador elite that had allowed the US to dominate Canadian industry and, as a result, to exert powerful influence over Canadian policy. Fundamental to this position was the assumption that Canada's freedom to control its own policies was limited by US ownership of Canadian enterprises.[35] This claim has, at times, been popular among Canada's opposition parties; McQuaig herself is a member of the NDP and her position has been repeated by Elizabeth May, leader of the Green Party, who has argued that "Canadian environmental law [is] unguarded against motivated US corporate lobby interests."[36] The problem with this argument is that Canadian environmental laws (among others) are vulnerable to not just US but predominantly Canadian corporate interests. Many very thoughtful and critical Canadian scholars and activists have adopted versions of this argument: in the 2007 collection *Whose Canada?,* Bruce Campbell calls Canada a "colonial supplicant;"[37] Murray Dobbin claims that we are in the final stage of the "assimilation of the Canadian economy into that of the US;"[38] and even editors Ricardo Grinspun and Yasmine Shamsie highlight "the loss of policy autonomy resulting from trade and investment agreements."[39]

It needs to be noted that there is a shared critical spirit that is reflected in both sides of this debate. One might be tempted to ask whether it makes any difference, since everyone in this debate agrees that Canada is projecting a foreign policy that is damaging and unjust. But the implications of this debate are significant, insofar as they suggest very different strategies of resistance: one which asserts Canadian independence as a progressive step, the other which insists upon direct confrontation with Canadian nationalist politics. Thus, it is out of respect for the importance of these questions, and all who undertake answering them, that I insist upon getting to the heart of the matter.

As such, it remains an important fact that Canadian capital was increasingly concentrated following the Second World War, and that process of concentration accelerated during the 1980s, a decade in which there were 7,732 mergers and acquisitions in the Canadian economy.[40] That is, the ownership of Canadian firms became increasingly interlocked and concentrated in the hands of a small, powerful Canadian capitalist class.[41] According to William Carroll's critical 2004 study of the Canadian corporate elite, *Corporate Power in a Globalizing World*, Canada's largest 250 firms have typically had fewer than 500 different individuals on their boards of directors, making the Canadian national bourgeoisie one of the most concentrated in any advanced capitalist economy.[42] In fact, Canadian firms have a much higher concentration of controlling shareholders than does the United States, and have a relatively small number of transnational ownership links that interrupt the intra-Canadian matrix of ownership.[43] The overlapping and interlocking networks of corporate ownership demonstrate that Canada hosts what could arguably be called an oligarchy, a small network of incredibly powerful and wealthy capitalists who, by virtue of their concentration of corporate power, exert significant pressure on the Canadian state.[44] Put simply, the fact that a small number of individuals personally control most of Canada's wealth makes it very easy for those individuals to organize themselves to marshal their collective resources to influence and infiltrate the state.

Furthermore, with respect to the left nationalist fear of foreign ownership, Jerome Klassen demonstrates that, by 2007, Canada's GDP was the ninth largest in the world and US firms only owned around 12 percent of Canadian assets.[45] Canadian firms have relatively few foreign interruptions in their ownership networks, especially the largest and most profitable among them, and this dynamic has been steadily increasing since the early 1980s.[46] Indeed, American–Canadian trade has actually served to strengthen the Canadian capitalist class *vis-à-vis* other international competitors. By 2006, Canada was the ninth-highest source of foreign direct investment (FDI) flows in the world, and Canadian firms had more money invested abroad than there was foreign capital invested in Canada. While in 2006 around $500 billion in Canadian assets were owned by foreign firms, almost $515 billion in foreign assets were owned by Canadian firms, pointing towards the fact that, as the Canadian bourgeoisie has consolidated, it has looked outward in order to cash in on the spoils of neoliberal globalization.[47] As of 2015, Canada was reporting over $1 trillion in outward FDI, with an FDI surplus of well over $2 billion.[48]

In 2008, Canada recorded its first-ever surplus in bilateral FDI with the United States, investing some $17 billion more in the US than the US did in Canada. By 2015, Canadian firms had over $60 billion more invested in the US than American firms had in Canada.[49] As Todd Gordon points out, the Canadian capitalist class itself is proud of its accomplishments; a University of Toronto-based corporate think-tank claimed that, in 2006, seventy-two Canadian firms were among the "global leaders," up from thirty-three in 1985, cutting across a wide variety of sectors beyond simply resource extraction.[50] To the extent that Canada has sought deeper integration with the United States, it has not been a function of dependency but, rather, as Henry Heller has argued, a conscious and active strategy of Canadian foreign policy.[51]

A SHORT HISTORY OF CANADIAN FOREIGN POLICY

Mainstream accounts of Canadian foreign policy fail to adequately explain how Canadian policy has been generated and to what ends. Instead, we must dig into the critical traditions that are not hampered by a naïve insistence that the Canadian state inherently wants to be "helpful." In so doing, we can build a history of Canada's foreign policy that makes it much easier to comprehend how Canada came to behave with such callous disregard for its neighbours in Honduras and elsewhere.

As noted above, Canada's first experience of "foreign policy" was with the Indigenous people upon whose land Canada was built. The decimation of Indigenous nations was a seminal event in world history and the trajectory of the Canadian state cannot be separated from it. Early French and British colonial relations with Indigenous nations, while they were often exploitative and violent, did not actually reach their most terrifying genocidal heights until the late nineteenth century. To be sure, the Europeans arrived uninvited and set up their farmsteads and trading posts without regard for the effects that their presence would have on the nations whose land they had invaded. What is more, those effects were disastrous, as the unleashing of smallpox on Indigenous nations led to catastrophic death rates, which subsequently created food crises by ravaging the very people who would have been responsible for hunting.[52] As European penetration into the west proceeded, so too did the scourge of disease, and Indigenous life was increasingly reorganized around the new trade relationships that flowed through European trading posts. Nevertheless, for the first 200 years of the significant European presence in what is now Canada, the settler colony was established primarily for the purpose of mercantile trade—the extraction of raw materials, especially furs, to be sold in Europe—and thus did not seek to establish direct dominion over Indigenous people. Rather, they were the primary source of labour for the fur trade, and were used as agents in the conflicts between the English and French.

This dynamic shifted around the time of Confederation in 1867, which was designed by the emerging capitalist class of British North America as a way to cement its position on the continent—rather than being absorbed into the United States—and was predicated on the significant emergence of capitalist social relations after the 1840s, as waves of immigration from Ireland provided a reserve army of labour.[53] As the new social relations in Canada took shape, the growing capitalist class sought to industrialize production and consolidate the vast territory it could potentially transform into private property. John A. Macdonald's National Policy was designed to precisely this end, and this necessitated a more complete colonization of the country. The construction of the transcontinental railway and the complete subjugation of Indigenous peoples under the dominion of Canada would become central preoccupations of the state after Confederation.[54]

Indeed, the cumulative effects of Canadian policy towards Indigenous people following Confederation can only be described as genocide, since these policies had as their intention the complete destruction of Indigenous nations. The Indian Act, the creation of the reserve system, the residential schools, and indeed the forced starvation of Indigenous communities were just a few of the darkest aspects of Canada's brutal colonial policy during this period.[55] It is worth emphasizing that the Canadian capitalist class always prioritized its needs over the lives of Indigenous people: in the 1880s, when famine ravaged the plains (due in part to the disappearance of the bison after the introduction of European cattle ranching), the Canadian state selectively offered relief to communities willing to submit to the treaty process.[56] That is, the state withheld food rations from those who refused to give up their lands and allowed them to starve to death. Such was the extent to which Canada's priority was gaining access to Indigenous land and, needless to say, it has echoes in Canada's willingness to facilitate violence in Honduras in order to assert its businesses' control over land there.

The roots of Canada's colonial project run very deep indeed. Of course, Canadian statesmen did not consider the settling of the west to be a matter of foreign policy; even before they had signed the deeply problematic treaties, they considered all of the territory north of the forty-ninth parallel to belong to Canada. From the standpoint of the Canadian elite, foreign policy after Confederation was largely about carving out space for an independent—from Great Britain—foreign policy. That goal was more or less achieved over the course of the World Wars, after the Canadian state demonstrated its willingness and ability to send its own working-class people to their deaths in Europe. At the outbreak of WWI, then-Prime Minister Robert Borden used the war to try to increase his voice in British politics; the Dominion of Canada sent some 500,000 soldiers to war—about one of every sixteen Canadians—and over 60,000 of them never returned.[57] Many were conscripted—sacrificed by the Canadian state against their will—to fight for Great Britain, after Borden and the leader of the opposition Wilfrid Laurier enthusiastically declared, "Our answer [to the outbreak of war] goes at once, and it goes in the classical language of the British answer to the call of duty: Ready, Aye, Ready!"[58]

Canada was even willing to intervene in the Russian Revolution to assert its role in international politics, though it is worth noting that the interests of private capital were present in Canadian statecraft even then; Canada invaded Russia in 1917 at Archangel and Murmansk and, in 1919, an army of nearly 5,000 Canadians landed in Siberia to try to destroy the new workers' state.[59] Joining the mission was Canadian Trade and Commerce official Dana Wilgress, who "had great hopes for a huge Russian market after the Revolution was defeated."[60] The defeat of Russia's revolution did not work out, but at the end of two great wars, Britain was exhausted, Canada had asserted its independence, and the US was unquestionably at the head of the capitalist world. Subsequently, Canada's foreign policy would seek to cultivate the "Middle Power" image, actively protecting its independence by working to establish an international architecture that would allow for Canadian capitalist development.

As such, the immediate post-war moment in Canadian foreign policy was characterized most dramatically by the push for the creation of NATO. Indeed, far from being roped into an American project, it was Canada which pushed hardest for the creation of the military alliance. The hope was that NATO would serve to strengthen Canada's independence by creating an infrastructure that would protect Canada from being folded into the United States. Lester Pearson, then minister of external affairs, was clear about the advantages NATO held for Canada, arguing that a defence treaty including the North American and European powers:

> would help to ensure that Canada was not pushed out ahead of the United States in the event of war. In the last two wars Canada has gone to war more than two years before the United States. A treaty commitment by the United States instead of a congressional resolution would lessen the danger that this might happen again.[61]

Indeed, a 1948 visit to Ottawa by the US Secretary of Defence elicited his surprise at the "curious fact" that Canada was pushing fervently the idea for a North Atlantic alliance.[62] That Canada should have been the driving force behind the agreement suggests not dependence on the US but, rather, an active strategy for protecting its independence.

NATO served to facilitate the shift in Canadian foreign policy to what Paul Kellogg calls "military parasitism," which characterized much of the post-war era. With defence alliances firmly in place with the United States, Canada could rely on the US Cold War machine to protect western access to markets in its "sphere of influence," while Canada would not need to maintain the high military budgets that characterized the US and Soviet Union during that period. Though Canada's military budget in the early 1950s remained high, and Canada was an active participant in the Korean War, the following two decades saw a significant turn away from military spending; in 1951 the military represented some 40 percent of Canadian state expenditure, but by 1971 it was down to around 10 percent.[63] In the meantime, Canada locked in the Defence Production Sharing Agreement (DPSA) in 1959 to guarantee that Canadian small-scale arms manufacturers would have a steady customer in the US military.[64]

Even while Canada kept out of the Cold War spotlight, it was nevertheless an active benefactor of the US wars of empire. Latin America offers a particularly revealing window here; on the one hand, Canada was relatively uninvolved in the near-constant US aggression in Latin America during the Cold War. Nevertheless, Canadian capital often benefited from it, especially beginning in the 1970s. Ricardo Grinspun and Yasmine Shamsie describe Canadian Latin American policy at the time:

> Since the late 1970s, Canadian foreign policy has followed a liberal economic philosophy that emphasizes economic competitiveness, the enhancement of trading opportunities, and fiscal responsibility. These goals are in full harmony with the outward-oriented, market-driven strategy that Ottawa has pursued in the region. Its support for [structural adjustment policies] has been evident in its active participation in the region's key multilateral organizations, through its bilateral relations with individual

> countries, and through its vigorous support of Canadian corporations active in the region. In fact, by 1989, Canada's International Development Agency (CIDA) had unreservedly adopted this policy set and "came to regard support for structural adjustment as a first priority."[65]

Canada stubbornly continued to promote these policies throughout the disastrous decades of the 1980s and '90s and Canadian companies reaped the benefits where they could, as the Honduran case described. But with the United States doing all of the "dirty work" of empire, Canada was able, more or less, to slip under the radar while it grew its capital in the blood-soaked earth of the Americas.[66]

What is more, the rewards of a "military parasitism" were also manifest in the realm of international diplomacy, where Canada was able to cultivate its image as a force for peace and multilateral dialogue in global affairs, an image that still retains its ideological power. As Canada mostly withdrew from direct participation in America's secret and not-so-secret wars, it avoided the political "taint" that came with them; Washington's aggression in Iran, Guatemala, Chile, Vietnam, Cuba, Nicaragua, Afghanistan, and elsewhere made it an obvious target for anti-imperial discontent. Canada, by contrast, was perceived as having no active role in Cold War aggression,[67] and it earned political and diplomatic capital, especially among the emerging post-colonial states, that gave it a stronger voice at international forums and made it a more important ally for the United States. This period, arguably ushered in during Canada's mediation of the Suez Crisis in 1956, represented the fruition of Canada's "military parasitism," and created what is perhaps best described as the "peacekeeping moment" in Canadian foreign policy. Notably, this course was plotted in contradiction to the wishes of the United States; as Kellogg argues:

> Interestingly, the Canadian government made these decisions despite considerable pressure from its principle ally, the United States, to go the other direction – to become a warfare, not a welfare, state. But successive Canadian governments successfully resisted this pressure ... thus the "leaders of a secondary state," Canada, accommodated themselves to the military preoccupations of the hegemon. But they did so in such a way as to advance Canada's economic interest at the expense of the hegemon.[68]

Canada, then, adopted strategies that allowed it to take advantage of its relationship with the United States to further its own aims, most notably the development and consolidation of Canadian capital, a project which was so successful, in fact, that it ultimately dictated the shift in Canadian foreign policy underway today.

THE CONTEMPORARY TURN: MILITARISM AND IMPERIALISM

The transition from the "peacekeeping moment" to an openly imperialist politics is the crucial period for the purposes of this book, and, in order to understand it, we must briefly return to the question posed at the start of this chapter: what is Canada? More specifically, it is crucial that we understand what compels the Canadian state to act, and what factors determine the nature of that action. Jerome Klassen puts it succinctly:

> The state is structurally connected to the relations of exploitation that constitute the capitalist mode of production. The state guarantees private property, issues the money form, regulates class relations, mediates all cross-border transactions and taxes various points of exchange.[69]

The state in capitalism acts fundamentally as a representative of the dominant capitalist class, albeit with much differentiation in how that plays out, depending on the country and the class forces in a given moment.

Indeed, the modern state form emerged alongside the rise of capitalism, as the rising bourgeois classes of Britain and France in the seventeenth and eighteenth centuries battled their respective monarchies to gain supremacy and build governmental arrangements that better suited their needs.[70] Of course, as the state form developed, it had to adapt to a variety of class interests that sought representation; at different moments, the state finds it expedient to make greater or lesser allowances to groups outside the dominant capitalist class.[71] Indeed, for capitalism to function effectively, some degree of stability and labour peace is required. As such, the liberal capitalist state would fail to serve its purpose if it acted transparently and exclusively as an arm of capital. Furthermore, even states that are thoroughly dominated by a particular class are subject to contestation from outside; a Canadian state held solidly by a concentrated Canadian capitalist class still has to contend with the forces that would struggle against it, from working-class organizations to civil society institutions to popular media, and so on. The point is not to deny that the state is a profoundly complicated network of interests. Rather, it is to assert that the modern nation state is, at its core, a formation designed to protect and promote the interests of capital in general and national capital in particular.

Typically, the modern capitalist state facilitates the privatization of the production process and the regulation of the macroeconomy, acting as the "guarantor and ultimate manager" of capitalist production.[72] Capital and the state are interdependent, and exercise only relative autonomy from one another. Thus, while we cannot draw a straight and direct line between state policy and the capitalist class forces it represents, we can operate from the fundamental premise that state policy reflects, most often, the interests of its capitalist classes. In Canada's case, this has been particularly pronounced since the mid-1970s, when the Canadian capitalist class began a major consolidation as a class and built institutions to express those class interests at the state level. These included the Business Council on National Issues (BCNI) formed in 1976, the Canadian Chamber of Commerce, and the Canadian Council of Chief Executives (CCCE), which structured and amplified the voice of the Canadian capitalist class at the level of the state, and helped successfully establish and maintain a neoliberal consensus in Ottawa since the 1980s.[73]

With the capitalist class in the driver's seat, Canadian foreign policy saw a shift that began in the early 1990s and manifested most dramatically in the past decade. Canada's participation in peacekeeping, for instance, went into rapid decline in the 1990s and has all but disappeared completely from Canadian policy today. In 1991, Canada contributed around 10 percent of UN peacekeeping personnel; by 2006, that number had dropped to less than 0.01 percent.[74] To the extent that "peacekeeping" is still mobilized rhetorically to justify Canadian militarism, it has gone from an exaggeration to an outright myth.

Beginning in the early 1990s, Canada became increasingly engaged in aggressive military adventures beyond its borders. Canada was an active participant in the war against Iraq in 1991, though it expressed reservations, and it also played a role in the continuous bombing campaigns in that country throughout the decade. In 1993, Canada intervened in Somalia, ostensibly in a peacekeeping role, and left in disgrace after its soldiers were implicated in sadistic torture of Somali prisoners.[75] Canada took a lead role in NATO's bombing of the former Yugoslavia in 1999, became a prominent part of the occupation of Afghanistan in 2001, and made a variety of contributions to the US invasion of Iraq in 2003, despite a rhetorical stance that suggested otherwise.[76] In 2004, Canada played an active and crucial military role in the overthrow of Haitian President Jean-Bertrand Aristide, and subsequently stayed on as a semi-permanent force, propping up the regime that replaced

Aristide and training the Haitian police to carry out violent counter-insurgency actions against Aristide supporters.[77] In 2011, a Canadian general led the NATO attacks against Libya, and nearly 500 Canadians participated in the dismantling of the Libyan state that left the country in a chaotic and calamitous civil war that claimed tens of thousands of lives and sent over two million people fleeing to Tunisia. In 2013, the Canadian military was in Mali supporting a French invasion.[78] In 2014, Canada joined the war against ISIS in Iraq. In 2015, that bombing was extended to Syria. In the early months of 2016, Prime Minister Trudeau first expanded Canada's role in the campaign (February), then denied that Canada was actually at war with ISIS (March). Canada was definitely still at war in Iraq and Syria, and made much ado of its plan to "liberate" the city of Mosul a few months later.[79] Most recently, Canadian troops were deployed to support the Ukraine in its disputed border with Russia, in what is likely to mark a dangerous escalation of that conflict.

There is much to say about each of these interventions: the scale of civilian casualties and human suffering inflicted, the degree of institutional and infrastructural damage doled out, the range of spurious justifications offered in each case, the colonial "freedom, democracy, and good governance" that Canadian politics and policy typically deploys. Moreover, this is simply a sketch of the most obvious examples where Canada has used direct military intervention as a tool of foreign policy. They do not cover the wide range of imperial relationships that Canada has cultivated—around mining operations in Africa, for instance—without resorting to using its own military forces. The Honduran case at the centre of this book is, indeed, a perfect encapsulation of the latter category.

It is no coincidence that as Canadian capital has turned outward, Canadian foreign policy has become increasingly focused on the creation and protection of market-friendly regimes in the Global South. It is similarly unsurprising that this project has necessarily entailed closer collaboration with the United States, whose government has more or less the same macroeconomic goal, even if its capitalists find themselves periodically in competition with Canadian firms. Indeed, the consolidation of Canadian capital has seen it expand into the Global South in the hopes of procuring ever-greater profits, a process that is necessarily and inherently violent.

Consider Marx's descriptions in the first volume of *Capital,* of the violence—physical, structural, material, and spiritual—at the heart of "so-called primitive accumulation," or the creation of conditions for capitalist production:

> In actual history, it is a notorious fact that conquest, enslavement, robbery, murder, in short, force, play the greatest part ... the capital-relation presupposes a complete separation between the workers and the ownership of the conditions for the realization of their labour. As soon as capitalist production stands on its own feet, it not only maintains this separation, but reproduces it on a constantly expanding scale.... So-called primitive accumulation, therefore, is nothing else than the historical process of divorcing the producer from the means of production ... the history of their expropriation is written in the annals of mankind in letters of blood and fire.[80]

This description resonates both with the colonial practices that established Canada in the first place, and many of the ongoing dynamics of Canada's involvement in Honduras. While some of the specific circumstances have changed, the overarching dynamics Marx describes remain embedded in Canada's foreign enterprises today. The very act of investing capital abroad is predicated on the idea that there are greater profits to be made there than by comparable investments at home, and this calculation is almost always based on the availability of cheap and easily exploitable labour.[81]

Naturally, the violence of the profit-seeking behaviour of Canadian corporations abroad engenders resistance virtually wherever it goes, and the Canadian state now employs all manner of underhanded tactics to smother the dissent generated by its corporations' behaviour. Interventions in local politics, including the overthrowing of governments, assassinations of activists organizing against Canadian firms, support for repressive institutions that defy popular will, and even military intervention, are part of Canada's toolkit in those places where its capital is invested.

A few scattered examples from across the Americas demonstrate that the case of Honduras is not unique, and that we can, indeed, generalize from the Honduran experience of Canadian imperial politics. In April 2013, Alberto Rotondo, head of security for the San Rafael mine in Guatemala, owned by Canadian mining company Tahoe Resources, ordered the assassination of Guatemalan activists protesting the company's social and environmental record.[82] Similar stories dog the activities of Canadian companies across Latin America; in Mexico, after a leading community activist against Calgary-based Blackfire Exploration was murdered, the Canadian government ignored some 1,400 letters of concern about the Blackfire-sanctioned murder. Instead, DFAIT worked with the company to help it sue the local Mexican government that had suspended its activities after the assassination. According to a Mining Watch report:

> Mere days after a damning report about the company was circulated to the highest echelons of the Canadian government, Canadian authorities sought advice for the company about how to sue the [Mexican subnational] state of Chiapas under NAFTA for having closed the mine.[83]

Canadian companies operating in Central America appear to have plenty of support from the Canadian state in asserting their rights against local governments, even when their behaviour is engendering all manner of social harm and opposition. Environmental codes in Costa Rica were strengthened by its government in 2011, leading to the halt of operations of the Las Crucitas gold mine, owned by Calgary-based Infinito, which did not meet the new environmental criteria set by the government. The company is currently building momentum to launch a $1 billion lawsuit against the government of Costa Rica under the terms of the Canada-Costa Rica free trade agreement.[84] Even CIDA—the Canadian government organization that was ostensibly most committed to doing "development" work abroad until its disbanding in 2013—was implicated in imperial violence; a growing portion of CIDA funding was diverted over the past two decades to firms—sometimes themselves Canadian—that built the military hardware that repressed activists struggling against Canadian mining companies.[85]

In the meantime, Canada's participation in the occupation of Afghanistan has to be considered one of the most significant imperial adventures in Canadian history and the degree of human suffering that it has provoked is almost impossible to calculate. The occupation spanned two decades and left Afghanistan devastated, with tens of thousands of civilians killed and some 70 percent of surviving Afghans living in poverty under the NATO–approved Afghan government. Against the wishes of some 70 to 90 percent of Afghans who wanted an end to the Canadian presence,[86] Canada established a semi-permanent Strategic Advisory Team (SAT-A) that was embedded in the Karzai government, and helped write the policies—and even the speeches—of that government. Members of SAT-A boasted that "no other country was as strategically placed as Canada with respect to influencing Afghanistan's development," and, in fact, SAT-A was responsible for crafting legislation like the Afghanistan Compact and the National Solidarity Program, which directly benefited Canadian companies, including Kilo Goldmines, Lockheed-Martin, Canaccord Financial, SNC-Lavalin, and SRK Consulting.[87] Meanwhile, the Karzai government that Canada so effectively influenced reintroduced many of the most conservative social policies the war was ostensibly fought to eliminate, including laws that allow husbands to rape their wives.[88]

Far from rebuilding Afghanistan, Canada helped oversee the neoliberal dismantling of a state that had achieved some economic growth and social equality in the 1970s and '80s, including some redistribution of land, sweeping new measures for gender equality, and a comprehensive education and literacy program for Afghans of all ages and genders.[89] Much of that work was undone in the civil wars that followed US and Soviet intervention, and what remained was totally undermined by the NATO invasion and occupation that began in 2001. After dropping billions of tons of bombs and reducing Afghan infrastructure to rubble, Canadian aid for reconstruction was paltry and directly tied to the military occupation itself, as part of campaigns to win the "hearts and minds" of Afghans.

What is more, much of the money that Canada spent on Afghanistan went directly to Canadian companies operating in the new neoliberal framework that the Karzai government pushed through; at least 50 percent of reconstruction money was recycled right back into Canadian corporate profits and salaries.[90] Not surprisingly, the extreme violence of the occupation actually filled the ranks of the Taliban and other armed resistance groups who, quite reasonably, did not consider the foreign presence benevolent; Canada, for instance, is directly implicated in the torture of civilian detainees who have been stripped, beaten, frozen, electrocuted, deprived of sleep, sexually assaulted and humiliated, attacked with dogs, and often ultimately killed.[91] In 2016 it was revealed that Canadian military personnel were not simply facilitating or turning detainees over to be tortured by Afghan soldiers; they were themselves taking part in these acts directly.[92]

As Sherene Razack has argued, Canada's involvement in the torture of Afghan detainees, as in Somalia in 1993, demonstrates the deep colonial logic and nature of the occupation. Razack refuses to accept what she calls the "instrumentalization" of torture, eschewing the idea that Canadian soldiers submitted their victims to torture simply to gain military information. Rather, she insists that the violence of the torture act is designed to mark the colonized body with its "savage" status. The message, Razack argues, is that the "civilized" world of the colonizer is considered important enough to justify destroying "uncivilized" bodies in order to protect it, even when the intervention is rhetorically premised on humanitarian aims:

> The West understands peacekeeping and humanitarian interventions as an encounter in which "civilized" nations confront the savagery of cultures and peoples that have not yet entered modernity.... Canadian soldiers imagined themselves as disciplining and

> keeping in line, through practices of violence, uncivilized Somalis whose resentment and anger at western peacekeepers who had come to save them they could not comprehend.[93]

In the case of Somalia in 1993, the actions of Canadian torturers were more or less forgiven in the Canadian public for being driven by heat exhaustion, poor leadership, and the ungratefulness of those they had gone to protect. This suggests, to Razack, "a nation that ultimately remembers the torture as a moment of its own kindness and superiority," which partially explains the underwhelming response in the Canadian public to accounts of torture in Afghanistan and other acts of violence by the Canadian military abroad.[94]

Razack's argument resonates in the Honduran context, if one considers the collusion between the Honduran military—which describes its project as "modernizing" even while it tortures its own people—and the Canadian state, which has endeavoured to facilitate and legitimize the regime committing such violent acts. As this book demonstrates, the Canadian state has had to work hard to ignore the widespread reports of repressive—sometimes shocking and brutal—violence in Honduras since the 2009 coup. The Canadian state has similarly accepted torture as part of the "mission" in Afghanistan and elsewhere. What is more, returning briefly to Razack's point, the extent to which the broader Canadian public has accepted torture as part of the toolkit of imperial benevolence is, itself, a striking demonstration of a colonial frame of mind. No less striking is the openness with which that mindset is proclaimed, as when a right-wing columnist asserted in a major newspaper in 2001 that "what the Afghans need is colonizing."[95]

REORGANIZING THE IMPERIAL MACHINE

While the attention of Canadian imperialism has been most typically focused on those places where significant amounts of capital are invested, the shift in Canadian foreign policy is far deeper than simply working to protect particular firms' investments. The Canadian state has made a conscious decision to integrate more deeply with the machine of US imperialism, on the understanding that Canadian firms will benefit from that co-operation. While "military parasitism" was once an effective strategy for building the capacities of the Canadian capitalist class and mediating class conflict at home, three factors have worked to change that. First, the consolidation and growth of Canadian capital has meant that it, like all capitalist classes, has had to contend with periodic crises of over-accumulation, setting in whenever there are not immediately available sources of profitable investment. As David Harvey details in *The New*

Imperialism, one solution to this problem is geographic expansion into Global South states where a variety of violent practices can make possible an "accumulation by dispossession," whereby profits can be sustained and expanded on the basis of plunder, bullying of governments, and greater exploitation.[96]

Second, a sustained neoliberal assault has flattened out the prospects for working-class organizing in Canada, leaving the state in a position to worry far less about protecting the welfare state and freeing up resources to expand its military. This point is well articulated by Thom Workman and Geoffrey McCormack in *The Servant State*, who highlight the ways that the Canadian state has squeezed its working classes, especially in the past two decades.[97] Finally, the end of the Cold War put the United States in a position to redefine the nature of its alliances; no longer facing existential danger in the spectre of an international communist revolution, the United States is now able to discipline its allies by insisting that they contribute to the military aggression that is necessary to maintain the inequalities of the world market system.[98] Canada, anxious to ensure that it continues to have access to the markets where its firms make some of their greatest profits, has made it a priority to demonstrate to the United States that it is a willing and able component of the new imperial order, such that it may reap its rewards.[99]

Canada, then, has emerged as a secondary component of the new imperialism. As Greg Albo concludes:

> The Canadian state recognized the continental relationship as the means by which it preserves a secondary position in the world order and, therefore, the necessity of following US dictates and doctrines in matters of foreign policy. In fact, in recasting its foreign policy after 9/11, the Canadian state had the support of a wide range of economic interests – notably the Canadian Council of Chief Executives and the C.D. Howe Institute … to this end, Canadian governments sought to increase the operational capacity of the military, to subordinate other international activities to concerns of national and continental security, and to reorganize the administrative apparatus of the state accordingly.[100]

Crucial here is the nuanced way in which Albo addresses continental integration—which is an undeniable development of post-Cold War and especially post-9/11 Canadian foreign policy—as a function not of Canada's weakness but, rather, as a conscious strategy of a capitalist state seeking to position itself most effectively for its own reproduction. This is an important corrective to the position which saw this integration as being primarily imposed on Canada from outside, rather than chosen from within.

Nevertheless, both sides of this debate agree that the changes inherent in the "deep integration" project are profound and structural, and are designed to recast Canadian foreign policy for years to come. Over the past decade, institutional power has been increasingly centred around the Prime Minister's Office (PMO) and the Department of National Defence (DND) as a variety of other state structures have been forced to fall into subordinate positions, most notably the Department of Foreign Affairs and International Trade (DFAIT) and CIDA, whose merger into one organization was announced—to the dismay of many—in 2013.[101] As early as 2006, Canadian policy-making was being actively embedded in continental security projects and placed under the oversight of the security apparatus, even as the DND has dramatically increased its funding for strategic studies in Canadian universities through the Security and Defence Forum,[102] buttressing an increasingly influential, right-wing, pro-military stream within the discipline of International Relations, especially in Canadian Foreign Policy and Security Studies.

As Canadian foreign policy is being brought under the control of the military, that apparatus is engaged in the much-maligned "deep integration" project with the US defence apparatus, especially in the "Fortress North America" linkages designed to securitize the geography of capital accumulation at home.[103] Canada has joined the United States in missile defence system planning, has harmonized much of its maritime security apparatus with the US, and has entered into a variety of intensified continental military command chains at the recommendation of the Bi-National Planning Group (BPG), an advisory council established under NORAD to concretize many of the "deep integration" plans.[104] The BPG and much of the Canadian military intelligentsia argued throughout the 2000s that the Canadian Forces needed to increase its "interoperability" with the US military, which has, in fact, given the Canadian state a greater role in the imperial order.

The Canadian military itself is growing faster than ever; in the most obvious manifestation of the growing militarization of the Canadian state, the actual number of soldiers has steadily increased and has now reached over 100,000 in regular and reserve forces. Meanwhile, the military itself has seen substantial renovation and reformulation, both in terms of its operational capacity (increasingly organized to fight urban counterinsurgency wars on multiple fronts) and the networks of interoperability (devised to make the Canadian military adaptable to collaborating with continental allies as well as local military and police forces wherever it may be deployed.) In addition, the last decade has seen the most dramatic escalation of military budgeting since the Second World War, with the Canadian state spending over $18 billion on the military in 2008/09 alone and sparking some controversy with a proposal to spend an additional $25 billion on a new fleet of fighter jets.

As noted above, this spike in military spending has taken place alongside a concerted imposition of austerity on working Canadians in the aftermath of the 2008 financial crisis; jobs have been slashed, wages have been hammered down, and strikes have been broken.[105] The Canadian corporate elite continues to enjoy relatively lax taxation, but user-fees and taxes have been raised for everyone else, ranging from transit systems to privatized health services and rising tuition fees. Federally funded organizations that provide valuable services to communities are being scuttled or starved of resources; Indigenous, environmental, LGBT, and women's organizations have been particularly targeted.[106] Direct support for people is diminishing, as reflected in decreases in social housing and assistance; for instance, after significant structural changes, less than half of unemployed Canadians today even qualify for Employment Insurance (EI). Working poverty and precarity are becoming more and more common—over 10 percent of Canadians are now living below the poverty line and almost half of the Canadian workforce works precariously—even as there is less and less support for those who are struggling.[107]

The disjuncture between increased military spending and support for working Canadians has aroused some criticism, but that criticism has been muted and diluted by a variety of factors. Notable among them is the militarization of Canadian popular culture, which has manifested in a new Canadian patriotism and a "support the troops" discipline hitherto absent in Canadian popular consciousness. Perhaps the best example of this dynamic is to be found in the spectacle of Canadian hockey, and the collaboration between the military, the National Hockey League (NHL), the individual franchise owners, and the Canadian media, especially the public Canadian Broadcasting Corporation (CBC), in relentlessly celebrating the Canadian Armed Forces at hockey games, a cultural phenomenon undeniably woven into the fabric of Canadian popular culture.[108] We will return to the matter of Canadian popular culture in the following chapter.

A VERY CANADIAN ENGAGEMENT

Canada's role in the world has undeniably changed in the past two decades. For those who continue to ascribe to Canada a degree of benevolence in its foreign interventions, the reality of Canada's increasing international presence are surely disappointing. In 2007, Canada declared itself to be "re-engaging" with the Americas. Despite proposing three key priorities for the region that included the promotion of democracy and the advancement of social justice, Canada has only actually pursued one goal: the deepening of the neoliberal development model that has so consistently and completely failed to bring equitable or sustainable economic growth for Latin America. Ricardo Grinspun and Yasmine Shamsie assessed that re-engagement in 2010:

> We contend that Canadian support for democracy, human rights, and sustainable development is being weakened by (1) the government's persistent adherence to a neoliberal development model and (2) its steadfast support for US geostrategic interests in the continent, even when they run counter to humane internationalist objectives.[109]

Nevertheless, the primary institutions of the Canadian ruling class continue to talk about Canadian engagement in Latin America as if it were a great act of kindness. The *Canadian Military Journal* boasts that Canada is a positive role model in Latin America and that it collaborates with Latin American militaries because they are often "the only reliable organ of government that has the ability to maintain order or mount a credible force against transnational threats." The Canadian Forces, they insist, "help build operational and institutional capacities" of the countries to which they are sent, and "have a role to play in advancing the government's agenda under the security pillar of [Canada's] engagement [in Latin America]."[110]

Grinspun and Shamsie, by contrast, articulate what many in the community of Canadian scholarship on Latin America and the Caribbean have been saying since 2007: that Canada has prioritized its commitment to its own neoliberal agenda over its other stated goals in Latin America and that the Canadian military is often used to bolster that agenda. That is, they argue that the role of the military has increasingly been to support the imposition of neoliberalism, especially as Canada has quickly become the world's third largest investor in the region.[111] Grinspun and Shamsie rightly critique Canadian emphasis on neoliberal development models and view Canada's decision to prioritize the promotion of neoliberalism as a "missed opportunity" to support the burgeoning social movements in Latin America—sometimes described as the "Pink Tide"—seeking to reverse the destructive policies of the past decades.[112] They are certainly not wrong to flag Canada's failure to support those movements, but it may be worth asking whether it is even conceivable that a Canadian government in the neoliberal era would contradict the wishes of the Canadian corporate elite.

For nearly a decade, much of the Canadian left emphasized the role of the ruling Conservative Party in carving out a foreign policy with such harmful effects around the world. There is no question that the Harper years were marked by a gleeful embrace of neoliberal policy, but now that the government has changed hands, any expectation that Canada will revert to a kinder, more benevolent role in the world rings hollow. "Canada is back!" declared the new prime minister, Justin Trudeau, at one of his first international summits.[113] Thunderous applause for the mythological Canada that had supposedly returned; but will anything really change under the Liberal Party that presided over much of the neoliberal shift in the first place?

The argument in this book is that Canadian foreign policy is shaped by the dynamics of global capitalism and the position occupied by the Canadian capitalist class therein. In this light, the twists and turns of party politics may tilt the ship in one direction or another, but they do nothing to significantly change course. Canada has not simply *prioritized* the goals of neoliberal capital accumulation over other, more humanitarian, goals. Rather, the project of capital accumulation at the heart of Canadian foreign policy is in fundamental contradiction with the advancement of true democracy or social justice. Canadian policy, stemming as it does from the relations of production in which Canada is embedded, has long been invested in reaping the benefits of an imperial world order. But, as a result of changes in the global political economy in which Canadian capital is located, Canadian policy has become increasingly aggressive in its particular adaptations of imperialism, and Canada has emerged as a crucial, secondary component in the imperial system. This has manifested in a whole variety of policy shifts over the past two decades and in the dramatic restructuring of the Canadian state and military to facilitate an escalation and institutionalization of those shifts.

Mainstream understandings of Canadian politics have consistently failed to acknowledge or comprehend these dynamics. Left nationalist analyses have correctly critiqued Canada's increasingly harmful foreign policy, but too often misread its genesis, leading to conclusions that would seek to strengthen Canadian sovereignty and independence in the realm of policy-making. What they miss is that Canada is already sovereign and independent and is using that power to pursue an imperialist foreign policy that adapts, foments, creates, and relies upon profound social injustice in order to accomplish its aims. No left project in Canada can hope to achieve any sustainable progress if it fails to recognize this fact and mobilize against Canadian imperialism.

That being said, this book is not proposing a detailed program for confronting Canadian imperialism. Instead, it is gesturing toward the need to build a political challenge that would go beyond asserting Canadian nationalism, and would, instead, recognize the need for profound and radical change that would delink Canada from the network of capitalism. This would necessarily have to be part of a broader global break from the imperatives of capitalism and a shift to a different mode of production that would offer greater prospects for radical democracy, personal freedom, creative expression, and social justice. Sustained discussion of this ambitious objective is beyond the scope of this book. Nevertheless, to the extent that this study suggests certain policy changes, they should be understood as precursors to the broader changes that will be necessary if there is to be any long-term change. Greg Albo offers a useful articulation of this compromise. After detailing five points of action that the Canadian state should take, which include immediate withdrawal from Afghanistan and support for stronger international regulations on capital, Albo argues:

> This platform would reinforce democratic sovereignty and advance the struggle for an equalizing world order.... To put forward such a democratic and egalitarian agenda in the current world order means confronting US hegemony and, more directly, *the domestic political and social relations that underpin Canadian imperialism*. Avoiding the need for radical social transformation in the hope of returning to a more UN-centred multilateralism is to fall prey to the fictions of a liberal world order. Indeed the belief that Canadian foreign policy has been – or can be – a force for a more just or balanced world has been one of the most crippling illusions of political life in Canada, particularly in progressive circles.[114]

Indeed, while Albo's particular demands of Canadian policy—reducing the military, separating foreign aid from foreign investment, etc.—are shared by many progressive-minded Canadians, his broader project cuts much deeper, based on his critical understanding of the Canadian state. For Albo, foreign policy is a direct manifestation of domestic and international social relations, a product of the dynamics of global capitalism. As a result, changes to that foreign policy can only be superficial and short term if they are not part of a broader contestation of the social relations from which they are derived. It is a truth as old as capitalism itself and, while it makes the challenge more difficult, it also compels a more profoundly emancipatory and international project into which we could place our hope for a truly better world.

6 CONCLUSION
Mythologies Old and New

In early 2016, I received the news that Berta Cáceres had been assassinated in her home in western Honduras. Berta, whom I interviewed several times between 2009 and 2016, was one of the most respected and recognized figures in the Honduran resistance. She was a co-ordinator of COPINH, a national Indigenous organization that remains a foundational presence in the Honduran social movement. She was a pillar of strength in the struggle of the Lenca communities around Rio Blanco, defending their land against hydroelectric dam projects that threatened to carve up and contaminate the earth upon which the Lenca live. She was also an internationally recognized activist, having won the Goldman Environmental Award for her work in Rio Blanco. Her speech upon accepting the award was a clear articulation of the feelings of many Hondurans at this critical juncture:

> We must wake up, humanity. We're out of time. We must shake our conscience free of rapacious capitalism, racism, and patriarchy that will only assure our self-destruction. The Gualcarque River has called upon us, as have other gravely threatened rivers. We must answer the call. Mother Earth—militarized, fenced-in, poisoned, a place where basic rights are systematically violated—demands that we take action.[1]

Berta's prominence in Honduras and her international reputation seemed to suggest that she was insulated from violent reprisal for her activist work, even despite her receiving over thirty death threats in recent years. But evidently no one is untouchable in Honduras.

¡BERTA VIVE!

Berta was killed on March 3, 2016, by men associated with the hydroelectric company trying to gain access to the land in Rio Blanco. One of the men worked as private security for this company, Desarrollos Energéticos,

SA (DESA), another was a company engineer, and two were active members of the Honduran military. Shortly thereafter, another co-ordinator of COPINH, Nelson García, was killed in similar fashion.[2] They were not the first members of the community to be killed in conflicts over the hydroelectric developments, which are designed to provide energy for the intensive, mostly Canadian, mining operations popping up in this part of the country. But the murder of Berta Cáceres sent a very clear message to activists across the country: if they can kill Berta, they can kill anyone.

While the murder of Honduras' most prominent activist did generate a media reaction outside the country—perhaps the largest since the coup itself—it did little to shake Canada's steadfast support for the regime. The Canadian government released a short and inconsequential statement urging the Honduran government to "clarify" the murder of Berta Cáceres and "ensure the protection of human rights defenders who have been threatened."[3] The statement did not mention that the last death threat Berta had received came from men connected to Blue Energy, the Canadian company that was also trying to build a hydroelectric dam in Rio Blanco.[4] Nor did it reference the support Canada had provided for seven years to the perpetrators of such violence in Honduras.

Meanwhile, on the home front, Canadian culture continued to propagate the myth that Canada is a kind-hearted underdog, trying to do good in a world that doesn't appreciate it. "Blame Canada," cried a *National Post* headline in 2013, offering a list of recent indignities: "Brazil says we're spying, the Maldives says we're mean, Sri Lanka says we're out of line."[5] In fairness, leaked NSA documents demonstrated that Canada was indeed spying on the Brazilian mines and energy ministry, through the Communications Security Establishment Canada (CSEC).[6] This comes as no surprise, given Canada's increasing investment in Brazilian mining and oil and gas, especially in the context of a Brazilian government which was led by a centre-left coalition—at least until that government was overthrown in a parliamentary coup in 2016. Canada didn't issue a statement on the coup but, a week later, quietly invited the head of the Brazilian military to bilateral talks with the Canadian armed forces, to "strengthen our military cooperation" as they negotiate a comprehensive Defence Cooperation Agreement.[7]

If Brazilians were upset by Canadian espionage and destabilization of their country, they appear to be perfectly justified, just as Hondurans are upset by Canadian support for the coup, Guatemalans by the violence of Canadian mining companies, Afghans by the Canadian occupation, and many in the

Middle East by Canada's arming of the repressive conservative monarchy in Saudi Arabia.[8] These frustrations are increasingly being manifested in Canada's exclusion from international organizations. Most notably for this study, Canada and the United States were the only two countries cut out of the Comunidad de Estados Latinoamericanos y Caribeños (Community of Latin American and Caribbean States, CELAC), a body created in response to the manipulation of the OAS in the aftermath of the coup in Honduras, which was denounced by the rest of the hemisphere. Nevertheless, Canadians often remain mystified that anyone should have a beef with our peace-loving country.

DON CHERRY AND CANADIAN MILITARISM

This sentiment is best expressed by Canada's intentionally inarticulate, widely known, right-wing hockey pundit Don Cherry. "Canadian people are so naïve ... we love everybody and everybody hates us," says Cherry, lamenting the fact that Canada is so magnanimous in a world full of ingrates.[9] In the 1980s, when Canada was less prominent as a military power in the world, he bemoaned it as weakness: "I am sick and tired of Canada cow-towing to the rest of the world ... we're weak, spineless."[10] But the times have changed, and Don Cherry's weekly instalments of chest-beating nationalism and hyper-conservatism as a commentator on *Hockey Night in Canada* are, remarkably, one of the most enduring manifestations of Canadian popular culture. Cherry was a runner-up in a 2004 CBC contest searching for the "greatest Canadian," and one would be hard-pressed to come up with a more recognizable name in the country. Indeed, the former hockey coach—who is now into his fourth decade as a TV commentator—has never been closer to the pulse of Canadian culture.

There was a time when Don Cherry seemed anachronistic; a strange relic from a world that we had thankfully transcended.[11] And yet, his xenophobic rants about foreigners, his rampant sexism and homophobia, and, especially, his championing of aggressive Canadian nationalism and militarism are, today, more reflective than ever of the shifting political culture of Canada. Don Cherry's Canada is a humble, but muscular and gun-toting, farm boy who would happily stay home and play hockey but is driven—by an innate sense of right and wrong—to go out and make the world better. His is a simple world, where right is always whatever the troops are doing, and wrong is anyone who doesn't line up behind them. The Canadians, he exalts while pounding his desk, are "the good guys."[12] It is not dissimilar from the kind of jingoistic American patriotism we are accustomed to, except that it is skilfully adapted to the Canadian context to frame Canadians as "underdogs." The world may view Canada as a little guy, but Don Cherry knows that Canadians will always rise to the occasion and fight off the bad guys when no one else has the guts to do it.

In a segment promoting the Vimy Ridge memorial, Cherry proclaimed Canada's troops "the best of all time" after boasting of how effectively they stormed Vimy Ridge in 1917:

> The French and English tried to take Vimy Ridge for three years ... we took up under General Arthur Currie and four divisions of Canadians, 35,000 guys ... and he said gimme the four divisions of Canadians, the Canadians took it in three days, they actually took it in one day, it was unbelievable, with General Currie, it was great. And you know, everybody says it was the birth of a nation ... we're the best troops of all time.[13]

The Canadians who actually participated in the First World War did not come back with such tales of glory and gallantry. Many returned to Canada jaded by the experience of being sent into a veritable hell on Earth for the sake of an abstraction called the British Empire. Near the end of the war, Canadian veteran Frederick Varley painted the poignant *For What?,* which pointedly asked why so many working-class bodies were sacrificed in a grotesque war between competing nations' ruling classes. Many other soldiers returned to Canada committed to politics that rejected militarism and nationalism, joined trade unions and left-wing political parties, and played a significant role in upheavals like the Winnipeg General Strike of 1919.

Wider public opinion remained against the war for decades following it, and early commemorations of battles like Vimy Ridge were patently anti-war events; average Canadians remembered the war as a catastrophe that broke bodies and tore apart families.[14] One returning Canadian, Tommy Burns, articulated that sentiment: "[L]et [any proponent of war] spend five minutes in a trench listening to the blurred wailing of a comrade shot through the belly, and if he thinks of patriotism at all it will only be to curse it."[15] Indeed, many had opposed the war even while it was in full swing, including the four working-class Quebecois demonstrators killed in Quebec City by Canadian soldiers during a protest against conscription in 1918.[16]

Don Cherry's memory of the war he didn't fight, then, is very selective. But his history lessons are among the most prominent in this country, as millions of Canadians tune into his segments every Saturday night, wherein he weaves together a patchwork of right-wing populism that is expertly designed to tap into the Anglo-Canadian cultural tradition. Cherry glorifies the violent aspects of hockey—in spite of an increasing body of evidence connecting hockey violence to long-term brain injuries—and repeatedly compares hockey to war. Meanwhile, he celebrates the masculinity of those players who perform the appropriate form of structured violence that, notably, places a high value on loyalty to their team/company and coaches/officers. "It was war, like it should be," said Cherry glowingly of a playoff game in 2015, in a refrain that is now routinely parroted by other Canadian sports broadcasters, even in ostensibly non-violent sports like baseball.[17]

Meanwhile, Cherry explicitly celebrates and honours symbols of militaristic authority like soldiers and police officers, hosting hockey-related segments with them—like travelling to Afghanistan to play road hockey with the troops—and holding unscripted "memorials" for them when they die. On Christmas Day 2010, he went to Afghanistan with a CBC crew to apply his signature to Canadian bombs, joking with a soldier that he should write "this is for you, the Taliban."[18] He encourages no remembrance of the many people—Taliban or otherwise—killed by Canadian soldiers and police, nor does he memorialize Canadians killed in other professions, like construction workers who fall from scaffolding or prostitutes murdered by their clients.

SUPPORT THE TROOPS

Don Cherry's performance is a prominent and conspicuous aspect of the new Canadian militarism, but he is only the most visible figure in a project that has been growing rapidly over the past decade and shows no signs of slowing. Every Canadian city with a professional hockey team now hosts annual "military appreciation" nights, in which an elaborate pre-game ceremony honours the soldiers' bravery and heroism. The televised spectacles often feature paratroopers rappelling to the ice from the rafters, loud music designed to pump up the crowd, tanks carrying former hockey stars; they are performances carefully planned in co-ordination with the military itself to promote the image of the armed forces in venues—hockey arenas—where many of its values are likely to find potentially sympathetic audiences. Meanwhile, individual teams have introduced their own special military promotions, like the Toronto Maple Leafs' "Luke's Troops" campaign. The program initially featured Maple Leafs player Luke Schenn donating a fraction of his salary to buy tickets for the families of Canadian soldiers, providing an ideal opportunity for a seemingly spontaneous in-game commemoration of the troops' bravery and sacrifice. When Schenn was traded, the team quickly renamed the program "Lupe's Troops" and gave the honour to Joffrey Lupul.

These types of promotions are part of an explicit public relations campaign carried out by the armed forces of both Canada and the United States (the latter of which spent $6.8 million on contracts with six NHL teams to conduct patriotic military-themed ceremonies and celebrations at games and during telecasts).[19] In Canada, the DND spent nearly half a million dollars on promotional military-themed pucks and jerseys between 2007 and 2012,[20] to say nothing of the now common practice of producing professional team merchandising, like shirts and sweaters, with a military camouflage-style background. Players are often given such military-themed jerseys to wear during warm-ups and at special events. The NHL itself gushes over its relationship with the military, acknowledging that the league's "fan demographics fit perfectly" with military recruitment and marketing targets.[21]

When my hometown of Winnipeg lost its professional franchise, the Winnipeg Jets, in 1996 to a business consortium in Arizona, I was among the many Winnipeggers who were devastated. So it was with much fanfare that Winnipeg announced its return to the national stage with the return of the Winnipeg Jets in 2011. But what had once been a commercial jetliner on the crest of our players was replaced, in the new iteration of the team, by a CF-18 fighter jet. The unveiling of the new jerseys and logos was made at 17 Wing Air Force Base in Winnipeg, and the Jets' new owner thanked the military for its input into the design of the logo, which was developed in consultation with the DND to look similar to the insignia of the Canadian Air Force. In fact, it was revealed later that year that the team was contractually obligated to use its merchandising "in such manner as to protect and preserve the reputation and integrity of Her Majesty the Queen in Right of Canada, as represented by the Minister of National Defence, and the Canadian Forces."[22] When I wrote an article for a local magazine criticizing the team owner's decision to link the image of the team to the Canadian military, I was personally rebuked in the *Winnipeg Sun*, for daring to criticize the honour of the Canadian military.[23] I had so offended the editors of the right-wing newspaper that they brought me back at the end of 2011 for a "dishonourable mention," as a reminder that criticism of the military would not be tolerated in the new Canada without considerable public shaming.

Professional sports, and hockey in particular, is fertile ground for promoting the Canadian military, but it is by no means the only place this shift is taking place. As Alyson McCready has documented, the increased presence of Canadian troops in the Middle East in the decade of the 2000s saw a requisite increase in the ubiquity of the "yellow ribbons," on cars, windows, and winter jackets, carrying the "support the troops" message that feels more like a command than a suggestion.[24] Meanwhile, a stretch of highway in southern Ontario was rechristened the "Highway of Heroes"; the bodies of Canadian soldiers killed in the wars would be driven in procession down the highway and Canadians were encouraged to line the highway, waving flags and laying flowers. These exercises in patriotic grief and disciplined support for the military are designed to leave no room for asking why Canadians are being sent to fight, and whether their actions abroad are, indeed, heroic at all. They are deemed heroes simply because they fought with the Canadian military.

The Canadian military has spent significant resources making itself a more permanent and seemingly benevolent presence in Canadian society. Though it is unclear what percentage of Canada's multi-billion-dollar military budget is spent on marketing and public relations each year, we do know how much money is spent on military advertising over and above the regular military budget. In 2012, Canada spent nearly $5 million on advertising to commemorate the War of 1812, and $1 million on advertising to promote "Support for Canadian Business in Foreign Markets."[25] In 2013, Canada budgeted $4 million for a series of military remembrance vignettes with titles like "Brave and Proud" and "Legacy of a Nation."[26] In 2014, the total reached $12 million in direct government advertising for National Defence and Veterans Affairs, and data for the first two quarters of 2015 showed that already $5.5 million had been spent on recruitment ads and remembrance vignettes.[27]

There is no question that the military is making its public presence felt: in 2008, the military had even tapped into the gaming world, spending $200,000 on a series of in-game recruitment ads embedded within a military-themed "Call of Duty" video game for the Xbox game system.[28] In 2015, the military rolled out a massive new marketing venture, featuring a cinematic sixty-second video advertisement, which purchased airtime in movie theatres, on television (including a highly coveted and expensive spot during the Super Bowl), and on a variety of online media. A spokesperson for the campaign bragged that "every Canadian [would] see it."[29] Head down to a summer street festival in any major Canadian city and one is as likely to see a juggler and a bouncy castle as one is likely to see an anti-aircraft missile and a military recruitment table. In 2013 I stopped by the Polish festival in the west end of Toronto and saw children playing on a tank. A soldier in full regalia stood nearby explaining to a few of the kids what the different parts of the tank were used for. I interrupted him to ask whether he had any misgivings about teaching small children about machines used to kill people from other countries and his answer, not surprisingly, was that the Canadian military was here "for our protection."

However, it is increasingly evident that Canada's aggressive new foreign policy is designed for the protection of Canadian capital, not average Canadian citizens. In the meantime, Canada's deeper imperial engagement in the world has come at great cost for its victims, be they Afghan, Iraqi, Haitian, or Honduran. The emphasis that this book has placed on Honduras serves to demonstrate that, even in Canada's less direct imperial campaigns, the consequences of Canada's behaviour are deeply troubling and represent a rupture from anything resembling its rhetorical mobilization of peace, freedom, democracy, or human security. What is more, they represent a significant escalation of Canada's efforts to seize upon the advantages of the global capitalist world order and play an ever-greater role in shaping and perpetuating that order. Far from being a "middle power," a neutral or sensible arbiter of relations between imperial powers and peripheral states, Canada has emerged as a secondary component in the US-led empire of capital, with a ruling class that is coherent and organized and that has fully signed on to its role in international class struggle. To the extent that individual Canadians would reject this imperial politics, they have a marginal impact on state policy, which is powerfully shaped by the interests of a small network of wealthy Canadians.

"WE'RE BETTER THAN YOU"

What should be most alarming is that the analysis provided in this book details only one example of the new Canadian imperialism. While Honduras, the central case study here, has taken on greater significance for Canada since the opening that the 2009 coup provided, it remains a relatively minor component of Canada's broader imperial agenda. While Canada is Honduras' second largest foreign investor, that country represents only a fraction of total Canadian investment; the Latin American region as a whole received some $27.9 billion in 2007, still representing only 20 percent of all Canadian FDI, with the highest amounts going to Argentina, Brazil, Mexico, and Chile.[30] Honduras, in fact, receives as little as 0.1 percent of Canadian investment. Meanwhile, the patterns of support that the Canadian state provides to its capital in Honduras are replicated—with adaptations for the particular dynamics in different countries and regions—in most of the places where Canadian capital has gone.

For the many victims of Canadian imperialism, the need to identify and combat this dynamic is urgent. It may be urgent for Canadians, too, as the changes inherent in the Canadian state's greater participation in imperialism are affecting a dramatic and wholesale shift in Canada's perception in the world and—even more troubling—in Canadians' perception of the world. Imperialism, being so profoundly in contradiction with the values most associated with social justice, requires a variety of delusions and deceptions to be made palatable to people who might otherwise recoil at its naked assertion of the power of one over another. Colonizers seek to convince themselves—and sometimes those they are colonizing—that their colonization is necessary, benevolent, well intentioned, or otherwise just.[31] Imperialist powers typically project narratives about themselves that justify their actions and, as Canada has delved deeper and deeper into imperial politics, Canadian culture has increasingly produced the ideological material necessary to justify it.[32]

There may be no better example of this than the winner of the 2008 Governor General's Literary Award, *National Post* columnist Christie Blatchford, who is a key figure in the new Canadian right and whose award-winning book, *Fifteen Days*, represents perhaps the most straightforward—and offensive—justifications of the new Canadian imperialism. Blatchford's book, written as a series of vignettes of her experiences embedded with the Canadian military in Afghanistan, opens with a quotation drawn from one of the great cheerleaders of classical imperialism, Rudyard Kipling, and the first line of the first chapter blusters, "by July 2006, Task Force Orion was a killing machine."[33] Blatchford is signalling from the get-go that she is not interested in denying Canadian imperialism, as some liberal apologists might; she is celebrating it.

A few pages later, Blatchford narrates a scene between a Canadian solider and an Afghan citizen, wherein the Canadian stumbles upon a wounded Afghan and decides to take him in for medical support, but not before asserting Canadian superiority:

> "Willy had to calm me down because I was pissed," he says ... [To the wounded Afghan,] 'if I was under the bush there, bleeding, and you came across me, what would you do to me?' And he said, 'Oh I'd take you back to my compound and heal you up,' and I said, 'that's bullshit.... That's bullshit. *Because I'm better than you, because we're better than you,* I will heal you up and patch you up and take you back.'"[34]

In Blatchford's tale, the Canadian military is in Afghanistan because Afghanistan needs an imperial power. Afghans need people who are better, to show them how to themselves be better. The extent of Blatchford's colonial arrogance is matched only by the soldiers she idolizes, whose comments are as clear an articulation of imperial logic as one could possibly imagine and make it hard to view the Canadian occupation as anything *but* imperialist. Consider the following from Canadian soldier, Ash Van Leeuwen, quoted by Blatchford:

> We're not saving Afghanistan so that we can do free trade with them after; I mean, you can import rugs to Canada, but it's not an industrial country. We build infrastructure, provide education for children. The girls never had it. And it's not taking away from their culture; it's kind of showing they're being empowered. Look how long it took to get women's rights in North America, and we're in a country [Afghanistan] that's back two thousand years. It's like walking with people out of *National Geographic*.[35]

There is much to unpack in these statements. Clearly, Van Leeuwen had been prepared to effectively deny the claim that Canada is motivated by economic concerns. He is also trained to speak to Canada's advancement of education and women's rights in Afghanistan, though his suggestion that Afghanistan "never had" infrastructure, education, or a women's rights movement is simply inaccurate; in the late 1970s Afghanistan had a complicated political scene that came to be dominated by a secular left coalition that was accomplishing a great deal of what Van Leeuwen falsely attributes to the Canadian occupation.[36] But, most telling is his conclusion that Afghans are "back two thousand years." That, in his mind, they have walked out of the pages of *National Geographic* is a disturbingly patent and straightforward articulation of colonialism that would be right at home with the Rudyard Kiplings of a century ago.[37] This casual assertion that Afghans are obviously and essentially backwards, tribal, and pre-modern speaks directly to the imperial character of Canada's occupation, as manifest in its foot soldiers. If it looks like imperialism, functions like imperialism, and is justified using imperial logic, it seems rather straightforward to assert that this is, indeed, imperialism.

It is the increasing willingness of average Canadians—be they soldiers, policy-makers, or newspaper columnists—to declare Canada an imperial power, with the caveat that Canadian imperialism is good and necessary, that should raise serious alarm bells for those Canadians who imagine themselves to be committed to social justice. Indeed, of all the further studies that this book suggests, among the most urgent is a reassessment of Canadian social and political culture that takes seriously the notion that imperial politics, as Albert Memmi argued, change both the imperial power and the targets of its aggression: "for if colonization destroys the colonized, it also rots the colonizer."[38] The dramatic ruptures from human sociality that are required to justify the colonization of another people cause profound and sometimes existential harm even to colonizers themselves. As Aimé Césaire so astutely noted in 1955, the fascism that tore Europe asunder in the 1930s and '40s was a manifestation of colonialism come home.[39]

COLONIAL PAST, IMPERIAL PRESENT

The shift in Canada to an openly imperialist politics renders impossible the prospects for Canada's promotion of a somehow less exploitative global capitalist system and that, in turn, reflects back on Canada's domestic politics, which are becoming increasingly unequal, exploitative, and cruel.[40] In the early 1990s, Canadian popular culture was mobilized to think through questions of Canada's identity. We were typically encouraged to assert that Canadian identity was rooted in being something different from the United States; that we were kinder, gentler, more thoughtful, and more considerate, both as individuals and in the foreign policies of our country. However mythical this may have been, it is significant that the political moment required a citizenry who believed in that particular idea of Canada. Flash forward a decade or two and Canadian identity is increasingly rooted in an aggressive patriotism; Canadians are encouraged by the state, by the media, by public institutions, in sporting spectacles, and increasingly by one another to loudly and proudly represent a bigger, stronger, tougher Canada.[41]

One of the most arresting trends in Canadian opinion polls is the steadily rising support for the military. In 1984, 22 percent of Canadians had a "very favourable" opinion of the armed forces; by 2008 that number had almost doubled to 38 percent.[42] The election of Justin Trudeau in 2015, who mobilized the old language of a kinder, more caring Canada in his campaign, suggests that there remains a wide section of Canadians who want to be a "nice guy" in the world. But early in Trudeau's tenure, the contradiction between his language and practice is apparent, most notably in his conclusion of a multi-billion-dollar arms deal with the repressive Saudi monarchy[43] (which, ironically, supplies weapons to ISIS, with whom Canada is presently at war), to say nothing of the warm welcome he gave to Mexican President Enrique Peña Nieto at the precise moment that the Mexican state was murdering striking teachers in Oaxaca.[44] Given Canada's imperial role in the world, Trudeau's rhetoric seems unsustainable. His foreign policy will likely necessitate a shift back to hawkish language, which may be even more effective than that of his predecessor, Stephen Harper, coming as it will from a younger face with fluffier hair and a bizarre penchant for spontaneous shirtless public appearances.[45]

As such, in spite of the temporary shift in the tone from Ottawa, Canadian culture is undergoing a transformation requisite to the structural changes in the Canadian political economy that are manifesting visibly in the new Canadian imperialism. This transformation not only serves to ideologically sustain a Canadian state that behaves in profoundly different ways than it used to, it also complicates the picture of who gets to be included in "Canada." If Afghans are "two thousand years behind," where does that leave Afghan-Canadians? If Haiti is a "basket case" that should be thanking Canada for its intervention, are Haitian-Canadians the saviours or the saved? If Canada is exporting prosperity and development to Honduras, how do we address the Hondurans who spend half of their time working for less than minimum wage on Ontario farms as part of migrant worker programs, driven to this work by the utter lack of other opportunities in the Honduras that Canada is helping to create?

Finally, and perhaps most importantly, what does the new Canadian imperialism tell us about the original Canadian imperialism? The Canadian government's claim that Canada has "no colonial history" is a remarkable denial of the genocide that marked Canada's origins, and it obscures the fact that the original colonization of Indigenous nations is an ongoing project that plays out in the daily, "domestic" politics of Canada. The new assertion of Canadian patriotism consistently finds expression in conflicts between Indigenous communities and white settlers; at the site of a land conflict in southern Ontario, for instance, white settlers at Caledonia have mobilized counter-protests against Indigenous demonstrations in which they wave Canadian flags and sing "Oh Canada" at Indigenous protestors who quite rightly claim that the Canadian state is breaking the treaties it signed with them.[46]

Not surprisingly, the links between Indigenous struggles in Canada and the social movement in Honduras are growing; in the wake of Berta Cáceres' assassination, a delegation travelled from Canada to Honduras to participate in a celebration of Berta's life and her struggle. Prominent among the delegation were Indigenous women who recognized in the crisis in Honduras many of the same dynamics at work in their own communities. Bev Sellers, a Xat'sull survivor of a Canadian residential school, returned from the delegation noting that "the impacts that communities face around Canadian mining projects in Honduras are not much different from what we confront in Canada."[47] Canada is a settler colony that has blossomed into an imperial power, with a thread of colonial logic that connects its ignominious past to its shameful present.

Canada's emergence since the Cold War as a full-fledged imperial power is rooted in shifts in the deeper political economy of Canada and it would be wrong to imagine that this change is simply a function of different people, different political parties, or different ideas; Canada's brief peacekeeping moment was not motivated by benevolence or some natural Canadian predisposition to "do good," even if many individual Canadians were and are well-intentioned and progressive. Nevertheless, it would be similarly wrong to assume that Canadian policy is wholly predetermined by political-economic dynamics; activist organizing—whether in trade unions, in radical political parties, in social movements, in civil society, or elsewhere—can have and has made an impact on Canadian politics in the past. Indeed, if there is any hope that Canadians can be a force for a better world, it is surely rooted in the prospects of those activist organizations gaining traction and, ultimately, provoking a rupture in the Canadian state that would radically transform the Canadian polity.

As such, there is inspiration to be taken from the Honduran social movements that are at the centre of this book. In contrast to the colonial logic that sees Canada as the ideological guide for its colonial dominions to follow, the Canadian left should be seeking to learn from and adapt movements like those in Honduras, which have mobilized around particular and immediate community needs with a vision of radically transforming the Honduran state. The Honduran social movement has always understood that we must fight for immediate victories while building the capacity to win larger, truly revolutionary struggles. In life, Berta Cáceres articulated this as clearly as anyone.[48] In death, she has become a symbol of the urgency of building—and winning—that larger struggle. An embattled social movement in Honduras has declared that "Berta did not die, she multiplied." It is imperative that her spirit live on, not just in Honduras, but in the activist networks of the North as well. The Canadian government is on the wrong side of history, but individual Canadians need not be. It is my sincere hope that this book will compel greater collaboration and solidarity between the social movements and organizations confronting imperialism in Honduras and those in Canada. The need has never been greater.

NOTES

INTRODUCTION

1. Rick Hillier, quoted in "Hillier surprised that many didn't know a soldier's job is to kill," *Calgary Herald*, October 29, 2009.
2. Doug Saunders, "Canada's African adventure takes a colonial turn," *The Globe and Mail*, February 2, 2012.
3. Yves Engler, *The Black Book of Canadian Foreign Policy* (Black Point, NS: Fernwood Publishing, 2009), 4.
4. For instance, "Death to Canada" chants have become ubiquitous in Afghanistan, and folk songs in Central America increasingly feature Canada as the chief antagonist. Jerome Klassen, "Introduction: Empire, Afghanistan and Canadian Foreign Policy," in Jerome Klassen and Greg Albo, eds., *Empire's Ally: Canada and the War in Afghanistan* (Toronto: University of Toronto Press, 2013), 9.
5. Michael Ignatieff, "Peace, Order and Good Government: A Foreign Policy Agenda for Canada," DFAIT, Jules Leger Library. Available at international.gc.ca
6. Interestingly, the key rhetorical pieces here—promotion of peace, freedom, democracy, and stability—only feature in minor ways in Canada's stated foreign policy goals, which, today, typically emphasize free trade and security. For instance, Canada's foreign policy in the Americas claims to be founded on three pillars: "increasing economic opportunity," "strengthening security and institutions," and "fostering lasting relationships." www.international.gc.ca/americas-ameriques/stategy-stratege.aspx?lang=eng
7. Harjit Sajjan, quoted in Steven Chase, "Nature of peacekeeping no longer fits demands of conflict zones: Sajjan," *The Globe and Mail*, August 10, 2016.

1 IMPERIAL LEGACIES

1. Decades of exhaustive research on population decline, most notably by Woodrow W. Borah and, later, Nicolás Sánchez-Albornoz, have lent strong credence to the claim that when Columbus arrived in the Americas, there were as many as 100 million people living there. Within 150 years, that number was reduced to as few as 10 million, a catastrophe that Sánchez-Albornoz called "hard to grasp." Nicolás Sánchez-Albornoz, *Population of Latin America* (Berkeley: University of California Press, 1974). Please see also Sherburne F. Cook and Woodrow Borah, *Essays in Population History: Mexico and the Caribbean,* Vol. I (Berkeley: University of California Press, 1971). There is not space here to detail the debates around the causes of such a drastic decline, but suffice it to say that although

disease—not direct massacre—was the primary cause of death, European conquerors encouraged the decimation of Indigenous civilizations both intentionally (in the "gifting" of smallpox-infected blankets, for instance) and indirectly (through colonial practices, like slavery and displacement, that left Indigenous societies broken, such that bodies were unable to fend off diseases old and new). Sánchez-Albornoz addresses this, and fuller treatment of this problem can also be found in Roxanne Dunbar-Ortiz, *Indians of the Americas* (London: Zed Books, 1984). See also Ward Churchill, *A Little Matter of Genocide: Holocaust and Denial in the Americas, 1492 to the Present* (San Francisco: City Lights Books, 1997). For the Canadian context, see James Daschuk, *Clearing the Plains* (Regina: University of Regina Press, 2013).

2. Stephen Harper, quoted in David Ljundgren, "Every G20 nation wants to be Canada, insists PM," *Reuters*, September 25, 2009.
3. For details, see the final report of the Truth and Reconciliation Commission of Canada at: trc.ca
4. James A. Morris, *Honduras: Caudillo Politics and Military Rulers* (Boulder: Westview Press, 1984) 1.
5. This was his first arrival on the mainland, and the episode gave a name to the contemporary Honduran department (province) of "Gracias a Dios" (Thanks to God). Robert S. Chamberlain, *The Conquest and Colonization of Honduras, 1502–1550* (New York: Octagon Books, 1966) 10.
6. Ralph Woodward Jr, *Central America: A Nation Divided* (New York: Oxford University Press, 1999) 10. See also Linda Newson, *The Cost of Conquest: Indian Decline in Honduras Under Spanish Rule* (London: Westview Press, 1986).
7. Justin Jennings, Martha Cuevas García, and Roberto López Bravo, *Maya: Secrets of their Ancient World* (Toronto: Royal Ontario Museum Press, 2011).
8. For more detail on the complex tributary society of the Maya, please see David Freidel, "Lowland Maya Political Economy: Historical and Archaeological Perspectives in Light of Intensive Agriculture," in Murdo J. MacLeod, ed., *Spaniards and Indians in Southeastern Mesoamerica: Essays on the History of Ethnic Relations* (Lincoln: University of Nebraska Press, 1983).
9. Freidel, "Lowland Maya Political Economy," 43.
10. Many scholars consider the vast plunder of "New World" riches to have been a crucial foundation for world capitalism, insofar as it was this tremendous transfer of wealth that was seized upon by the emerging capitalist classes in Europe and turned towards the establishment of unequal class relations that is so central to capitalism. As Marx notes, "the treasures captured outside Europe by undisguised looting, enslavement, and murder flowed back to the mother country and were turned into capital there." Karl Marx, *Capital*, Vol. I (London: Penguin, 1990) 918. Jim Blaut has argued that "[the conquest] inaugurated a set of world historical processes that gave European protocapitalists enough capital and power to dissolve feudalism in their own region and begin the destruction of competing protocapitalist communities everywhere else." James M. Blaut, "Political Geography Debates No. 3: On the Significance of 1492," *Political Geography*, Vol. 11, Issue 4, July 1992, 355. Recent scholarship has called Blaut's position into question. Ellen Wood has insisted that the conquest of the Americas cannot be a causal factor in the emergence of capitalism since Spain, the dominant early colonial power, "amassed huge wealth from South American mines, and was well-endowed with 'capital' in the simple sense of wealth, [but it] did not develop in a capitalist direction," instead expending its massive colonial wealth "in essentially feudal pursuits." Ellen Wood, *The Origin of Capitalism: A Longer View* (New York: Verso, 2002) 148. David McNally agrees that Spanish metal wealth was used not to develop capitalism but "to finance wars." David

McNally, *Another World is Possible: Globalization and Anti-Capitalism* (Winnipeg: Arbeiter Ring, 2006) 144. Henry Heller concurs; though his explanation for the rise of capitalism diverges significantly from Wood's, he agrees that the conquest of America is not what created capitalism: "the power of colonial expansion," he insists, "depended on the growing strength of capitalism." Henry Heller, *The Birth of Capitalism: A Twenty-First Century Perspective* (Winnipeg: Fernwood, 2011) 168. Samir Amin, nevertheless, accuses the entire tradition of western social science of downplaying the role of colonialism in establishing the unequal power relations that are maintained by capitalism: "the dominant currents of Western social thought stress the internal transformations of European society [in the establishment of capitalism] and are content to note that identical transformations were not realised elsewhere, placing the blame almost exclusively on factors internal to those non-European societies." Samir Amin, *Eurocentrism*, 2nd ed. (New York: Monthly Review Press, 2009) 185. It is unclear precisely what role the colonization of the Americas—and, in particular, the early Spanish zeal for precious metals—played in the establishment of a world capitalist system. But it is clear this tremendous transfer of wealth played *some* role; it was, arguably, a necessary condition for the rise of capitalism, though most certainly not a sufficient condition.

11. Sánchez-Albornoz, *Population of Latin America*, 38.
12. Murdo J. MacLeod, *Spanish Central America: A Socioeconomic History, 1520–1720* (Austin: University of Texas Press, 2008) 49.
13. MacLeod, *Spanish Central America*, 50-51.
14. Longino Becerra, *Evolucion Historica de Honduras* (Tegucigalpa: Baktun Editorial, 1983) 54-55. (Translated from Spanish. All translations by the author unless otherwise indicated.)
15. Bartolomé de las Casas, *A Short Account of the Destruction of the Indies* (New York: Penguin, 2004) 32–33. To be sure, his critique was limited by the fact that he, himself, was a missionary who sought to convert Indigenous people to Christianity and who was granted land in the Americas by the Spanish crown. He endorsed a more peaceful brand of colonialism, in which Indigenous people "might be properly ruled and governed," a benevolent occupation that has echoes in much of Canada's contemporary language regarding Honduras.
16. Las Casas, *A Short Account*, 33.
17. MacLeod, *Spanish Central America,* 50–55.
18. I have chosen, here, to skip over much of the narrative describing the wrangling between various Spanish *conquistadors* for control over this part of Central America. Much detail on this can be found in Robert S. Chamberlain's *The Conquest and Colonization of Honduras*, a largely celebratory study of Columbus, Cortés, Alvarado, and the other conquerors. A more critical but less detailed account can be found in Murdo MacLeod's *Spanish Central America.*
19. Newson, *The Cost of Conquest,* 178.
20. Ibid., 183.
21. Ibid., 188.
22. Ibid., 187–188.
23. Ibid., 188. This should call to mind the important passages in Volume I of Marx's *Capital* on "so-called primitive accumulation," in which Marx describes the absolute refusal of many peasant farmers in England during the fifteenth, sixteenth, and seventeenth centuries to submit themselves to wage labour and market-dependence. In these stirring passages, Marx describes the process by which capitalist property relations were forced upon people "under circumstances of ruthless terrorism," and describes the "bloody legislation" that was enacted to impose violent punishment on dispossessed peasants who refused to enter into wage labour. Marx, *Capital* Vol. I, 873–904. This is further taken up and

elaborated in David McNally's *Another World is Possible,* in which he demonstrates that people faced with any alternative to capitalist wage labour have overwhelmingly pursued those alternatives, even when they have imposed all manner of hardship and difficulty. McNally, *Another World,* 90-91. In the case of Spanish Central America, many Indigenous people chose death; suicide and infanticide were not uncommon responses to the idea of life under Spanish rule. Dunbar-Ortiz, *Indians of the Americas,* 8.

24. MacLeod, *Spanish Central America,* 50.
25. Newson, *The Cost of Conquest,* 96–97.
26. Julio César Pinto Soria, in Edelberto Torres Rivas, ed., *Historia General de Centroamérica, Tomo 2* (Madrid: Sociedad Estatal Quinto Centerario, 1993) 64–65.
27. Lempira, quoted in Chamberlain, *Conquest,* 80.
28. Chamberlain, *The Conquest and Colonization of Honduras,* 69–99.
29. Naturally, Chamberlain is just one example of the standard European framing of Indigenous people. J. L. Stephens was an American archaeologist who travelled in Central America in the 1840s and whose descriptions of the sites of abandoned Mayan cities are still popular (and are featured in the ROM exhibit described above); he brags about the fact that he "bought" the ruins at Copan for fifty dollars and has the following to say about Indigenous people in 1843: "the North American Indian is by drinking made insolent, ferocious and brutal, and with a knife in his hand he is always a dangerous creature; but the Indians of Yucatan when intoxicated are only more docile and submissive. All wear machetes, but they never use them to do harm." J. L. Stephens, *Incidents of Travel in Yucatan* (New York: Dover Publications, 1963) 203. These types of descriptions were typical of the colonial and post-colonial era and remain popular among settlers and their descendents today, serving, as they do, the purpose of justifying the colonial project itself. A useful collection of some of these racist assertions can be found in Robert F. Berkhofer, Jr., *The White Man's Indian* (New York: Vintage Books, 1978).
30. Chamberlain, *The Conquest and Colonization of Honduras,* 220–226. See also Newson, *The Cost of Conquest,* 116.
31. Newson, *Cost of Conquest* ,189.
32. John A. Booth, Christine J. Wade, and Thomas W. Walker, *Understanding Central America: Global Forces, Rebellion, and Change,* 5th ed. (Boulder: Westview Press, 2010) 48.
33. Booth, Wade, and Walker, *Understanding Central America,* 48.
34. MacLeod, *Spanish Central America,* 148.
35. Booth, Wade, and Walker, *Understanding Central America,* 50.
36. Edelberto Torres Rivas, *History and Society in Central America* (Austin: University of Texas Press, 1993) 1.
37. Héctor Pérez Brignoli, in Edelberto Torres Rivas, ed., *Historia General de Centroamérica, Tomo 3* (Madrid: Sociedad Estatal Quinto Centerario, 1993) 84.
38. Dating the abolition of slavery in Great Britain and the United States is necessarily imprecise, since it was a gradual and complicated process; I have used here the Slavery Act of 1843 in Britain and the Thirteenth Amendment in the United States as the key moments. In Central America, slavery would re-emerge only briefly in 1855 in Nicaragua under the dictatorship of US adventurer William Walker, who also made English the official language, despite there only being a tiny minority in the country who spoke it. In 1857 Walker was toppled by an alliance of the Central American states and fled with American protection, but when he returned to try to orchestrate another takeover in 1860 he was captured by Honduran authorities and executed. See Booth, Wade and Walker, *Understanding Central America,* 54.
39. Alison Acker, *Honduras: The Making of a Banana Republic* (Toronto: Between the Lines, 1988) 40.

40. Woodward Jr, *Central America,* 104.
41. Ibid., 103.
42. British agent Frederick Chatfield was a key player in the failure of a Central American union. Knowing that each state would be more easily manipulated if they were divided, Chatfield manipulated leaders of various states and factions against one another, fomenting the crisis that broke up the first union attempt, as well as efforts to rebuild the union in the 1850s. See Mario Rodríguez, *A Palmerstonian Diplomat in Central America: Frederick Chatfield, Esq.* (Tucson: University of Arizona Press, 1964).
43. Acker, *Honduras,* 53.
44. Becerra, *Evolucion Historica,* 118.
45. Robert H. Holden, *Armies Without Nations: Public Violence and State Formation in Central America, 1821-1960* (Oxford: Oxford University Press, 2004) 68.
46. William I. Robinson, *Transnational Conflicts: Central America, Social Change, and Globalization* (New York: Verso, 2003) 119.
47. Victor Bulmer-Thomas, "Honduras since 1930" in Leslie Bethell, ed. *The Cambridge History of Latin America,* Vol. 7 (Cambridge: Cambridge University Press, 1990) 284.
48. Morris, *Honduras,* 4.
49. Becerra, *Evolucion Historica,* 151.
50. Bulmer-Thomas, "Honduras since 1930," 284–286.
51. Acker, *Honduras,* 59.
52. One of many examples of this attitude can be found in the gushings of American writer William Sydney Porter, pseudonym O. Henry, who escaped from the United States, where he was a fugitive, to Honduras in 1895. His *Cabbages and Kings* is a romantic account of great adventures undertaken by Americans—usually connected to the fruit companies—in Central America, replete with all manner of racist and Orientalist discourse, comparing Afro-Caribbean workers to "black panthers," and describing an Indigenous man as possessing "inherited sloth." As for American "free enterprise," he describes its arrival as follows: "The little *opera bouffe* nations play at government and intrigue until some day a big, silent gunboat glides into the offing and warns them not to break their toys. And with these changes comes also the small adventurer with empty pockets to fill, light of heart, busy-brained – the modern fairy prince, bearing an alarm clock with which, more surely than by the sentimental kiss, to awaken the beautiful tropics from their centuries' sleep." O. Henry, *Cabbages and Kings* (New York: Doubleday, 1904) 9.
53. Roger Burbagh and Patricia Flynn, *Agribusiness in the Americas* (New York: Monthly Review Press, 1980) 159.
54. Becerra, *Evolucion Historica,* 147.
55. Bulmer-Thomas, "Honduras since 1930," 286.
56. Smedley D. Butler, quoted in Eduardo Galeano, *Open Veins of Latin America* (New York: Monthly Review Press, 1997) 108.
57. Daniel Faber, *Environment Under Fire: Imperialism and the Ecological Crisis in Central America* (New York, Monthly Review Press, 1993) 34.
58. "Tegucigalpa, New National Capital Has No Railroad: Honduras Has Mules And Carts To Convey Its Travellers," *Schenectady Gazette,* November 18, 1921.
59. James Dunkerley, *Power in the Isthmus: A Political History of Modern Central America* (New York: Verso, 1988) 526.
60. Victor Meza, *Historia del Movimiento Obrero Hondureño* (Tegucigalpa: Guaymuras, 1980) 13.
61. Meza, *Historia del Movimiento,* 208.
62. Faber, *Environment Under Fire,* 38.
63. Ibid., 38.
64. Acker, *Honduras,* 74.

65. William Krehm, *Democracies and Tyrannies of the Caribbean* (Westport, CT: Lawrence Hill & Co, 1984) 91.
66. Krehm, *Democracies and Tyrannies*, 91.
67. Holden, *Armies Without Nations*, 78.
68. Ibid., 78–79.
69. Acker, *Honduras*, 82.
70. Dana Frank, "Hondurans' Great Awakening," *The Nation*, April 5, 2010.
71. Dunkerley, *Power in the Isthmus*, 529.
72. Acker, *Honduras*, 83.
73. So named as a consequence of the dynamics of the 1954 strike, which was anchored in many ways by the strategically positioned railroad workers.
74. The institutionalization of labour relations into codes of law both protects workers from certain forms of exploitation but also reifies, naturalizes and codifies the labour relation itself, thus weakening the ability of labour movements to think—and act—outside of the logic of the labour relation. Thom Workman builds a compelling case for this contradictory consequence of codified labour laws in the Canadian context, wherein he celebrates the victories that protected workers against the harshest and most inhumane expressions of labour exploitation but also laments the fact that the increasingly complicated legal apparatus in which labour operates lends itself to the creation of labour bureaucracies and enmeshes workers' organizing efforts in a whole host of legal spider webs designed to contain workers' demands and clearly delineate (and limit) the strategies they can use to achieve them. Please see Thom Workman, *If You're In My Way, I'm Walking: The Assault on Working People Since 1970* (Winnipeg: Fernwood Books, 2009).
75. The American Federation of Labour (AFL)—a bureaucratic business union organization in the US—established itself among Honduran labour, ostensibly as an ally, in order to encourage a passive and non-confrontational line within the Honduran labour movement. First, they helped convince the workers at Standard Fruit to accept a deal that satisfied a few demands but left many others ignored and which, crucially, failed to include language that would protect union activists from post-strike reprisals. The AFL set up shop permanently in Honduras, through its preferred instrument in Central America, the Inter-American Regional Organization (ORIT). ORIT advisors cultivated good relationships with the directors of the fruit companies and with the emerging military as it was being reorganized under the auspices of the United States. It was significantly funded by the CIA and USAID, the latter spending tens of thousands of dollars building offices for the now ORIT-controlled unions at both United Fruit and Standard Fruit. While militant workers tried to fight for independence, compliant and co-operative workers were offered lucrative positions as union leaders and given expensive training in the United States. Independent unions were largely squeezed out, and the labour code of 1959 made it illegal for more than one union to operate at any workplace; one of the contradictions noted above was that the labour code, which ought to have helped protect Honduran workers from American employers, actually left them at the mercy of American trade unionists with an imperialist agenda. For more on this, please see Tom Barry and Deb Preusch, *AIFLD in Central America: Agents as Organizers* (Albuquerque: The Inter-Hemispheric Education Resource Center, 1986). And for the broader picture of the AFL in Central America, see Kim Scipes, *AFL-CIO's Secret War against Developing Country Workers* (Toronto: Lexington Books, 2010).
76. Holden, *Armies Without Nations*, 179.
77. Ibid., 179.
78. Whiting Willauer, quoted in Holden, *Armies Without Nations*, 180.
79. Holden, *Armies Without Nations*, 178–186.

80. In neighbouring countries, the establishment of a well-defined local ruling class had, by the opening of the twentieth century, emerged around the expanding coffee-growing industry. By contrast, the Honduran ruling and subordinate classes were less coherent and stable, well into the twentieth century, owing to a lack of rich volcanic soil and chronic labour shortages. In the absence of a consolidating oligarchy seizing land for agri-business, land remained relatively available to *campesino* communities well into the 1940s and '50s, especially since the banana growing enclaves were located in the northern swamplands and didn't occupy much fertile land. Thus, the peasantry had come under less pressure than elsewhere—in 1952 some 85 percent of Hondurans still lived off the land—and had not yet been significantly compelled to organize as a class. Torres Rivas, *History and Society in Central America.*
81. Bulmer-Thomas, "Honduras since 1930," 300–306.
82. Liisa North and CAPA, *Between War and Peace in Central America* (Toronto: Between the Lines, 1990) 85.
83. Ibid., 74.
84. For instance, since ANACH was sponsored by the US trade unions and worked closely with the Honduran state, it was able to offer *campesinos* a certain amount of land without the threat of violent repression (which was often the case when FENACH occupied lands), thus drawing *campesinos* into its orbit with the promise of peaceful land reform that would ultimately prove to be limited in scope and undermine and further isolate the more politicized FENACH and the broader platform of emancipatory struggle it offered. For more on ANACH's undermining of FENACH, see Dunkerley, *Power in the Isthmus,* 538–565.
85. Booth, Wade, and Walker, *Understanding Central America,* 162.
86. Marvin Barahona, *Honduras en el siglo XX* (Tegucigalpa: Editorial Guaymuras, 2005) 220–226.
87. Dunkerley, *Power in the Isthmus*, 542.
88. Becerra, *Evolucion Historica,* 197–198.
89. Acker, *Honduras,* 97.
90. Dunkerley, *Power in the Isthmus*, 557.
91. Richard Lapper, *Honduras: State for Sale* (London: Latin America Bureau, 1985) 80.
92. North and CAPA, *Between War and Peace*, 83.
93. Booth, Wade, and Walker, *Understanding Central America,* 169.
94. Ibid., 163.
95. See Lapper, *Honduras,* 46-103 and Robinson, *Transnational Conflicts*, 120–123.
96. Joaquín A. Mejía, Victor Fernández, and Omar Menjívar, *Aspectos históricos, conceptuales y sustanciales sobre el proceso Constityente en Honduras* (Tegucigalpa: Movimiento Amplio por la Dignidad y la Justicia, 2009) 20.
97. Lapper, *Honduras,* 77–92.
98. Negroponte, who later served as US Ambassador to Iraq in the immediate aftermath of the US invasion, was a notable endorser of the presidential campaign of Hillary Clinton in 2016. Charles P. Pierce, "Why is Hillary Clinton Bragging About This Endorsement?" *Esquire*, August 10, 2016.
99. Juan Almendares, interview by Tyler Shipley, May 4, 2012.
100. Ibid.
101. Margarita Oseguera de Ochoa, *Honduras hoy: sociedad y crisis política* (Tegucigalpa: CEDOH, 1987) 27–35.
102. North and CAPA, *Between War and Peace,* 87.
103. Ibid.
104. Barahona, *Honduras,* 269–275.
105. Quoted in North and CAPA, *Between War and Peace,* 83.

106. Bulmer-Thomas, "Honduras since 1930," 313.
107. *El Tiempo*, March 31, 1987.
108. There is no shortage of material on the neoliberal globalization project. David Harvey's *A Brief History of Neoliberalism* is perhaps one of the best systematic overviews of neoliberalism, though it is by no means the only one. David Harvey, *A Brief History of Neoliberalism* (Oxford: Oxford University Press, 2005). David McNally's *Global Slump* offers a compelling picture of neoliberalism—as located in the broader history of world capitalism—that informs my own understanding of this period of capitalist development. David McNally, *Global Slump: The Economics and Politics of Crisis and Resistance* (Winnipeg: Fernwood, 2011).
109. Adrienne Pine, *Working Hard, Drinking Hard: On Violence and Survival in Honduras* (Berkeley: University of California Press, 2008) 137.
110. Ibid., 137.
111. Kent Norsworthy and Tom Barry, *Inside Honduras* (Albuquerque: Inter-Hemispheric Education Resource Center, 1993) 54.
112. Claudia Virginia Samayoa, *Ejecuciones Extrajudiciales de jovenes estigmatizados en Centroamérica* (San Salvador: Programa Seguridad Juvenil en Centroamérica, 2011) 218–219.
113. Booth, Wade, and Walker, *Understanding Central America,* 172.
114. Andy Thorpe, "Honduras: The New Economic Model and Poverty," in Victor Bulmer-Thomas, ed., *The New Economic Model in Latin America and its Impact on Income Distribution and Poverty* (Basingstoke, UK: MacMillan, 1996) 223-248.
115. Donald E. Schultz and Deborah Sundloff Schultz, *The United States, Honduras, and the Crisis in Central America* (Boulder: Westview Press, 1994) 273–277.
116. Thorpe, "Honduras," 223–248.
117. Roger Marin, quoted in Jesuit Reflection, Research, and Communication Team (ERIC), "Maquila: The Swallow That Lays Golden Eggs," *Envio*, vol. 16, no. 194, September 1997, 24.
118. ERIC, "Maquila," 16–22.
119. Thorpe, "Honduras," 223–248.
120. Booth, Wade, and Walker, *Understanding Central America,* 171.
121. Schultz and Schultz, *The United States*, 298–303.
122. Woodward Jr., *Central America,* 273.
123. Pine, *Working Hard,* 4.
124. Booth, Wade, and Walker, *Understanding Central America,* 171.
125. Ibid.
126. Adrienne Pine's 2008 book *Working Hard, Drinking Hard* describes the creation of Honduran subjectivities in the context of a daily life that is regularly punctuated by hyper-violence. In particular, she describes the ways that Hondurans in the 2000s were often encouraged to blame the victims of violence—physical, social, and economic—rather than the perpetrators, which reinforces the cycle of shame and violence. Her book demonstrates that part of the class project of the Honduran elite has been to criminalize and individualize poverty, just as its policies have been imposing that poverty on people at ever greater levels. On the responses to Hurricane Mitch, see Pine, *Working Hard,* 89.
127. Booth, Wade, and Walker, *Understanding Central America,* 172.
128. Ibid., 172–173.
129. Pine, *Working Hard,* 58.
130. Casa Alianza came up with 1,569, while groups associated with the Catholic Church estimated over 4,500. Virginia Samayoa, *Ejecuciones Extrajudiciales,* 241.
131. Pine, *Working Hard,* 60.
132. Virginia Samayoa, *Ejecuciones Extrajudiciales,* 220.
133. Booth, Wade, and Walker, *Understanding Central America,* 172–173.

134. Pine, *Working Hard,* 60–63.
135. Ibid., 63.
136. Booth, Wade, and Walker, *Understanding Central America,* 173.
137. Ibid.
138. Pine, *Working Hard,* 198.
139. Ibid., 195.
140. That promise would be emphasized as part of the presidential campaign of Porfirio "Pepe" Lobo in 2005, who would lose the election to Manuel Zelaya, but was elected in the fraudulent coup-sponsored elections of 2009. Booth, Wade, and Walker, *Understanding Central America,* 173.
141. Ibid., 175. See also Al Giordano, "Honduras Coup General Was Charged in 1993 Auto Theft Ring," *The Narco News,* July 4, 2009.
142. Booth, Wade, and Walker, *Understanding Central America,* 173.
143. Mike Davis and Justin Akers Chacon offer an excellent starting point on these issues in *No One Is Illegal: Fighting Racism and State Violence on the U.S.-Mexico Border* (Chicago: Haymarket Books, 2006).
144. Booth, Wade, and Walker, *Understanding Central America,* 174–175.
145. The extent to which this was a moment of rupture was emphasized to me in a three-hour conversation I had with Marcelino Borgas, whose parents were veterans of the 1954 strike, and who was deeply involved in the organizing the took place between the 1960s and 1980s. As Borgas narrated a lifetime of struggle, he insisted that the failure of Honduras' social movement to launch an effective guerilla struggle alongside the Sandinistas led to its utter decimation by the forces of reaction in the 1980s. Borgas himself is among the few Hondurans who remained politically active after the 1980s, in part because he spent much of that period in Nicaragua supporting the Sandinistas; most of his contemporaries in the Honduran struggle were either killed, jailed, tortured, or otherwise withdrawn from political life forever. Interview with Marcelino Borgas, February 19, 2015.
146. Pine, *Working Hard,* 176-178.
147. Booth, Wade, and Walker, *Understanding Central America,* 173.
148. Robinson, *Transnational Conflicts,* 132.

2 THE PRESIDENT IN HIS PYJAMAS

1. Mario Mencía Gamero, *135 Dias que estremecieron a Honduras* (Tegucigalpa: Lithopress Industrial, 2009) 16.
2. Álvaro Cálix, "Honduras: de la crisis política al surgimiento de un nuevo social actor," *Nueva Sociedad,* No. 226, April/May 2010.
3. Ashley Holly McEachern, "Postcard from Honduras: Birth of the coup," *This Magazine,* April 7, 2010.
4. A. Cano, "Golpistas agradecen apoyo en mitin de autoconvencimiento," *La Jornada,* July 1, 2009.
5. T. Rogers, "Leftist Leaders Hold Emergency Meeting Over Honduras Coup: Hugo Chávez, Daniel Ortega, and Other Leaders Met in Nicaragua," *The Christian Science Monitor,* June 29, 2009.
6. Amnesty International, "Honduras: Submission to the UN Universal Periodic Review," November-December 2010.
7. "Rocky First Year for Zelaya," *Central American Report,* February 16, 2007.
8. Gilberto Rios, interview by Tyler Shipley, May 8, 2012.
9. Juan Barahona, interview by Tyler Shipley, May 10, 2012.
10. Gilberto Rios, interview by Tyler Shipley, May 8, 2012.

11. Tomás Andino, interview by Tyler Shipley, May 9, 2012.
12. Ibid.
13. Peter Peetz, "¿De hacendado a revolucionario? Mel Zelaya y el giro hacia la izquierda del gobierno hondureño," *Iberoamericana*, Nueva época, Año 9, No. 33, March 2009.
14. Thelma Mejía, "Minimum Wage Increase Bad For Economy," *Honduras News*, January 6, 2009.
15. Adrienne Pine, *Working Hard, Drinking Hard: On Violence and Survival in Honduras* (Berkeley: University of California Press, 2008) 135–191.
16. Miguel Cáceres Rivera, "Carta a un amigo hondureño que está lejos," *El Mercurio*, July 4, 2009.
17. Joaquín A. Mejía, Victor Fernández, and Omar Menjívar, *Aspectos históricos, conceptuales y sustanciales sobre el proceso Constityente en Honduras* (Tegucigalpa: Movimiento Amplio por la Dignidad y la Justicia, 2009) 22. It is worth noting that accusations of corruption made by the oligarchy against the Zelaya government often hinge around his relations with Venezuela. In particular, the claim is that Zelaya was using Venezuelan money to support particular communities that backed him politically—extending loans and subsidies selectively to his allies. It would not be altogether shocking if there were some truth in these claims; every government since the end of the military dictatorship has been accused of varying levels of petty corruption. That said, the Truth Commission struck by the coup regime to whitewash the coup in 2010 worked very hard to demonstrate that Zelaya's government was corrupt—as part of a broader project to legitimize the coup—and could only come up with rumours and hearsay. As such, it would not be a farfetched supposition that, while there was some level of petty corruption in Zelaya's government, it was not at levels that would make it a significant factor for this analysis.
18. "Wikileaks: Micheletti made pact with Zelaya on ALBA," *Honduras Weekly*, March 21, 2011.
19. "Honduras Politics: Mixed Report Card for Zelaya," *Economist Intelligence Unit*, London, 2009.
20. In 2010, a program on the US television station History Channel ranked it the second most dangerous airport in the world. In addition to being tucked into a valley among steep mountainous terrain, the two runways at Toncontín are among the shortest at international airports in the world. After these dangerous conditions led to the crash of Taca Flight 390, which overran the runway and careened into city streets in 2008, Zelaya suspended all large aircraft landings and announced plans to divert air traffic to the Soto Cano Air Base at Palmerola, jointly run by the Honduran and US militaries. Zelaya's efforts were consistently blocked and interpreted as an attack on US regional military power, and it is no small irony that when he was deposed in 2009, the first stop was Soto Cano. Plans for the diversion of air traffic away from Toncontín were scrapped after the coup.
21. Pedro Landa, interview by Tyler Shipley, May 4, 2012.
22. Harsha Walia, "Dissecting the Coup in Honduras," *The Georgia Straight*, July 6, 2009.
23. Zelaya's government had, in fact, prepared a draft of a new mining code that included higher taxation of foreign mining companies, a ban on open-pit mining using toxic chemicals, and stricter requirements regarding community consultations. The draft was presented in May 2009, the month before the coup, and was scheduled for debate in Congress in August 2009, which, of course, was scrapped by the coup government. The post-coup Lobo government brought forward its own new mining codes—with the full support and co-operation of Canadian authorities, who describe Zelaya's draft as "anti-mining" and Lobo's as "pro-sustainable mining"—which failed to enshrine any of the reforms Zelaya's draft had proposed, protecting instead the interests of foreign companies over Honduran workers and communities. See Jennifer Moore, "Canada's Subsidies to the Mining Industry Don't Stop at Foreign Aid," *Mining Watch Canada*, June 2012.
24. "Congress in Honduras prohibits abortion pill," *Catholic News Agency*, April 7, 2009.

25. Andrea Nuila, interview by Tyler Shipley, May 4, 2012.
26. John Smeaton, "Honduras votes to ban abortion-inducing morning-after pill," *Society for The Protection of Unborn Children*, April 10, 2009.
27. Katherine Ronderos, "Poverty Reduction, Political Violence and Women's Rights in Honduras," *Community Development Journal*, June 9, 2011. Martha Lorena Alvadaro was given the post of deputy secretary of state. See Adriana Maestas, "Women's Rights and Reproductive Freedoms Under Attack with Honduran Coup," *Latino Politics Blog*, November 16, 2009.
28. John A. Booth, Christine J. Wade, and Thomas W. Walker, *Understanding Central America: Global Forces, Rebellion, and Change*, 5th ed. (Boulder: Westview Press, 2010) 168–170.
29. In fact, for what it's worth, Booth, Wade, and Walker only locate the successful transition to civilian democracy in Honduras in 1996, after the police came fully under civilian control and the military was effectively placed under meaningful control by the civilian government.
30. Booth, Wade, and Walker, *Understanding Central America*, 169.
31. Mejía, Fernández, and Menjívar, *Aspectos históricos*, 7–8, 19.
32. Jari Dixon, interview by Tyler Shipley, May 10, 2012.
33. Ibid.
34. Berta Cáceres, "Speech in Gracias, Lempira," November 1, 2009. Transcript available at hondurasresists.blogspot.ca
35. Jorge Lara Fernández, quoted in Dawn Paley, "Towards Responsible Global Journalism: Transnational Theory, Foreign Reportage, and the 2009 Coup D'Etat in Honduras," Master of Journalism Thesis, Faculty of Graduate Studies, University of British Columbia, 2010, 62.
36. Mejía, Fernández, and Menjívar, *Aspectos históricos*, 47–74.
37. Ibid.
38. Rutilia Calderon, quoted in Matt Schwartz, "Honduran Resistance Calls for Deepening of Democracy," November 10, 2009.
39. Gilberto Rios, interview by Tyler Shipley, May 8, 2012.
40. Dana Frank, "Out of the Past, A New Honduran Culture of Resistance," *NACLA Report on the Americas*, May 3, 2010.
41. Jari Dixon, interview by Tyler Shipley, May 10, 2012.
42. For instance, Zelaya vocally supported both the neoliberal dictates of CAFTA and the alternative presented by membership in ALBA. He made senior appointments to neoliberals like Gabriela Nuñez, and supported measures to create differential wage zones in poor departments, which would have the effect of lowering the wage floor for *maquiladora* owners. He even got a thumbs-up from the US Millenium Challenge Corporation for stabilizing the Honduran currency. Booth, Wade, and Walker, *Understanding Central America*, 174.
43. Jesse Freeston, interview by Tyler Shipley, August 23, 2011.
44. Roberto Sosa, "In Honduras, The Walls Are Talking," *The Progressive*, November 2009.
45. Paley, "Responsible Global Journalism," 47.
46. "Be Like Washington," *The Globe and Mail*, July 6, 2009.
47. Speaking of fabrications, some of the most dramatic speculations came from the supposed centre-left, which imagined itself too progressive to support the coup, but too clever to support Zelaya, a position staked by popular liberal Canadian journalist Gwynne Dyer, whose October 2009 piece on the Honduran crisis suggested that Zelaya had intentionally provoked a coup d'état by pretending that he was going to use the *constituyente* to run for re-election, such that the military would react against him, thus provoking a crisis and creating a context in which rule of law would break down and he could use his new popularity to make himself president for life. Quite a story, though Dyer offers no

evidence to support it and it ascribes to Zelaya a degree of long-term diabolical cunning that seems rather far-fetched, especially to people familiar with Honduran politics in general and Manuel Zelaya in particular. Gwynne Dyer, "Manuel Zelaya's Game II In Honduras," *The Georgia Straight*, October 25, 2009. Perhaps most disappointing about Dyer's concoction is that, once upon a time, Dyer was a relatively progressive voice with respect to Honduras. In the early 1980s, he wrote against the US regional wars and took pains to highlight the ways that Honduras was set to be "trampled upon" by US occupation and counter-revolution. Gwynne Dyer, "Honduras is in the Same Position Today as Cambodia Was a Decade Ago," *Kingston Whig-Standard*, March 28, 1981.

48. The issue of presidential term lengths is a contested matter in Honduras as it is in many Latin American countries. The limitations on presidential power would, no doubt, have been part of the discussion had a *constituyente* been convoked. Many Honduran politicians, including Manuel Zelaya and subsequent *golpista* president Pepe Lobo, have spoken against both the four-year term length and the restriction on running for re-election. To which side one falls in this debate is a rather trivial matter; the point is that speaking against a four-year maximum is not the same as moving towards becoming "president for life," and this accusation against Zelaya in the North American media is made all the more absurd by the fact that the United States allows its presidents to run for re-election to one additional full four-year term and Canada sets neither a limit on term length nor any restriction on re-elections. Canada, in fact, theoretically allows for the possibility of being "prime minister for life" and, in practice, the most significant recent Canadian prime ministers, Jean Chrétien and Stephen Harper, were each in power for around a decade. For more detail on the paucity of the claim that Zelaya was making a play for power, see Cálix, "Honduras."
49. Rosemary A. Joyce, "Legitimizing the Illegitimate: The Honduran Show Elections and the Challenge Ahead," *NACLA Report on the Americas*, Vol. 43, No. 2, March/April 2010.
50. Michael Fox, "Honduran Coup: Same Story, Different Stage, New Reality," *Third World Resurgence*, No. 226, June 2009.
51. Booth, Wade, and Walker, *Understanding Central America*, 175.
52. Manuel Zelaya Rosales, quoted in Mencía Gamero, *135 dias,* 16.
53. One might reasonably ask to what extent it is useful to interpret the political situation by the standard of a legal system that was being rewritten in an ad hoc way in order to block one particular act (which sought to set into motion a project to re-establish that very legal system). The pillars of the Honduran legal system —the Congress and Supreme Court—were actively undermining the legitimacy of their own system of law in order to stop the referendum that might have threatened it. As such, I consider the relative legality or illegality of the referendum to be a rather misleading distraction. Nonetheless, the relevant legal points are as follows: under the Citizen Participation Law of 2006, Zelaya was justified in pursuing the referendum and Congress was acting against the Constitution in attempting to stop him. However, when Congress passed a law prohibiting referenda within six months of an election, it made Zelaya's poll illegal and justified his arrest if he pursued the project. When Zelaya dismissed Gen. Vásquez Velásquez, it was justified under Article 280 of the Constitution, which allows the President to assign or remove the head of the armed forces. When the Supreme Court had Vásquez Velásquez reinstated, it did so based on Article 323, which establishes that the head of the armed forces is not compelled to carry out an illegal order, which is how the Supreme Court characterized Zelaya's perseverance in pursuing the referendum. On the day of the referendum, it could be argued, then, that according to the laws Congress had thrown up over the previous three days, President Zelaya could be arrested for carrying out what was now deemed an illegal referendum, since it was within six months of an election. However, follow-

ing Article 102, there is no justification for the subsequent removal of Zelaya from the country and, of course, the later presentation by the armed forces—and acceptance by Congress—of a forged resignation letter was quite obviously illegal. Any persuasive force that the *golpistas*' shaky and ad hoc legal apparatus to justify Zelaya's removal might have had was utterly discredited by their subsequent behaviour, which bore no resemblance whatsoever to a constitutional transfer of power but, rather, looked every bit the part of a military coup. The legal analysis is drawn from interviews with Jari Dixon, May 10, 2012, and Nectali Rodezno, May 4, 2012, and from Angel Edmundo Orellana, "Artículos sobre el golpe de estado en Honduras," CEDOH Boletín Especial, No. 93, September 2009, and Victor Meza et al., *Golpe de Estado: Partidos, instituciones y cultura política* (Tegucigalpa: Lithopress Industrial, 2010).

54. William Booth and Juan Forero, "Honduran Military Sends President into Exile: Supportive Congress Names Successor," *The Washington Post*, June 29, 2009.
55. Ibid.
56. Ibid.
57. Amílcar Bulnes, quoted in Iván Vásquez, "Cohep respalda gobierno de Micheletti," *El Heraldo*, June 29, 2009.
58. Benjamín Bográn, quoted in Vásquez, "Cohep respalda."
59. Paley, "Responsible Global Journalism," 44-45.
60. Euraque, quoted in Paley, "Responsible Global Journalism," 45.
61. Luis Aguilar, interview by Tyler Shipley, November 26, 2009.
62. Berta Oliva, interview by Tyler Shipley, November 26, 2009. These figures will often vary, not because the documentation is sketchy, but, quite the opposite—because it endeavours to be airtight even under the most difficult circumstances. In a context where politically motivated violence can be easily masked as gang or narco violence (and where the two sometimes overlap), human rights documentation has to work very hard to assess which is which and, thus, the estimates tend to be much lower than the actual scope of political violence.
63. COFADEH, "Informe preliminar: violaciones a derechos humanos en el marco del golpe de estado en Honduras," June 15, 2009, 13–14.
64. Juan Barahona, interview by Tyler Shipley, May 10, 2012.
65. Marlon Hernández, interview by Tyler Shipley, October 21, 2012. Hernández is now a Toronto-based political advisor to the family of Manuel Zelaya.
66. Plataforma de Derechos Humanos (CODEH, COFADEH, FIAN, CDM, CPTRT, CIPRODEH), "Official Statement to the TSE," November 28, 2009.
67. Plataforma de Derechos Humanos, "Official Statement."
68. Victor Corrales Mejía, interview by Tyler Shipley, November 29, 2009.
69. The letter read: "the purpose of this letter is to request your support with the following: names and telephone numbers of the leaders of the community who support the Democratic Civil Unity and that work jointly with the municipality for the goodness of the people. Leaders' names and telephone numbers that support the resistance movement and that cause unrest in community projects. Mr. Mayor, we need this information as soon as possible so that we can be prepared each day in order to strengthen our democratic system." Republished by Rights Action, "Honduras Coup Alert #93," November 21, 2009.
70. Committee to Protect Journalists, "After Honduran Coup, reporters detained, signals blocked," June 30, 2009.
71. David Romero, quoted in Paley, "Responsible Global Journalism," 61–62.
72. Ibid., 62.
73. Reporters Without Borders, "Anti-Coup Media Resumes Broadcasting, But Closely Con-

trolled," October 21, 2009.

74. Sandra Cuffe, "The Snakes Sleep: Attacks against the Media and Impunity in Honduras," *Upside Down World,* November 23, 2010.
75. Delmer Membreño, quoted in Cuffe, "The Snakes Sleep."
76. Manuel Torres Calderón, "El poder de los señores mediáticos en Honduras," in *Poderes, Fácticos y Sistema Político,* 3rd ed., (Tegucigalpa: CEDOH, 2009) 137.
77. Ibid., 158–159.
78. "La Prensa de Honduras borra la sangre de la foto de Isis Obed Murillo," *Resistencia Morázan,* July 7, 2009. The writers who exposed the fraud by presenting both the original photo and the printing from *La Prensa* called it a "creepy and macabre manoeuvre."
79. Belén Fernández, "Freedom of the Press Acquires New Definitions," *The Narco News,* November 1, 2009.
80. Tamar Sharabi, "Independent Presidential Candidate and Liberal Party Vice-Presidential Candidate Among Those Who Withdrew from the Ballot," *The Narco News Bulletin,* November 22, 2009.
81. José Trinidad Sánchez, interview by Tyler Shipley, November 28, 2009.
82. "Is 21st Century Socialism a Project or a Boring Film?" pamphlet distributed by military reservists in La Esperanza, Intibucá, on November 14, 2009. Reproduced in El Frente Intibucano de Resistencia Popular Contra el Golpe de Estado, "Press Release," November 17, 2009.
83. The only event that comes close is a widely reported but routinely mischaracterized burning of a Popeye's Chicken location in Tegucigalpa during a demonstration on August 11, 2009. In what appeared to most observers as a fairly obvious case of police infiltration of the rally, a small group of protestors began throwing stones at the Popeye's Chicken and inciting others to violence against it. The demonstration was carefully and heavily marshalled, and most protestors ignored the provocation, while a small group chose to express their understandable enmity against the US fast food chain that exploits Honduran labour and pays no taxes to the Honduran state. During the vandalism of the store, Honduran police sat a block back and allowed the event to take place, a telltale sign that police provocateurs were behind the event, since acts of restraint by the Honduran police in this period were rare. The next day—and for many weeks following—the story was plastered all over the *golpista* media and was used to justify ever more violent repression in response. The Popeye's building was left notably untouched for years after the event, likely in order to reinforce the idea—especially among foreign reporters—that the FNRP was a violent organization. When Popeye's finally tore it down, it was rebuilt—in hydra-esque fashion—as a mega-complex with three additional fast food outlets. For more on the alleged vandalism, see Tyler Shipley, "Between a Bank and a Burger King: Election Farce in Honduras," *Canadian Dimension,* November 26, 2009.
84. "Votos nulos y blancos son tercera fuerza" *La Tribuna,* December 13, 2009.
85. *Fox News* in the United States was one of the few exceptions, reporting the absurd figure of 70 percent; no one has yet been able to explain where that number came from.
86. Todd Gordon, *Imperialist Canada* (Winnipeg: Arbeiter Ring Publishing, 2010) 380.
87. I spoke with a group of Honduran businessmen living in the United States who were flying back to Honduras to vote—because they wanted to support the "democratic process" that Micheletti was fostering—on November 22, 2009.
88. Felix Molina, interview by Tyler Shipley, May 2, 2012.
89. Jesse Freeston, "Exclusive: Honduran Elections Exposed," *The Real News,* December 6, 2009. Available at: www.youtube.com/watch?v=1O_0uJqoVtI
90. Cálix, "Honduras."
91. Enrique Ortez Sequeira and David Matamoros were members of Tegucigalpa City Coun-

cil and the National Congress, respectively, and therefore neither was constitutionally entitled to preside over the TSE.

92. Felix Molina, interview by Tyler Shipley, November 24, 2009.
93. Plataforma de Derechos Humanos, "Official Statement."
94. I had met a number of the elections observers a few days earlier, but my encounter with Edward Fox on December 1 was entirely coincidental, as we waited together at a luggage carousel in Miami after our respective flights out of Honduras.
95. Edward Fox, interview by Tyler Shipley, December 1, 2009.
96. Washington Senior Observer Group, "Statement on the National Elections in Honduras," December 1, 2009.
97. Ibid.
98. This interview was particularly illustrative of the flimsy edifice upon which the regime's legitimacy was being built. Fox was not especially careful in his statements with me, at least until he realized that I was well-informed, by which point the artificiality of his observation process had been plainly laid bare. As he backpedaled through his denial of state terror and violence, his denial of the coup itself, his demonstrably false claims that the *constituyente* process had been "overwhelmingly rejected," and his admittance that most of his investigation in Honduras was a conversation with the US ambassador, the result was a candid portrait of the right-wing, US ideologue gone back to Honduras to subvert its democratic processes yet again, this time using Hugo Chávez and Manuel Zelaya—instead of the Sandinistas and the FMLN—as the requisite bogeymen. (Fox claimed to have participated in electoral observation in the 1981 elections, held under the military dictatorship and designed to forestall growing social movement activity and secure Honduras as a base for US military operations in Central America.) Forced to defend his claims against real evidence, his construction of free and fair elections crumbled quickly and dramatically.
99. Jean-Guy Allard, "Honduras: Dictatorship Recruiting Right-Wing Extremists as 'Observers,'" *Granma International*, November 12, 2009.
100. The IRI's presence in legitimizing the coup in 2009 makes much more remarkable the Canadian government's donation of over $1 million to the IRI, earmarked for "Citizen Participation 2.0 for Citizen Security in Honduras," in December 2015. The timing is such that while the deal was likely made by the Harper government, it would have been approved by the incoming Trudeau Liberals. Government of Canada, Disclosure of Grant and Contribution Awards over $25,000, "International Republican Institute – Foreign Affairs," June 24, 2016. Available at acdi-cida.gc.ca
101. Herman and Brodhead originally described this process as: "a circus held in a client state to assure the population of the home country [the United States] that their intrusion is well received. The results are guaranteed by an adequate supply of bullets provided in advance." Edward S. Herman and Frank Brodhead, *Demonstration Elections: U.S.-Staged Elections in the Dominican Republic, Vietnam and El Salvador* (Boston: South End Press, 1984).
102. "International Mission denounces the brutal repression of pacific demonstrations," *Agencia Latinoamericano de Información*, July 30, 2009.
103. Carlos H. Reyes, quoted in Sharabi, "Independent Presidential Candidate."
104. Sharabi, "Independent Presidential Candidate."
105. Ibid.
106. Felix Molina, interview by Tyler Shipley, November 25, 2009.
107. Tomás Andino, interview by Tyler Shipley, May 9, 2012.
108. "Micheletti: Hundreds of Foreigners Coming In To Boycott Elections," *El Tiempo*, November 16, 2009.

109. "De 4 o 6 años de prisíon a quien infrinja Ley Electoral" *El Tiempo*, November 11, 2009.
110. Sharabi, "Independent Presidential Candidate."
111. José Miguel Cruz, "Estado y violencia criminal en América Latina," *Nueva Sociedad*, No. 226, April/May 2010.
112. Joyce, "Legitimizing the Illegitimate."
113. It was unclear what motivated Zelaya's last-minute call for the people to take to the streets. Zelaya was the nominal co-ordinator of the FNRP, but his being barricaded into the Brazilian Embassy made him somewhat disconnected from the movement itself. Some speculated that his call out, defying the official FNRP position, was designed to test the movement's allegiance. Others insist that it was a miscommunication among the leadership. In any event, few people responded to Zelaya's call, and the overwhelming majority of Hondurans simply stayed home.
114. Honduran polling stations use an ink stamp on the pinky finger to demonstrate that a person has voted. As such, the waving of an un-inked finger became the visible sign of the boycott.
115. Tyler Shipley, "Where Are The People?" *Canadian Dimension*, December 1, 2009.

3 THE VIEW FROM OTTAWA

1. Cameron MacKay, quoted in "Canadá y Honduras, trabajando juntos," *El Heraldo*, July 1, 2011.
2. "World Reaction: Honduran Crisis," *BBC News*, June 28, 2009.
3. D-FAIT, "Statement by Minister of State Kent on the Situation in Honduras," No. 184, June 28, 2009. (Emphasis added.)
4. Peter Kent, quoted in M. Lacey and G. Thompson, "Envoy Prepares to Visit Honduras Warning of Obstacles," *The New York Times*, July 3, 2009.
5. D-FAIT, "Situation in Honduras."
6. Grahame Russell, "In Response to Mr. Peter Kent: Canada's Increasingly Complicit Role in Honduras," *The Dominion*, August 2, 2009.
7. D-FAIT, "Canada Calls for Restraint and a Negotiated Settlement in Honduras," No. 268, September 22, 2009. (Emphasis added.)
8. D-FAIT, "Canada Committed to Advance Peaceful and Prompt Resolution of Political Crisis," No. 298, October 7, 2009.
9. D-FAIT, "Canada Plays Leadership Role in OAS Efforts to Initiate Dialogue in Honduras," No. 303, October 9, 2009.
10. D-FAIT, "Minster of State Kent Calls for Peaceful Elections in Honduras," No. 360, November 27, 2009.
11. D-FAIT, "Canada Congratulates Honduran People on Elections," December 1, 2009.
12. Annie Bird, "Disappearing Truth in Honduras: Commissions Cover Up Demands for New Constitution," *Upside Down World*, April 13, 2010.
13. "Declaran a Micheletti diputado vitalicio," *La Tribuna*, January 14, 2010.
14. D-FAIT, "Statement by Minister of State Kent on Inauguration of Honduran President," January 28, 2010.
15. D-FAIT, "Canada Concerned Over Venezuelan Suspension of TV Stations," January 28, 2010.
16. D-FAIT, "Inauguration of Honduran President."
17. In fact, meetings with the actual government of Venezuela weren't even on the itinerary. D-FAIT, "Minister of State Kent to Visit Venezuela and Bolivia," No. 31, January 19, 2010.
18. Todd Gordon and Jeffrey Webber, "Canada's Long Embrace of the Honduran Dictatorship," *The Bullet*, No. 330, March 20, 2010.

19. Peter Kent, quoted in Cindy Chan, "Minister Kent defends free speech rights in Venezuela," *Epoch Times*, February 9, 2010.
20. An incomplete list of the names of assassinated journalists that year includes Gabriel Fino Noriega, Joseph Hernandez Ochoa, David Meza Montesinos, Nahum Palacios, Jose Bayardo Mayrena, Manuel Juarez, Jorge Alberto Orellana, Luis Arturo Mondragon, and Israel Zelaya Diaz.
21. Luis Galdámez, quoted in Jackie B. Diaz, "Freedom of the Press Threatened in Honduras," *Infosurhoy*, March 23, 2011. Available at infosurhoy.com
22. Felix Molina, interview by Tyler Shipley, May 2, 2012.
23. Alejandro Velasco, "NACLA condemns attack on 2012 Chavkin Award winner Felix Molina," *NACLA Report on the Americas*, May 7, 2016. Available at nacla.org
24. D-FAIT, "Minister of State Kent Concludes Successful Visit to Honduras," February 22, 2010.
25. Belén Fernandez, "Honduran newspaper discovers murder after 3 days," *Pulse Media*, February 27, 2010.
26. "Strange Fruit" was, of course, the title of Billie Holiday's famous song, written by American Marxist Abel Meeropol in 1936 in response to the continued practice of white supremacist lynchings in the American South. That Peter Kent should describe his visit to Honduras as "fruitful," just three days after a young girl was hanged in a politically motivated killing, should be a reminder of the macabre indifference with which imperial powers regard the victims of their machinations.
27. Sandra Cuffe, "The Snakes Sleep: Attacks against the Media and Impunity in Honduras," *Upside Down World*, November 23, 2010.
28. Peter Lackowski, "A State of Siege in Northern Honduras: Land, Palm Oil and Media," *Upside Down World*, November 30, 2010.
29. FIAN-Honduras, "Violence and Death in the Aguán Valley," November 16, 2010.
30. In October 2009, the UN Special Rapporteur on the use of mercenaries reported that Honduran landowners had hired forty members of the Self-Defence Forces of Colombia (AUC), classified as a terrorist organization by the US government.
31. FIAN-Honduras, "Violence and Death."
32. Joni Rivas, interview by Tyler Shipley, May 3, 2012.
33. Peter Lackowski, "A State of Siege."
34. Joni Rivas, interview by Tyler Shipley, May 3, 2012.
35. "Update and Action for the *Campesinos* of Rigores, Aguán," *Honduras Resiste*, July 13, 2011.
36. "Latest News," *Honduras Resiste*, July 23, 2011.
37. This number, however, is still growing, despite being the lowest possible estimate, since many deaths can only be indirectly attributed to political repression. It also excludes the many people victimized as a result of circumstances created by the violence and insecurity, as in the case of five Honduran Pepsi employees, killed on August 15, 2011, by security guards who mistook them for members of MUCA.
38. Daniel Altschuler, "Between Resistance and Co-optation: The Politics of Education in the Honduran Crisis" in *NACLA Report on the Americas*, Vol. 43, No. 2, March/April 2010, pp. 23-29.
39. Kari Lydersen, "Fired for Opposing Coup, Honduran Educators Go On Hunger Strike," *Working In These Times*, July 5, 2010.
40. Kari Lydersen, "Angered by President 'Pepe,' Teachers Strike Again in Honduras" *Working In These Times*, November 5, 2010.
41. Maquila Solidarity Network, "New Wave of Repression Targets Opponents of Honduran Coup," *The Bullet*, May 6, 2010.
42. According to COFADEH, police reported the death as caused by a "traffic accident."

In fact, Velázquez Rodriguez was part of a group of teachers attacked by police during a peaceful demonstration; as police fired tear gas into the crowd, people became asphyxiated and confused and a forced evacuation route became blocked. In the melee, Velázquez Rodriguez was hit in the face by a tear gas canister, knocking her out; she fell to the street and while laying unconscious on Boulevard Francia, she was hit by a car. As such, COFADEH declares Velázquez Rodriguez a victim of state repression, not a traffic accident. "Urgent Action from COFADEH," *Honduras Resiste*, June 16, 2011.

43. Lydersen, "Angered by President 'Pepe'."
44. Some, like the Federación de Asociaciones de Padres y Madres de Familia por la Educación de *Honduras* (Federation of Parents' Associations for Education in Honduras, FAPAMEH) have made efforts to present themselves as "politically neutral" and interested only in bettering the Honduran education system, while others like Volvamos a Clases (Let's Return to Class) are transparently pro-coup and anti-union.
45. Altschuler, "Between Resistance and Co-optation."
46. Todd Gordon and Jeffrey Webber, "From Cartagena to Tegucigalpa: Imperialism and the Future of the Honduran Resistance," *Upside Down World*, July 4, 2011.
47. Felix Molina, interview by Tyler Shipley, May 2, 2012.
48. Peace Brigades International (PBI), "Report of the Short-Term Mission to Honduras," October 2011.
49. Felix Molina, interview by Tyler Shipley, May 2, 2012.
50. COFADEH, "Urgent Action: Human Rights Defender Threatened and Given Ultimatum," March 7, 2011.
51. José Trinidad Sánchez, interview by Tyler Shipley, November 28, 2009.
52. US Labor Education in the Americas Project (USLEAP), "Honduras News Labor Update," March 2011. Available at usleap.org
53. Miriam Miranda, "Honduras: El golpe de Estado, sus herederos y la criminalización de la protesta social," *Honduras Resiste*, March 29, 2011.
54. Claiming, for instance, that COFADEH's efforts to document the violence against organized *campesino* movements in the Aguán constitutes support for terrorist activities, since those groups are increasingly being labelled "terrorist" groups in order to justify their repression. COFADEH, "Informe: Situación de defensores de derechos humanos en Honduras," Tegucigalpa, December 2011.
55. A quick scan of COFADEH's regular reports demonstrates these patterns and, indeed, when I've travelled and worked with COFADEH, FIAN, and other human rights documenters, I've heard these types of stories over and over again.
56. From a COFADEH report: "Defenders of human rights, especially women working in poor communities, are also themselves victims of abuse on the part of agents of the state. It has become common for the authorities to refuse to offer any protection and to fail to comply with their responsibility to investigate or sanction those responsible for the attacks." COFADEH, "Situación de defensores" 26.
57. Gladys Lanza, interview by Tyler Shipley, May 7, 2012.
58. COFADEH, "Situación de defensores," p. 27.
59. According to Lanza, there were over 18,000 complaints of domestic violence in 2010, of which more than 11,000 were never investigated.
60. Gladys Lanza, interview by Tyler Shipley, May 7, 2012.
61. Claudia Virginia Samayoa, *Ejecuciones Extrajudiciales de jovenes estigmatizados en Centroamérica* (San Salvador: Programa Seguridad Juvenil en Centroamérica, 2011) 227.
62. Ibid., 229.
63. Berta Oliva, "A Real Truth Commission for Honduras," *Huffington Post*, July 4, 2010.
64. DFAIT, "Canada Supports Creation of Honduras Truth and Reconciliation Commis-

sion," April 15, 2010.

65. Ibid.
66. Hugh McKinnon, "Bennett-Jones Welcomes Michael Kergin As Senior Advisor," January 5, 2009.
67. Bennett-Jones LLP, "Practices." Available at bennettjones.com
68. Andrew Ross, quoted in Yves Engler, *The Black Book of Canadian Foreign Policy* (Black Point, NS: Fernwood, 2009) 99–100.
69. Engler, *The Black Book*, 100–101.
70. Government of Canada, "Michael Kergin." Available at canadainternational.gc.ca
71. Engler, *Black Book*, 19–21.
72. McKinnon, "Bennett-Jones Welcomes Michael Kergin."
73. Bennett-Jones, LLP, "Our Work." Available at bennettjones.com
74. Jennifer Wells, "Ponzi Canadian Style," *Toronto Star*, September 20, 2009.
75. Thelma Mejía, "Honduras: Disputed Truth Commission to Investigate Coup," *Inter Press Service*, May 5, 2010.
76. Annie Bird, "Disappearing Truth in Honduras."
77. CEJIL, "Reflections on the Opening of the Honduran Truth Commission."
78. Porfirio "Pepe" Lobo, quoted in Radio América, "Presidente Lobo instala Comisión de la Verdad," May 5, 2010.
79. CEJIL, "Reflections."
80. Michael Kergin, "The Honduran Truth and Reconciliation Commission (2010–2011)," *Optimum Online*, Vol. 42, No. 3, September 2012, p. 42–45.
81. Ibid.
82. Ibid.
83. Ibid.
84. Kergin is referencing Zelaya's two attempts—the first unsuccessful—to re-enter Honduras after being kidnapped and exiled. Even the framing of these attempts at "testing the borders" serves to suggest that Zelaya was engaged in some sort of provocation. Ibid., 55.
85. Adrienne Pine does well to interrogate the notion of a violent Honduran subjectivity in *Working Hard, Drinking Hard.*
86. It is well outside the scope of this project to dig into the myriad cultural manifestations of colonialism, but it is worth briefly highlighting this point. Of course, there *is* a culture of violence in Honduras, which this book has described in some detail. But that culture cannot be separated from the successive waves of violent colonial interventions, subjugations, and impositions. Describing a "culture of violence" as a product of centuries of colonialism is very different from suggesting that there is something *inherently* violent in a given community, the latter of which has been a central component of colonialism for hundreds of years. The so-called *mission civilisatrice* upon which the colonizers embarked, supposedly to bring the "darker" nations into the "light," to bring them out of "primitive savagery" into "rational enlightenment," is obviously reliant on the assumption that the people who were the subjects of colonial interventions were inherently backward. The material purposes of the colonial project—thievery, expansion, exploitation—are subsumed into the cultural justifications that give it true form. The victims of colonialism are blamed for it; "it may be painful but it is for their own good," say the colonizers. "They must be broken from their backwards, violent, ignorant, savage ways." The colonizers insist that they aren't stealing land and riches and labour, they are simply spreading the best of civilization to those who need a helping hand. The violent destruction of entire cultural forms, the disrupting of human societal bonds, and the forced re-education into the culture of the colonizer, are common manifestations of this discourse. They can be seen in colonial projects ranging from the Canadian residential schools—designed to

"beat out the Indian" from surviving Indigenous people in Canada—to the banning of local customs, ceremonies, family and community structures, and even languages, in the European conquests of Latin America and Africa. Naturally, this discourse, and the practices that flow from it, take a variety of different forms in different times and places, but they are a consistent and insidious element of the colonial project and one can see the discourse at work very clearly in Michael Kergin's discussion of Honduras' "traditional culture of violence." This analysis is drawn from post-colonial scholarship, a few different articulations of which can be found in: Frantz Fanon, *The Wretched of the Earth,* New York: Grove Press, 2004; Albert Memmi, *The Colonizer and the Colonized*, Boston: Beacon Press, 1991; and Edward Said, *Culture and Imperialism*, New York: Vintage Press, 1993.

87. Kergin, "Honduran Truth and Reconciliation Commission," 54.
88. Again, this echoes the colonial justifications described above, though it represents a slightly different version; in this case, the colonizer relies on the discourse of its subjects' "backwardness" to justify supporting anti-democratic or otherwise reactionary local leadership. The notion is that the colonized subjects are not yet "ready" for democracy, wealth, autonomy, or whatever else popular social movements might be demanding. Think of the responses colonial powers always give to assertions of anti-colonial struggle; the French couldn't possibly leave Algeria; what would become of the Algerians? Or the Israeli answers to Palestinian liberation struggles, which have consistently claimed that Palestinians were not capable of responsibly governing their own state. The same discourse justifies Canada's ongoing colonization of Indigenous people, whose demands for self-government are always countered by claims that they would govern themselves irresponsibly and, as such, still need the Canadian state to take care of them. Indeed, Canada extends the same logic to Afghanistan, which it occupied ostensibly because it would fall into chaos and violence if Canadian troops weren't there to take care of things. Albert Memmi is particularly poignant on this: "whenever the colonizer adds, in order not to fall prey to anxiety, that the colonized is a wicked, backwards person with evil, thievish, somewhat sadistic instincts, he thus justifies his police and his legitimate severity. After all, he must defend himself against the dangerous, foolish acts of the irresponsible and, at the same time—what meritorious concern!—protect him against himself!" Memmi, *The Colonizer*, 82.
89. D-FAIT, "Canada Pleased With Release of Honduran Truth and Reconciliation Commission Final Report," July 7, 2011.
90. Todd Gordon and Jeffery R. Webber, "The Cartagena Accord: A Step Forward for Canada in Honduras," *The Bullet*, No. 526, July 13, 2011.
91. The full text of Cartagena can be accessed through the website of *La Tribuna*. "Acuerdo para la Reconciliación Nacional y la Consolidación del Sistema Democrático en la República de Honduras," *La Tribuna*, May 22, 2011. Available at: www.latribuna.hn/2011/05/22/acuerdo-para-la-reconciliacion-nacional-y-la-consolidacion-del-sistema-democratico-en-la-republica-de-honduras/
92. Dana Frank, "Ousted President's Return to Honduras Doesn't Mean Repression Is Over," *The Progressive*, May 27, 2011.
93. Jari Dixon, interview by Tyler Shipley, November 26, 2009.
94. Some claim the number to be as high as one million people, which would represent some 12 percent of the entire Honduran population. See Jesse Freeston, "Massive Turnout for Zelaya Launches New Chapter of Honduran Struggle," *The Real News*, June 23, 2011.
95. As Berta Cáceres explained at the time: "Everyone is happy that Zelaya has returned ... his right of return should have always been unconditional. He's a human being and he has a right to return to his country. However, we believe the Cartagena Accord is in accordance with US strategy ... the Resistance is not reducible to Mel Zelaya." Berta Cáceres, quoted in Gordon and Webber, "From Cartagena to Tegucigalpa."

96. Morgan Lee and Alexandra Olson, "Honduran Coup Shows Business Elite Still In Charge," *Associated Press*, August 5, 2009.
97. Carlos Amador, quoted in Gordon and Webber, "From Cartagena to Tegucigalpa."
98. COFADEH, "Human Rights are not subject to political negotiation," *Friendship Office of the Americas*, May 24, 2011.
99. "Acuerdo para la Reconciliación Nacional."
100. Berta Oliva, quoted in Gordon and Webber, "From Cartagena to Tegucigalpa."
101. Gordon and Webber, "From Cartagena to Tegucigalpa."
102. I offer fuller treatment of the complicated politics of this moment in Tyler Shipley, "Left International Solidarity in Post-Coup Honduras," *Upside Down World*, September 26, 2012.
103. The tortures he experienced while barricaded in the Brazilian embassy with Zelaya were—by his own admission—limited to sound cannons and bright lights that made it difficult to sleep. Very unpleasant treatment, to be sure, and these tactics have been known to have long term psychological effects on their victims. Nevertheless, it speaks volumes about his relationship to the social movement and to the resistance at large that he should decry these discomforts without mentioning the much more extreme levels of violence meted out to less-privileged movement activists.
104. Rasel Tomé, interview by Tyler Shipley, May 9, 2012.
105. In my experience, movement activists had little regard for Tomé, considering him a political opportunist who had conveniently jumped into LIBRE as a gamble that it would be a better bet for his own personal ambitions. The day that I spoke with Tomé, I fell rather ill and had to postpone a few other interviews; several people joked that speaking to Rasel Tomé had, quite literally, made me sick.
106. Juan Barahona, interview by Tyler Shipley, May 10, 2012.
107. Ibid.
108. Gilberto Rios, interview by Tyler Shipley, May 8, 2012.
109. Dana Frank, "US Underwrites Corruption and Violence in Honduras," *Al-Jazeera America*, June 1, 2015. Available at america.aljazeera.com
110. Center for Economic and Policy Research, "Honduran Elections: Live Blog," November 21–25, 2013. Available at: www.cepr.net/blogs/the-americas-blog/honduran-elections-live-blog
111. Leo Gabriel, quoted in Mark Weisbrot, "Why the world should care about Honduras' recent election," *The Guardian*, December 3, 2013.
112. Alberto Arce, "Deposed Honduran leader's wife leads in polls," *Associated Press*, June 22, 2013. See also Noé Leiva, "A un mes de las elecciones, la izquierdista Xiomara Castro encabeza las encuestas," *El Faro*, October 24, 2013. Available at elfaro.net
113. Eric Sabo and Isabella Cota, "Debut Honduran Bonds Rally as Polls Show Tighter Election," *Bloomberg Business*, October 31, 2013. Available at bloomberg.com
114. Weisbrot, "Why the world should care"
115. Giorgio Trucchi, "Honduras Finds Itself on the Edge of a Social Explosion Again," *Vice*, May 19, 2014. Available at vice.com
116. Tracy Wilkinson, "A Honduran Coup Comes Full Circle," *Los Angeles Times*, April 27, 2015.
117. Victor Meza, interview by Tyler Shipley, February 18, 2015.
118. Leticia Salomón, interview by Tyler Shipley, February 20, 2015.
119. David Gagne, "Organized Crime Turmoil in Honduras Extends to Politics," *In Sight Crime*, June 19, 2015. Available at insightcrime.org
120. Karen Spring, "Scandal in the Social Security Institute in Honduras," *Aqui Abajo*, May 14, 2015. Available at desdeaquiabajoabajo.blogspot.ca
121. Elisabeth Malkin, "Wave of Protests Spread to Scandal-Weary Honduras and Guatemala," *The New York Times*, June 12, 2015.

122. Karen Spring, "Berta Cáceres, the Murdered Honduran Activist, Did Not Die. She Multiplied," *Huffington Post*, March 23, 2016.
123. Oscar Alvarez, quoted in Cuffe, "The Snakes Sleep."
124. Adrienne Pine's above-mentioned *Working Hard, Drinking Hard* provides an excellent overview of the complicated terrain of gang violence in Honduras, prior to the 2009 coup. Even before the coup, Pine notes that Honduran police exaggerated the extent and severity of gang violence in order to bolster their own power and that the problem of gang violence in Honduras is both a product of poverty and isolation in poor communities and, at the same time, is used to justify violent policies and practices towards Honduras' poor.
125. Vásquez Velásquez was arrested in 1993 for participation in a series of auto thefts connected to narco gangs and supposedly called himself part of a "gang of 13." It isn't entirely clear that this was a reference to MS-13, but Vásquez Velásquez has undoubtedly been implicated in gang and narco activity for decades. Berta Cáceres said in 2009: "He's a car thief from the '13's' gang. This country has become a narco-politics country." Al Giordano, "Honduras Coup General Was Charged in 1993 Auto Theft Ring," *The Narco News*, July 4, 2009.
126. Ismael Moreno, "Insecurity, Criminality, Hidden Powers and Visible Roots," *Envío* 312, July 2007.
127. Victor Meza, interview by Tyler Shipley, May 10, 2012. Meza, whose scholarly work on the Honduran labour movement is the most thorough and important work of its kind, has been critical of the coup from the beginning. Nevertheless, aware of the very real danger in being a public figure with a critical view, he walks a careful line in his public statements. Regarding the police reform commission, he both acknowledged the deep, structurally rooted nature of the problems in Honduras while, simultaneously, expressing a curious and contradictory optimism with respect to the prospect of resolving Honduras' problems through semi-official organs like the commission. I asked him, if the police and the state are as corrupt as he thinks they are, won't they surely respond with violence to any attempt to meaningfully reform it? His response was, "yes, I recognize the danger and difficulty. In fact, a journalist was kidnapped 20 metres from this office yesterday." Yet, in the same breath, he insists that a coalition of civil society groups have come together around the commission and that he believes it can work. I return to the matter of police reform—and Canada's role in that process—in Chapter 5.
128. All of this is reminiscent of Charles Tilly's 1985 assessment of statecraft as organized crime; Tilly argues that war-making and state-making can be described as "protection rackets" in which "banditry, piracy, gangland rivalry, policing and war-making all belong on the same continuum," and where the same coercive force that creates danger (i.e., the state, the police, organized crime) offers itself as the protection from it. In a case like contemporary Honduras, Tilly's comparison of the state to a crime syndicate actually becomes real; no longer simply an analogy, the state is more or less a criminal organization and the criminal gangs are more or less the state. See Charles Tilly, "War Making and State Making as Organized Crime," in Peter B. Evans, Dietrich Rueschemeyer, and Theda Skocpol, eds., *Bringing the State Back In* (New York: Cambridge University Press, 1985) 169-192.
129. Chrystia Freeland, House of Commons, January 29, 2014. Transcript available at: openparliament.ca/debates/2014/1/29/chrystia-freeland-1/only/
130. Bill Fairbairn, Tara Ward, and Stacey Gomez, "Canada-Honduras Free Trade Agreement," *Embassy Mag*, July 9, 2014.
131. "Berta Caceres received death threats from Canadian company," *Telesur*, March 4, 2016. Available at telesurtv.net

4 A FRUITFUL PARTNERSHIP

1. Todd Gordon, *Imperialist Canada* (Winnipeg: Arbeiter Ring Publishing, 2010) 177.
2. Todd Gordon, "Canada Backs Profits, Not Human Rights, in Honduras," *Toronto Star*, August 16, 2011.
3. A reliable and consistent source for information on Canadian mining operations is the organization Mining Watch Canada, which publishes seasonal newsletters and, periodically, larger investigative reports. Please see miningwatch.ca
4. Ashley Holly, "Shame on Canada, Coup Supporter," *The Tyee*, July 9, 2009. The influx of foreign capital after Hurricane Mitch follows the patterns described in Naomi Klein's important *The Shock Doctrine*. Klein's argument is that capital seeks and seizes upon natural or social disasters in order to take advantage of the dislocation and weakness of the affected peoples and states, in order to move into otherwise blocked spaces or establish new spaces for profitable investment (by coercing states to sign free-trade agreements, rewrite legislation around investment, labour, or environmental codes, or simply moving in at a moment of need and offering services that local companies can no longer functionally offer, thus displacing them semi-permanently.) Klein makes a convincing case for what she calls "disaster capitalism," and while I think she overemphasizes the need for natural disasters, she does acknowledge that capital also finds ways to construct these "shock" conditions whenever it sees a need. Her "disaster capitalism" could be better described simply as "capitalism," since the history of capital has been propelled forward by precisely the dynamics she describes; the dramatic and violent uprooting of the peasantry in England, the shock and dislocation of colonial invasions and occupations, or the fomenting of debt crises in the Global South are all examples of unnatural disasters, created in large part *by* capital, that created "shock" conditions upon which capital seized and turned to its advantage. Naomi Klein, *The Shock Doctrine: The Rise of Disaster Capitalism* (Toronto: Vintage Books, 2007).
5. Holly, "Shame on Canada."
6. Karen Spring and Sandra Cuffe, "Canada and Chile Meddling in Honduras's Economic and Security Policies," *Upside Down World*, May 21, 2012.
7. Canadian Council for International Cooperation (CCIC), "Honduras: Democracy Denied," Report from the CCIC's Americas Policy Group with Recommendations to the Government of Canada, April 2010, 17.
8. Mary Durran, "Honduran Partners Mobilize Against New Mining Law," Canadian Catholic Organization for Development and Peace, January 22, 2012.
9. Harvey Beltrán, "Coup Leaves Nation Without Mining Law," *Business News Americas*, September 25, 2009.
10. Jen Moore, "Honduran organizations fight to have Canadian-backed mining law declared unconstitutional," Mining Watch Canada, February 26, 2015. Available at miningwatch.ca
11. Pedro Landa, interview by Tyler Shipley, May 4, 2012.
12. "Breakwater Resources agrees to $663 million all-cash takeover by Nyrstar," *Proactive Investors USA & Canada*, June 15, 2011.
13. All this information, summarized by Pedro Landa in our interview, comes from a series of documents that CEHPRODEC was able to obtain from Dirección Ejecutiva De Fomento a la Mineria (DEFOMIN) which detail each concession (prior to 2009) specifically, by department, including the names and companies represented by the applicants for the concessions. DEFOMIN, "Listado de solicitudes metálicas otorgadas, departamento de Francisco Morazán," Registro público de derechos mineros, April 15, 2010.
14. Michael Marsh, "From Québec to Copan: Globalization and the Case of San Andrés

Minas," *Mining Watch Canada*, June 25, 2001. Available at miningwatch.ca

15. Agatha Christie's *Sparkling Cyanide*, for instance, involved a murder disguised as suicide in which the killer used a few drops of cyanide in a glass of sparkling wine. These stories are significant only because they illustrate that it is rather common knowledge that even a drop of cyanide is lethal, putting into sharp relief these mining companies' use of thousands of tons of cyanide in their operations on or around communities that may or may not have agreed to their presence.
16. Aura Minerals Inc., "San Andres Technical Report," March 28, 2012, 7-15. Available at auraminerals.com
17. Xiomara Orellana. "La ruptura de un tubo de la minera Yamana ocasionó la muerte de peces," *La Prensa*, March 20, 2009.
18. Canadian Mining in Honduras, "Case Study, San Andres, Copan," Available at mininginhonduras.wordpress.com
19. Aura Minerals, "San Andres Technical Report," 131.
20. "Urgent Action: What does Aura Minerals have to hide?" Mining Watch Canada, April 17, 2016. Available at miningwatch.ca
21. Rights Action, "Goldcorp Staff Face Criminal Charges Over Mine Pollution After CAFOD Investigation," *Upside Down World*, August 16, 2010.
22. Honduras Accompaniment Project (PROAH), "Press Conference about Health Impacts of San Martin Mine and Honduras' Proposed Mining Law," August 28, 2012.
23. Carlos Amador, interview by Tyler Shipley, May 8, 2012.
24. Ibid.
25. Ibid.
26. Lauren Carasik and Grahame Russell, "Honduras: Goldcorp Inc and the Death of Lesly Yaritza," *Indigenous Peoples Issues and Resources*, December 24, 2011. Available at indigenouspeoplesissues.com
27. "Awards and Recognition," Goldcorp.com. Available at goldcorp.com
28. Kady O'Malley, "Lobby Watch: MPs reveal cost details of Goldcorp-funded Guatemala trip," *CBC News Online*, October 22, 2012.
29. "Verdict," *Tribunal Popular Internacional de Salud*, July 15, 2012. Available at healthtribunal.org
30. "Overview," *Tribunal Popular Internacional de Salud*, July 15, 2012. Available at healthtribunal.org
31. Canadians involved in the project included Dr. David Heap from the University of Western Ontario, Judy Deutsch from the University of Toronto, and Claudia Campero from the Council of Canadians.
32. Fiona Anderson, "Goldcorp hits revenue high," *Vancouver Sun*, February 16, 2012.
33. Aura Minerals, Inc., "Management's Discussion and Analysis, For The Three and Nine Months Ended September 30, 2012," November 13, 2012. Available at auraminerals.com This online investor's guide, called "Happy Capitalism," advised prospective investors in 2011 to be careful with Aura: www.happycapitalism.com/2011/04/aura-minerals-inc-trying-to-reverse-a-steep-decline/
34. A complicating piece of the story here that doesn't fit into the central argument but needs to be remembered is that capital can leave Honduras as quickly as it enters. It is entirely possible that the coup regime could fail in its "race to the bottom" project of attracting further foreign investment; Canadian companies could discover that conditions for profitability in their Honduran operations might not be good enough and, as a result, they might choose to invest elsewhere. My argument that the Canadian state—in partnership with Canadian and Honduran capital—is supporting a compliant Honduran state in constructing conditions for profitability in Honduras is not disproven if those profitable

conditions are not created. That would simply mean that the project was unsuccessful, a very real possibility in the volatile world created by capitalist globalization.

35. Pedro Landa, interview by Tyler Shipley, May 4, 2012.
36. Todd Gordon, "Military Coups are Good for Canadian Business: the Canada-Honduras Free Trade Agreement," *The Bullet*, March 8, 2011.
37. DFAIT, quoted in Jennifer Moore, "Canada's Promotion."
38. *El Heraldo*, quoted in Jennifer Moore, "Canada's Promotion."
39. Marvin Palacios, "De cada 100 hondurenos y hondurenas, 91 se oponen a la mineria a cielo abierto," *Defensores en linea*, March 27, 2012. Available at defensoresenlinea.com
40. Jennifer Moore, "Honduran Mining Law Passed and Ratified, but the Fight is Not Over," Mining Watch Canada, January 24, 2013. Available at miningwatch.ca
41. Indeed, ANAMINH director Santos Gabino Carbajal reassured investors that the new laws would not interfere with their operations. Reuters reported that he "applauded the law and did not believe the caveat of giving locals a deciding say would be a problem," which suggests rather clearly that the law does not actually give locals a deciding say at all. "Honduras ends mining moratorium, approves taxes," *Rueters*, January 24, 2013.
42. Pedro Landa, interview by Tyler Shipley, March 3, 2013.
43. Ibid.
44. "Gildan Activewear Announces Record Quarterly Results and Projects Strong Earnings Outlook for Fiscal 2013," Gildan Press Release, November 29, 2012.
45. "Gildan Activewear Inc," *Bloomberg Business*. Available at bloomberg.com
46. "Gildan Activewear profit slips on price cuts," *The Globe and Mail*, July 31, 2015.
47. Steven Chase, "In a Bid to Enter New Markets, Harper Lands Free-Trade Deal with Honduras," *The Globe and Mail*, September 6, 2012.
48. Gildan, "Recognition," available at genuinegildan.com
49. Joel Bakan, *The Corporation* (Toronto: Penguin Books, 2004) 65–66.
50. Adrienne Pine, *Working Hard, Drinking Hard: On Violence and Survival in Honduras* (Berkeley: University of California Press, 2008) 140–155.
51. Canada was instrumental in the overthrow of the democratically elected government of Jean-Bertrand Aristide in 2004 and has subsequently become part of a semi-permanent occupation force in the country. See Yves Engler and Anthony Fenton, *Canada in Haiti* (Winnipeg: Fernwood, 2005).
52. The segment, titled "Sewing Discontent," was aired as part of the program *Disclosure*, but is no longer available at the CBC website, despite being referenced in the sidebar to related news articles, such as this one, published around the same time, on anti-sweatshop activism in Canada. Available at www.cbc.ca/marketplace/pre-2007/files/home/cutitout/index.html
53. Gordon, *Imperialist Canada*, 250–251.
54. Ibid., 251.
55. Workers Rights Consortium, "Case Summary, Star, S.A. (Honduras), October 1, 2008. Available at: www.workersrights.org/Freports/Case%20Summary%20-%20Star%20_Honduras_.pdf
56. Workers Rights Consortium, "Workers Rights Consortium Assessment, Star, S.A. (Honduras): Findings, Recommendations and Status" October 12, 2012. Available at: www.workersrights.org/Freports/WRC%20Assessment%20re%20Star%20%28Honduras%29%20-%2010.12.12.pdf
57. Ibid.
58. Ibid.
59. Maria Luisa Regalado, interview by Tyler Shipley, May 11, 2012.
60. Ibid.

61. Castillo struggled in the Honduran courts for over three years, with the support of CODEMUH, and was able to win her job back in 2016. Nevertheless, her case is the exception that proves the rule, as it took a massive effort to have her reinstated, and many others are not able to win these cases. In fact, even after the Supreme Court ruled in her favour, in March 2016, it took months of pressure before Gildan complied with the court order. See Karen Spring, "Gildan! Give Lilian Castillo her job back in Honduras!," *Aqui Abajo*, May 24, 2016. Available at aquiabajo.com
62. Pine, *Working Hard*, 159.
63. Maria Luisa Regalado, interview by Tyler Shipley, May 11, 2012.
64. Ibid.
65. In 2011, for instance, CODEMUH presented a comprehensive complaint to the Fair Labor Association (FLA) about Gildan's treatment of its workforce. Gildan responded by initiating an examination of its own practices which, not surprisingly, came back with a rosy picture of a socially responsible company. CODEMUH sent the complaint back to the FLA, but the response from that organization was disappointing to CODEMUH and its supporters in the North American-based Maquila Solidarity Network, which claimed that the FLA report ignored the root causes of the problems at Gildan factories and did not investigate the long-term health problems associated with working at Gildan. Please see Maquila Solidarity Network, "FLA investigation ignores root causes of workplace injuries," September 5, 2012. Available at en.maquilasolidarity.org
66. This event was related to me by two separate people, one who was present during some of the circumstances described. The sources are both trusted and the story was corroborated but, for their own reasons, both preferred to remain anonymous. This information was first shared with me in an interview on February 18, 2015.
67. Maria Luisa Regalado, interview by Tyler Shipley, May 11, 2012.
68. CODEMUH, "Open Letter," August 12, 2011.
69. Steven Chase, "Harper Exits Honduras With A New Free-Trade Deal," *The Globe and Mail*, August 12, 2011.
70. Peter Kent, quoted in Maxwell A. Cameron, "A Diplomatic Theatre of the Absurd: Canada, the OAS and the Honduran Coup," *NACLA Report on the Americas*, Vol. 43, No. 3, May/June 2010, 20.
71. CCIC, "Honduras: Democracy Denied," 19.
72. Tom Stollery, quoted in Rights Action, "Pro-Coup North Americans in Honduras," November 10, 2009. Available at rightsaction.org
73. Penelope Leigh, quoted in Rights Action, "Pro-Coup North Americans."
74. Dawn Paley, "Snowbirds Gone Wild! Canadian Retirees and Locals Clash in Honduras," *This Magazine*, November 4, 2010.
75. Soren Hvalkof, "Privatization of Land and Indigenous Communities in Latin America: Tenure Security or Social Security?" Danish Institute for International Studies, Working Paper No. 2008-21, 2008.
76. Tanya Krssen, *Grabbing Power: The New Struggles for Land, Food and Democracy in Northern Honduras* (Oakland: Food First Books, 2013) 76.
77. Kerssen, *Grabbing Power*, 76–77.
78. Ismael Moreno, quoted in Kerssen, *Grabbing Power*, 79.
79. Kerssen, *Grabbing Power*, 79–80.
80. "Public Statement," Triunfo de la Cruz Garífuna Pro-Improvement Community Council, Tela, Atlántida, Honduras, August 2, 2011.
81. Whether tourism can ever have positive local impacts is rather debatable. Julian T. Pinter's 2010 film *Land*, filmed in Nicaragua not far from the Honduran tourist enclaves, offers a bleak look at tourism and land development as neo-colonialism. Julian T. Pinter, *Land*,

7th Art, 2010.

82. Kerssen, *Grabbing Power,* 84.
83. Interview with Felix Molina, May 2, 2012.
84. This dynamic is reminiscent of my analysis in Chapter 1 of North American fascination with the "mysterious" Maya.
85. Karen Spring, "Canadian Porn Kings, Tourism 'Development' Projects, Repression and the Violation of Indigenous-Garifuna Rights in Honduras," *Rights Action Bulletin*, February 14, 2011.
86. Porfirio 'Pepe' Lobo, quoted in Life Vision Properties promotional video, available at: www.realestate-investments.co/caribbean-real-estate-for-sale/
87. Randy Jorgensen, quoted in Paley, "Snowbirds Gone Wild."
88. Evaristo Perez Ambular, quoted in Paley, "Snowbirds Gone Wild."
89. Karen Spring, "Canada's Ongoing Support for Honduras Regime," *Rights Action Bulletin*, January 10, 2011.
90. Jonathan Roberto Catracho, "First Big Cruise Ship to Visit Honduras' Banana Coast in Trujillo 'The Norwegian Jewel," Honduras.com, October 16, 2014.
91. Paul Jeffrey, "Sex Tourism Plagues Central America," *Response Magazine for United Methodist Women,* May 23, 2011.
92. For instance, the Pulitzer Center treats the problem as though it were rooted in a cultural naivety about the importance of using condoms. See Jens Erik Gould, "HIV and the Garífuna: Coming to Terms with a Virus," Pulitzer Center, January 30, 2013. In an article published a week earlier, the same author acknowledged that "the Garífuna have one of the highest HIV rates in the Western Hemisphere" and that "their culture and language are in jeopardy," but he insists that "HIV is one of the greatest threats to their survival" and says nothing about the assault on Garífuna social and cultural institutions that has led to the dramatic increases in prostitution and HIV. Jens Erik Gould, "The Forgotten: HIV and the Garífuna of Honduras," Pulitzer Center, January 23, 2013.
93. "Charged: Randy Jorgensen," *Maclean's*, December 3, 2001.
94. Paley, "Snowbirds Gone Wild."
95. Kerssen, *Grabbing Power,* 84–85.
96. OFRANEH, "Crisis en Vallecito (Colón): Aclaratión Pública ante Infundios del INA," August 29, 2012. Available at ofraneh.wordpress.com
97. Greg Albo, "Fewer Illusions: Canadian Foreign Policy Since 2001," in Jerome Klassen and Greg Albo, eds., *Empire's Ally: Canada and the War in Afghanistan* (Toronto: University of Toronto Press, 2013).
98. Jeremy Torobin, "How 'Charter Cities' Could Lift the Global Economy," *The Globe and Mail*, September 12, 2012.
99. Ibid.
100. OFRANEH, quoted in Tim Russo, "Vallecito Resists, Satuye Lives! The Garifuna Resistance to Honduras' Charter Cities," *Upside Down World*, September 18, 2012.
101. It also demonstrates a remarkable blindness to the degree of impunity and lawlessness that manifests in Canada in a variety of spheres. Though it is outside the scope of this project to critically assess the Canadian justice system, there is widespread doubt that Canada provides any measure of equality or justice in its policing and political-legal system. Organizations and communities that would question the Canadian justice system include: advocates for missing and murdered Indigenous women whose cases are rarely pursued; immigrant and migrant worker associations who are kept in vulnerable circumstances and, thus, excluded from access to social and legal institutions for fear of being deported; poor and racialized communities that are regularly subjected to police violence; left and activist organizations that are targeted for police infiltration and selectively run through

the time- and resource-consuming legal system on charges that rarely stick; victims of domestic and gender-based violence; and urban homeless and street-affected people who are routinely picked on for simply being impoverished.

102. The claim that most Chinese people would be glad that Hong Kong was seized by the British is unsubstantiated and ahistorical; Hong Kong was occupied in order to guarantee a controlling British influence in the opium trade, and marked a broader prying open of China to foreign concessioning that would last for nearly a century, culminating in fascist Japanese occupation in the 1930s and '40s. These dynamics were hotly contested at the time; British intervention in China was a major contributing factor in the largest peasant uprising against the Qing dynasty—the Taiping Rebellion—and the erosion of Chinese sovereignty and the catastrophic failures of governance that accompanied it—such as the great famine of the late nineteenth century—were among the grievances that ultimately led to the successful communist revolution in 1949. That Romer should use this as an example of a successful colonial intervention demonstrates a profound ignorance of the Chinese experience and it is clear that this ignorance extends to contemporary Honduras. Brandon Fuller and Paul Romer, "Success and the City: How Charter Cities Could Transform the Developing World," McDonald-Laurier Institute, Ottawa, April 2012. On the Taiping Rebellion and the dismantling of Chinese sovereignty, see Jonathan D. Spence, *God's Chinese Son: The Taiping Heavenly Kingdom of Hong Xuiquan* (New York: W.W. Norton and Co., 2006). On the colonial roots of the Chinese famine, see Mike Davis, *Late Victorian Holocausts: El Niño Famines and the Making of the Third World* (New York: Verso, 2001).
103. The *mission civilisatrice* was a central piece of the justification of French colonialism, and emerged as a rhetorical device in the great expansion of colonial empires in late nineteenth century. But the idea behind it—that colonial powers were actually providing a benevolent service to their occupied colonies by bringing "civilization"—dates back to the original "discovery" and occupation of the Americas. It manifests differently over time, but central to this idea is the assumption that European civilizations were more advanced and enlightened and that the colonized would ultimately benefit from the imposition of a more developed social structure. Rudyard Kipling infamously declared this "the white man's burden" and this dynamic can be traced through different generations of colonialism in Central America. The genocide in the Americas was justified, in part, by the claim that Indigenous people were "savage" or "barbaric," just as the imposition of US manifest destiny in the nineteenth century was framed as a way for a benevolent big brother to help a smaller, weaker one "grow up." American intervention in the region from the 1950s to the 1980s was often justified as a project to save Central Americans from themselves, when they made "foolish" and "backwards" decisions to support social reform and revolution. Even the discourse of "international development" that emerged prominently in the 1990s is rooted in the idea that the metropolitan power is "ahead" and that it should take efforts to help poorer countries to "catch up." Practitioners of this version of international development often express deep (and no doubt genuine) confusion when it appears that the communities they are trying to "develop" are not interested or refuse to do it the way that the developers expect. In all of these "civilizing" doctrines, there is always an assertion that the colonizers are providing a kind of painful medicine, "tough love," or "shock therapy;" people might resist them at first, out of backwardness, but that they will ultimately be thankful for the benevolent "helping hand." On the *mission civilisatrice*, see Robert J. C. Young, *Postcolonialism: An Historical Introduction* (Oxford: Blackwell, 2001). On US "manifest destiny," see William Appleman Williams, *The Tragedy of American Diplomacy* (New York: W.W. Norton & Co., 1972). On Canada's adoption of the *mission civilisatrice* in its foreign policy, see Sherene H. Razack, "Canada's

Afghan Detainee Torture Scandal," in Klassen and Albo, *Empire's Ally*, 367–387.
104. Faustino Ordóñez, "Honduras, a la vanguardia en atracción de capital," *El Heraldo*, July 25, 2011.
105. "Canadienses incentivan a la responsibilidad empresarial," *La Tribuna*, February 2, 2012.
106. Jari Dixon, interview by Tyler Shipley, May 10, 2012.
107. Ibid.
108. Sandra Marybel Sánchez, "Ni una revolución, mucho menos una elección revertirá las 'Ciudades Modelo' ¡Es ahora o nunca!," *Vos el Soberano*, August 8, 2012. Available at voselsoberano.com
109. Latin American and Caribbean Solidarity Network, "Harper Trades in Human Rights for Economic Concessions in Honduras," Press Release, August 9, 2011.
110. Latin American and Caribbean Solidarity Network, "Harper Trades in Human Rights."
111. Leticia Salomón, "Golpe de estado, clase política y proceso electoral," *LASA Forum*, Volume XLI, Issue 1, Winter 2010.
112. Nectali Rodezno, interview by Tyler Shipley, May 4, 2012.
113. A few brief examples include: 1) the pursuing and profiting from the ubiquitous "war taxes" that are charged by criminal gangs against people working in a variety of industries, like taxi-driving, as payment against the possibility of being targeted for violence; 2) the summary assassinations of people who run afoul of the criminal gangs, the state, or the police itself, without investigations; 3) the selective protection of politicians from physical violence, for those politicians who resist attempts to reform the police, thus reproducing the existing levels of corruption; 4) the managing of the penal system such that new arrivals in Honduran jails go through a "diagnostics" department, run by police, that charges taxes on inmates to determine whose cases will be investigated and who will be given preferential treatment in the prison system; 5) direct links between police and criminal gangs that are exemplified in cases like that of the "disappearance" of hundreds of state-owned guns which, eventually, were discovered in the hands of narco gangs. These are only a handful of the cases that could be discussed. As Rodezno concluded in our interview, the corruption functions as a "chain," in which one sphere of corruption feeds into another chain, such that the entire system is dysfunctional. Nectali Rodezno, interview by Tyler Shipley, May 4, 2012.
114. Maria Luisa Borjas, interview by Tyler Shipley, February 19, 2015.
115. Dana Frank, "Honduras in Flames," *The Nation*, February 16, 2012.
116. Alejandro Fernández, "A Sad Christmas Ballad," *Envío,* No. 378, January 2013.
117. Victor Meza, interview by Tyler Shipley, May 10, 2012.
118. Ibid.
119. The Chilean government named Aquiles Blu Rodriguez, a general in the national police who retired shortly after being implicated in a massive drug-trafficking cover-up, to the Honduran commission. Even members of the Honduran Congress have raised questions about having such a figure on a police reform commission.
120. Victor Meza, interview by Tyler Shipley, May 10, 2012.
121. Karen Spring and Sandra Cuffe, "Canada and Chile Meddling."
122. Ibid.
123. Ibid.
124. Victor Meza, interview by Tyler Shipley, February 18, 2015.
125. Maria Luisa Borjas, interview by Tyler Shipley, February 19, 2015.
126. "Detienen a cuatro efectivos de la Policía Militar por secuestro de comerciante," *El Tiempo*, February 12, 2015.
127. "Hondureña denuncia que fue violada por ocho miembros de la Policía Militar," *El Tiempo*, November 22, 2014.

128. Karen Spring, "The Future of Public Insecurity," *Aqui Abajo*, November 27, 2014. Available at desdeaquiabajoabajo.blogspot.ca
129. Berta Oliva, interview by Tyler Shipley, February 20, 2015.
130. Steve Rennie, "PM dismisses rights concerns as he touts trade pact with Honduras," *The Canadian Press,* August 12, 2011.
131. Chandra Lye, "Canadian Forces to undergo Spanish language training in Alberta," *Yeg-News*, August 29, 2011. Available at yegnews.com
132. Felix Molina, interview by Tyler Shipley, May 2, 2012.
133. Debbie Pestell, quoted in "International Forces train with and assist Hondurans during Beyond the Horizon 2012," video posted online by "armysouthPreview," May 10, 2012. Available at www.youtube.com/watch?v=3PqjvyFjUYA
134. Gordon, *Imperialist Canada*, 312.
135. Emma Feltes, "Laboratory, Honduras," *The Dominion*, June 8, 2012. This is a rather ironic development given that the Honduran military and police have essentially functioned as different branches of the same organization since the coup and, arguably, the collusion between the military and police has contributed to the overall degree of terror and impunity that has reigned in Honduras since 2009.
136. Adam Williams, "Operation Martillo Deemed a 'Complete Success' in Guatemala, Honduras," *Dialogo*, July 23, 2012.
137. "Canada and Honduras sign free trade pact," *AFP*, August 12, 2011.
138. The United States has, more or less, played a similar role politically to that played by Canada, though with rather less vigour. Greg Grandin, "Honduras, Obama and the Region's New Right," *LASA Forum*, Volume XLI, Issue 1, Winter 2010.
139. WikiLeaks, "Honduran Coup: SITREP #4 06/29/09 as of noon local," available at: wikileaks.org/plusd/cables/09TEGUCIGALPA514_a.html#par10 See also WikiLeaks, "TFH01: Who's Who of the Honduran Coup," available at: wikileaks.org/plusd/cables/09TEGUCIGALPA617_a.html
140. Hillary Clinton, quoted in Karen Attiah, "Hillary Clinton needs to answer for her actions in Honduras and Haiti," *Washington Post*, March 10, 2016.
141. Greg McCain, "The DEA and the Return of the Death Squads," *Counterpunch*, June 15, 2012.
142. Thom Shanker, "US turns its focus on drug smuggling in Honduras," *The New York Times*, May 5, 2012.
143. Ibid.
144. Annie Bird, interview by Tyler Shipley, May 10, 2012.
145. Not to be confused with the Secretaría de Integración Económica Centroamericana (Central American Secretariat of Economic Integration, SIECA) which is a regional organization with different roots.
146. Annie Bird, interview by Tyler Shipley, May 10, 2012.
147. Ibid.
148. The details of these projects are painstakingly laid out, in great detail, by Nieves Capote in *La Dictadura del Capital, No.2: Del P.P.P. al Projecto Mesoamérica* (San Cristóbal de las Casas: Otros Mundos A.C., 2010). Much of this infrastructure is in the process of being constructed, often by North American-based firms benefiting from subsidies from North American development agencies like the former CIDA and from host governments. Among the many developments that touch Honduras are the major inter-American highways—the Corredor del Pacífico and the Corredor del Atlántico—designed to bypass the busy Carretera Panamericana, as well as a series of highways cutting across the isthmus and the Corredor Turístico, which connects the Gulf Coast tourist destinations from Cancún to Trujillo. The Honduran sections of the highway, from Puerto Barrios

to Trujillo, were concessioned to the company Autopistas del Atlántico for thirty years in December 2012. The company is based in Spain but its majority shareholder is the US commercial and investment bank, Citigroup. "Gobierno concesiona por 30 años el corredor turístico de Honduras," *La Prensa*, December 12, 2012. Capote's analysis of the P.P.P. also details the construction of an inter-connected electrical system across Central America through the Sistema de Interconexión Eléctrica (SIEPAC) and the hundreds of hydroelectric dams and power stations being built across the region—some forty major hydroelectric facilities and over fifty microgeneration plants in Honduras—concessioned to private companies but massively subsidized.

149. Annie Bird, interview by Tyler Shipley, May 10, 2012.
150. Bird's analysis here is compelling, but it is by no means the whole story. Alexander Segovia's excellent three-part assessment of regional integration in Central America, for instance, complicates the picture by highlighting a significant shift in the regional power dynamics away from the old oligarchies connected to agroexport and towards the new transnational capitalist classes rooted in non-traditional sectors like *maquiladoras*, tourism, and the service industries. His 2007 assessment was prophetic insofar as it was a conflict between the old and new oligarchies that animated much of Manuel Zelaya's presidency and, arguably, helped pave the way for the right-wing coup in 2009. Segovia's analysis offers a useful reminder that the existence of predatory and imperialistic foreign powers does not preclude the possibility of local agents participating, benefiting, or even taking a lead role in establishing the apparatus that facilitates those imperial projects. See Alexander Segovia, "The Concentration of Power: More Integration and Inequality," *Envío*, No. 307, February 2007.
151. For more on the "Pink Tide," see Mark Weisbrot, *Failed: What the "Experts" Got Wrong About the Global Economy* (New York: Oxford University Press, 2015) 167–234.
152. Government of Canada, "Canada-Honduras Relations," February 2013. Available at canadainternational.gc.ca
153. Government of Canada, "Bilateral Relations – Honduras," May 2016. Available at canadainternational.gc.ca
154. Honduran historian Rodolfo Pastor Fasquelle reports, for instance, that the coup and its aftermath provoked discussion of the creation of a new Latin American Community of Nations that would include Cuba but exclude the United States and Canada. Canada's status as a pariah would come as a great shock to the "Middle Power" enthusiasts who, in the 1960s and '70s, imagined that Canada could mediate between US imperialism and Latin American development. Rodolfo Pastor Fasquelle, "The 2009 Coup and the Struggle for Democracy in Honduras," *NACLA Report on the Americas*, Vol. 44, No. 1, January/February 2011, 16–21.

5 MIDDLE POWER OR EMPIRE'S ALLY?

1. James Daschuk, *Clearing the Plains: Disease, Politics of Starvation, and the Loss of Aboriginal Life* (Regina: University of Regina Press, 2013).
2. Graeme Weardon, "Oxfam: 85 richest people as wealthy as poorest half of the world," *The Guardian*, January 20, 2014.
3. Credit Suisse, "Global Wealth Report 2014," October 2014. Available at: economics.uwo.ca/people/davies_docs/credit-suisse-global-wealth-report-2014.pdf
4. Jane Gerster, "Canada's richest 86 people have as much wealth as the poorest 11.4 million," *Toronto Star*, April 3, 2014.
5. David Harvey, *The New Imperialism*, (New York: Oxford University Press, 2003) 26–33.
6. David McNally, "Canada and Empire," *New Socialist*, No. 54, 2005/2006, 5.

7. Andrew J. Bacevich, *American Empire: The Realities and Consequences of US Diplomacy* (Cambridge, MA: Harvard University Press, 2002). Naill Ferguson, *Empire: How Britain Made the Modern World* (London: Basic Books, 2002). Michael Ignatieff, *Empire Lite: Nation Building in Bosnia, Kosovo, Afghanistan* (New York: Penguin, 2002).
8. Greg Albo, "Fewer Illusions: Canadian Foreign Policy Since 2001," in Jerome Klassen and Greg Albo, ed., *Empire's Ally: Canada and the War in Afghanistan* (Toronto: University of Toronto Press, 2013) 245.
9. Harvey, *The New Imperialism.*
10. David McNally, *Global Slump: The Economics and Politics of Crisis and Resistance* (Winnipeg: Fernwood, 2011) 61–85.
11. V.I. Lenin, *Imperialism: The Highest Stage of Capitalism* (New York: International Publishers, 2002).
12. Karl Marx and Friedrich Engels, *The Communist Manifesto* (Toronto: Penguin Books, 2002) 223.
13. Thomas D'Acquino, quoted in Henry Heller, "Review of Todd Gordon, Imperialist Canada," *Historical Materialism* 20.2, 2012, 224.
14. Ellen Meiksins Wood, *Empire of Capital* (New York: Verso, 2003).
15. David McNally, *Global Slump.*
16. Peter Gowan, *The Global Gamble: Washington's Faustian Bid for World Dominance* (New York: Verso, 1999).
17. A few useful examples include: David Dewitt and John Kirton, *Canada as a Principal Power* (Toronto: Wiley, 1983). Maxwell Cameron, "Round Table on Canadian Foreign Policy," *Canadian Foreign Policy* 6 (3) 1999, 1–24. Tom Keating, "Introduction: The Sources of Multilateralism in Canadian Foreign Policy," *Canada and World Order*, 2nd ed., (Toronto: OUP, 2002) 1–17. Lloyd Axworthy, *Navigating a New World: Canada's Global Future* (Toronto: Knopf, 2003). Jennifer Welsh, *At Home in the World: Canada's Global Vision for the 21st Century* (Toronto: Harper Collins, 2004). John Kirton, *Canadian Foreign Policy in a Changing World* (Toronto: Thomson Nelson, 2007).
18. Of course, both of these activities would, themselves, be critiqued by left and postcolonial scholarship for being liberal manifestations of colonial politics that assumes Canada should "help" other countries "develop" even while Canada participates in the construction of conditions that create the need for such assistance.
19. Eric Mintz, Livianna Tossutti, and Christopher Dunn, *Democracy, Diversity, and Good Government: An Introduction to Politics in Canada* (Toronto: Pearson, 2011) 496.
20. Ibid., 520–521.
21. This is a debate that, arguably, misses the point somewhat; as Colleen Bell argues, these traditions share a similar view on how national and international politics should function and differ only to the extent that they imagine different ways of protecting and policing the current order. Bell's work adds a key piece, focusing primarily on the post-9/11 security regime in Canada, and demonstrating the extent to which the entire apparatus of liberal democracy is being redefined in order to facilitate the colonial violence necessary —within and beyond Canadian borders—to maintain the capitalist world order. Colleen Bell, *The Freedom of Security: Governing Canada in the Age of Counter-Terrorism* (Vancouver: University of British Columbia Press, 2011).
22. Norman Hillmer and J.L. Granatstein, *Empire to Umpire* (Toronto: Irwin Publishing, 1994) 350–351.
23. Howard Adams, *Prison of Grass: Canada from a Native Point of View* (Saskatoon: Fifth House Books, 1989).
24. Andrew Cohen, *While Canada Slept: How We Lost Our Place In The World* (Toronto: McClelland and Stewart, 2003).
25. Ibid., 203.

26. Stephen Clarkson and Maria Banda, "Paradigm Shift or Paradigm Twist? The Impact of the Bush Doctrine on Canada's International Position," in Ricardo Grinspun and Yasmine Shamsie, eds., *Whose Canada? Continental Integration, Fortress North America and the Corporate Agenda* (Montreal: McGill-Queen's University Press, 2007) 118.
27. Levitt, *Silent Surrender* (Toronto: MacMillan, 1970) 39–40.
28. Ibid., 37.
29. For a sense of the history and dynamics of colonialism as a totalizing system, see Robert Young, *Postcolonialism: An Historical Introduction* (Oxford: Blackwell, 2001).
30. Steve Moore and Debi Wells, "Imperialism and the National Question in Canada," *Canadian Revolution*, No. 2, August-September 1975, 21–29.
31. Ibid., 37.
32. That assertion of US dominance within the imperialist camp was directed primarily at the growing power of Germany and Japan. Peter Gowan demonstrates that the US state worked to reconfigure the architecture of global capitalism and international relations in the 1970s to make itself an indispensable component of the functioning of global capitalism. According to Gowan and, later, David Harvey, this was a manifestation of inter-imperialist rivalry, undertaken in the context of a significant stagnation of US growth in the 1970s and the concurrent rise of Germany and Japan as competitors that threatened to outpace the United States. Peter Gowan, *The Global Gamble: Washington's Faustian Bid for World Dominance* (New York: Verso, 1999).
33. David McNally, "Staple Theory as Commodity Fetishism: Marx, Innis and Canadian Political Economy," *Studies in Political Economy*, No. 6, Autumn, 1981, 46.
34. William K. Carroll, "The Canadian Corporate Elite: Financiers or Finance Capitalists?" *Studies in Political Economy*, No. 8, Autumn, 1982, 106–109.
35. Mel Watkins, "A Staple Theory of Economic Growth," in G. Laxer, ed., *Perspectives on Canadian Economic Development* (Toronto: Oxford University Press, 1991) 96.
36. Elizabeth May and Sarah Dover, "Breaking the Free Trade Addiction: An Intervention on Environmental Grounds," in Ricardo Grinspun and Yasmine Shamsie, eds., *Whose Canada? Continental Integration, Fortress North America and the Corporate Agenda* (Montreal: McGill-Queen's University Press, 2007) 432.
37. Bruce Campbell, "Managing US-Canada Relations: An Alternative to Deep Integration," in Grinspun and Shamsie, *Whose Canada?*, 530.
38. Murray Dobbin, "Challenging the Forces of Deep Integration," in Grinspun and Shamsie, *Whose Canada?*, 503.
39. Grinspun and Shamsie nevertheless admit that the integration of Canadian and US politics has been carried out by and for the capitalist classes in both countries and that it is working people on both sides of the border who are increasingly hurting. As such, they still attribute much direct responsibility and agency to the Canadian elite. Ricardo Grinspun and Yasmine Shamsie, "Canada, Free Trade, and 'Deep Integration,'" in Grinspun and Shamsie, *Whose Canada?*, 5.
40. Jerome Klassen, "Canada and the New Imperialism: The Economics of a Secondary Power," *Studies in Political Economy*, No. 83, 2009, 180–181.
41. Murray E. G. Smith, "Political Economy and the Canadian Working Class: Marxism or Nationalist Reformism?," *Labour/Le Travail*, No. 46, Fall, 2000, 343–368.
42. William K. Carroll, *Corporate Power in a Globalizing World: A Study in Elite Social Organization* (Oxford: Oxford University Press, 2004) 17.
43. Ibid., 44.
44. Ibid., 57, 83. It is also worth noting that this concentrated Canadian capitalist class is overwhelmingly composed of Anglo-Saxon men. While a more gender-equitable and multi-ethnic capitalist class would not, in my opinion, lead to a less violent or imperialist politics, it is nevertheless significant that Canadian imperialism is driven by the needs of

primarily white men, while its painful and exploitative consequences fall disproportionately on women and people of colour. This dynamic adds even greater weight to the argument that Canada has embarked on what must be understood as a form of imperialism.

45. Klassen, "Canada and the New Imperialism," 177–179.
46. Todd Gordon, *Imperialist Canada* (Winnipeg: Arbeiter Ring Publishing, 2010) 17.
47. Klassen, "Canada and the New Imperialism," 177.
48. Canadian firms had $1,005,227,000,000 invested outside of Canada, while foreign companies invested $768,467,000,000 in Canada, for an FDI surplus of $236,760,000,000. Statistics Canada, Foreign Direct Investment Statistics, April 2016.
49. Canadian firms invested $448,513,000,000 in the United States, while US firms invested $387,691,000,000 in Canada. Statistics Canada, Foreign Direct Investment Statistics, April 2016.
50. The criteria for the list included, among other things, revenues of over $100 million and being among the top five most profitable firms in its market sector. Gordon, *Imperialist Canada,* 20.
51. Heller, "Review of Todd Gordon, Imperialist Canada," *Historical Materialism*, Vol. 20, No. 2, 228–230.
52. Daschuk, *Clearing the Plains*, 11-57.
53. Jerome Klassen, *Joining Empire: The Political Economy of the New Canadian Foreign Policy* (Toronto: University of Toronto Press, 2014) 9–12.
54. Klassen, *Joining Empire*, 11.
55. Direct quotations from Canadian officials make it clear that this was conscious policy. Said one colonial writer, "the Indians must disappear before the march of civilization." Duncan George Forbes MacDonald, *British Columbia and Vancouver's Island* (London: Longman, Green, Roberts, Longman and Green, 1862) 125. Describing the residential school system, which systematically kidnapped Indigenous children from their families to place them in abusive boarding schools where they were violently broken from Indigenous culture, one official proclaimed the schools' purpose "to kill the Indian in the child." Truth and Reconciliation Commission of Canada. Available at trc.ca. It has been widely observed that Adolf Hitler admired Canada's brutal project to destroy Indigenous nations, which is hardly surprising in light of comments like this one, from the then-deputy superintendant of the Department of Indian Affairs, which exercised sovereign power over Indigenous people: "I want to get rid of the Indian problem.... Our objective is to continue until there is not a single Indian in Canada that has not been absorbed into the body politic, and there is no Indian question." Duncan Campbell Scott, quoted in E. Brian Titley, *A Narrow Vision* (Vancouver: University of British Columbia Press, 1986) 50.
56. Daschuk, *Clearing the Plains*, 114–158.
57. Mintz, Tossutti, and Dunn, *Democracy, Diversity and Good Government*, 507.
58. Wilfred Laurier, quoted in Hillmer and Granatstein, *Empire to Umpire*, 53.
59. Yves Engler, *The Black Book of Canadian Foreign Policy* (Black Point, NS: Fernwood, 2009) 258–259.
60. Hillmer and Granatstein, *Empire to Umpire*, 70.
61. Lester Pearson, cited in Paul Kellogg, "From the Avro Arrow to Afghanistan: The Political Economy of Canadian Militarism," in Klassen and Albo, *Empire's Ally*, 189.
62. Kellogg, "From the Avro Arrow to Afghanistan," 189.
63. The story of the scuttling of Canada's "Avro Arrow" project—and the concurrent dismantling of Canada's defence industry in the 1950s—is often characterized in nationalist Canadian popular culture as a defeat, as inept Canadian politicians colluded with US military industrialists to bring down a project that provided jobs for Canadians and guaranteed military independence. However, this episode would be better understood as a strategic decision to reorient Canadian industry away from military aerospace in a

moment when there was no real foreign market for its products; the only buyer for the Arrow would have been the Canadian military, and with US protection guaranteed, Canadian capital stood to gain much more by developing alternative industries and keeping a low military budget in order to sustain a welfare state that would feed Canadian growth during the heyday of the Keynesian "golden age." Kellogg, "From the Avro Arrow to Afghanistan," 192.

64. Ibid., 181–209.
65. Ricardo Grinspun and Yasmine Shamsie, "Missed Opportunity: Canada's Re-engagement with Latin America and the Caribbean," in *Canadian Journal of Latin American and Caribbean Studies*, Vol. 35, No. 69, 2010, 175.
66. For more detail on the violence of Latin America's twentieth century, please see Eduardo Galeano, *Open Veins of Latin America* (New York: Monthly Review Press, 1997).
67. Of course, the claim that Canada has no colonial history is itself a manifestation of Canadian colonialism, insofar as it erases from history the very nations it colonized. Nevertheless, the claim is still ubiquitous in Canadian popular and political culture, and was famously reproduced by Prime Minister Harper at the G20 summit in Pittsburgh in 2009. David Ljunngrun, "Every G20 Nation Wants to be Canada, insists PM," *Reuters*, September 25, 2009. It is also parroted by the military, which insists that "with no history as a colonizer, [Canada is] a credible and trusted partner for the countries of the region." Walter Natyncyk and Nancy MacKinnon, "Canada and the Americas: Defending Our Backyard," *Canadian Military Journal*, Vol. 10, No. 3, Summer 2010, 9.
68. Kellogg, "From the Avro Arrow to Afghanistan," 198.
69. Jerome Klassen, "Introduction: Empire, Afghanistan and Canadian Foreign Policy," in Klassen and Albo, *Empire's Ally*, 17.
70. Henry Heller, *The Birth of Capitalism* (Winnipeg: Fernwood, 2011) 118–134.
71. The expansion of the welfare state after the Second World War is a good example, as Keynesian economic policy sought to protect capitalism from its own contradictions by redistributing some wealth to the working classes in order to sustain consumer demand. Thus, it was a series of policies that responded to the needs and demands of some sections of the working class, but which still fundamentally protected the primacy of the capitalist class. For more, see McNally, *Global Slump*.
72. Klassen, "Introduction," 18.
73. Klassen, *Joining Empire*, 92–98.
74. Steven Staples, "Marching Orders: How Canada abandoned peacekeeping – and why the UN needs us now more than ever," Ottawa, Report for Council of Canadians, 2006, 1.
75. Sherene H. Razack, *Dark Threats and White Knights* (Toronto: University of Toronto Press, 2004).
76. It is noteworthy that Canada refused to join the so-called "coalition of the willing" to invade Iraq. Indeed, it prompted an angry reaction from the Canadian far right, as evidenced in an impromptu live debate between hockey pundits Ron MacLean and Don Cherry, the latter of whom chastised the Canadian government for refusing to support the US invasion. Nevertheless, while Canada's decision not to join George W. Bush's war seems to be inconsistent with the pattern, it actually demonstrates the extent to which Canadian "deep integration" with the United States is limited by the actual independence of Canadian foreign policy. Canada's decision not to join the "coalition of the willing" illustrates that it could have similarly refused to participate in a variety of other military adventures with the United States. Canada's decision to distance itself from the war in Iraq, moreover, should not be overstated; Canadians did, in fact, participate in that campaign in a variety of capacities and it is well understood that Canada took on a larger role in Afghanistan to take pressure off US and British forces being re-deployed to Iraq.
77. Yves Engler and Anthony Fenton, *Canada in Haiti: Waging War on the Poor Majority*

(Black Point, NS: Fernwood, 2005).

78. Greg Shupak, "Canada's Forgotten War: Revisiting NATO's 'Humanitarian Intervention' in Libya," *Ricochet*, August 28, 2014.
79. Murray Brewster, "Canada to take part in Iraqi city of Mosul's liberation from ISIS with field hospital," *CBC News*, July 20, 2016.
80. Karl Marx, *Capital*, Vol. I, (London: Penguin Books, 1990) 874–875.
81. Of course, it is not only about labour. In the contemporary mining sector, for instance, the key component is, increasingly, the access to resources and the ability of foreign companies to access those resources in the cheapest and quickest way possible. This usually means employing mining practices that are devastating to the environment upon which local and regional communities rely, as the Honduran case demonstrated clearly.
82. "Alberto Rotondo ejecutivo de minera dio orden para matar," *La Hora Guatemala*, May 9, 2013.
83. Rick Arnold, quoted in Mining Watch Canada, "Report Reveals How Canadian Diplomacy Supported Deadly Blackfire Mining Project," May 6, 2013.
84. L. Arias, "Canadian firm threatens $1 billion lawsuit against Costa Rica," *Tico Times*, April 4, 2013.
85. Toby Moorsom, "Canada's tough-guy cop to 'aid' world's poor," *Al-Jazeera Online*, April 4, 2013.
86. A range of different polls reflecting this trend can be found in Klassen and Albo, *Empire's Ally*, 9.
87. Klassen, *Joining Empire*, 227.
88. Jerome Klassen, "Methods of Empire," in Klassen and Albo, *Empire's Ally*, 151.
89. John W. Warnock, "Afghanistan and Empire," in Klassen and Albo, *Empire's Ally*, 56–57.
90. Klassen, "Methods of Empire," 161.
91. Ibid., 167.
92. David Pugliese, "Out-of-control Canadian military police terrorized Afghan prisoners in Kandahar," *Ottawa Citizen*, June 30, 2016.
93. Sherene Razack, "From the Somalia Affair to Canada's Afghan Detainee Torture Scandal: How Stories of Torture Define the Nation," in Klassen and Albo, *Empire's Ally*, 378–379.
94. Ibid., 380.
95. Mark Steyn, "What the Afghans need is colonizing," *National Post*, October 9, 2001.
96. Harvey, *The New Imperialism*, 137–183.
97. Thom Workman and Geoffrey McCormack, *The Servant State: Overseeing Capital Accumulation in Canada* (Black Point, NS: Fernwood, 2015).
98. There is no consensus among scholars of contemporary empire on whether the US state can maintain its dominant position for much longer. Arguably, its adventures in the Middle East over the past decade have left it with less capacity to police that region, as perhaps evidenced by its inability to control the dynamics for the time being, but the United States remains central to the smooth functioning of global capitalism and, as such, it can still make significant demands upon those states which, like Canada, find themselves secondary components in the US-centred imperial order.
99. Greg Albo, "Empire's Ally," *Canadian Dimension* 40, No. 6, 2006, 54–60.
100. Albo, "Fewer Illusions," 255.
101. The McLeod Group, "CIDA's Dead-End Merger," May 18, 2013. Available at mcleodgroup.ca
102. Steven Staples, "Fortress North America: The Drive Towards Military and Security Integration and Its Impact on Canadian Democratic Sovereignty," in Grinspun and Shamsie, *Whose Canada?*, 162–163.
103. Greg Albo, "Empire's Ally," p. 55–59.
104. Steven Staples, "Fortress North America," 163–170.

105. In Ontario, for instance, a string of public sector unions had strikes ended by back-to-work legislation, beginning with part-time academic workers at York University, of which I was a member, whose targeting for strike-breaking legislation was condemned by the International Labour Organization as unwarranted. "Ontario Government condemned for abusing back-to-work legislation," Canadian Union of Public Employees, Press Release, June 20, 2011. Since that time, unions have been forced back to work by federal and provincial legislation, from pilots and flight attendants to transit workers to librarians to postal employees and teachers.
106. Among many organizations that have faced cuts: Climate Action Network, Native Women's Association, Sisters in Spirit, Canadian Child Care Federation, Centre for Spanish Speaking Peoples, Statistics Canada, Canadian Arab Federation, First Nations Child and Family Caring Society, Canadian Council for International Co-operation.
107. "It's More Than Poverty," report by United Way Toronto and McMaster University, February 2013. For more detail on the assault on working people in Canada, including immigrant and migrant workers, please see Thom Workman, *If You're In My Way I'm Walking: The Assault on Working People Since 1970* (Winnipeg: Fernwood, 2009).
108. Tyler Shipley, "The NHL and the New Canadian Militarism," *Canadian Dimension*, August 6, 2013.
109. Grinspun and Shamsie, "Canada's Missed Opportunity," 174.
110. Natyncyk and MacKinnon, "Canada and the Americas," 6–10.
111. Todd Gordon, "Positioning Itself in the Andes: Critical Reflections on Canada's Relations with Colombia," *Canadian Journal of Latin American and Caribbean Studies*, Vol. 35, No. 70, 56.
112. Grinspun and Shamsie, "Canada's Missed Opportunity," 179.
113. Rather fittingly, he was inadvertently stealing a line used by Stephen Harper when he became Prime Minister in 2006. Jessica Chin, "Justin Trudeau's Not The First Prime Minister To Say 'Canada is Back,'" *Huffington Post*, December 1, 2015.
114. Albo, "Fewer Illusions," 268. (Emphasis added.)

6 CONCLUSION

1. Berta Cáceres, acceptance speech, Goldman Environmental Prize, San Francisco.
2. Nina Lakhani, "Fellow Honduran activist Nelson García murdered days after Berta Cáceres," *The Guardian*, March 16, 2016.
3. Embassy of Canada to Costa Rica, "Canada urges Honduran authorities to clarify the murder of Berta Cáceres," March 3, 2016. Available at canadainternational.gc.ca
4. "Berta Caceres received death threats from Canadian company," *Telesur*, March 4, 2016.
5. Stewart Bell and Peter Koven, "Blame Canada," *National Post*, October 8, 2013.
6. Isabel Teotonio, "Brazil demands explanation over reports Canada spied on mine industry," *Toronto Star*, January 4, 2016.
7. Government of Canada, "Canadian Army hosts Brazilian Army Commander," June 1, 2016. Available at news.gc.ca
8. Steven Chase, "Canada now the second biggest arms exporter to the Middle East, data show," *The Globe and Mail*, June 14, 2016.
9. Don Cherry, quoted in Travis Hughes, "Don Cherry still can't believe they let Russians play hockey in Canada," *SB Nation*, December 26, 2012.
10. Don Cherry, quoted on CBC's *The Fifth Estate*, 1990. Available at www.youtube.com/watch?v=2-sG6u_Sats
11. A short sample of Don Cherry's comments: In 2015 he railed against "classless" Russians, after a lengthy diatribe about the "honour" of Canadians, which included claiming that,

"our heritage is being chipped away, chipped away, chipped away." It is evident that the heritage he means is that of the English colonizers, because later that same year, he referred to the Inuit seal hunt as "savage" and "barbaric," echoing the standard colonial slander against Indigenous people. In 2013 he shouted that women shouldn't be allowed to interview hockey players during the dressing room media scrum, in response to an incident where a player, Duncan Keith, made a dismissive and sexist remark towards a female reporter. Perhaps Cherry was sympathetic to the player, since two decades earlier he had joked that there should be "one woman in every dressing room," a thinly veiled reference to rape. His segments have always been peppered with sexism, from the relentless invocations of hockey as a "man's game" to his laughably patronizing lecturing of women to "stop chatting" and pay attention to the game when they come to the arena, lest they be hit by a puck. Even the most "manly" of men, the fighters, run afoul of Don Cherry if they don't stick to the script: in 2011 he responded to former hockey players who spoke out about their struggles with substance abuse after a career of hockey fighting and violence, calling them "pukes" and "hypocrites" for speaking out against violence. In 1998 he described Quebecois players as "whiners," in keeping with his record of near-constant abuse of who he calls "French guys," which included a tirade in 1991 about Quebec not wanting "our language." In 1989 he made fun of a Finnish coach on the Winnipeg Jets, saying his name sounded like a brand of dog food, and he has spent much of his television career engaging in homophobic mocking of European players, whom he routinely describes as "sweeties," or—in the case of the Swedish superstar twin brothers Daniel and Henrik Sedin—"the Sedin sisters." Indeed, one of his favourite topics in the 1990s was the "problem" of foreigners coming to Canada to steal Canadian jobs.

12. His message on this particular night was to the Canadian politicians who, in his words, were "more worried about the Taliban that's trying to blow us up" than the good Canadian boys in the military. Available at: www.youtube.com/watch?v=8RU2rzeMtvQ
13. The complete segment streams on the CBC website: www.cbc.ca/player/Shows/ID/2220528646/
14. Ian McKay and Jamie Swift have demonstrated this point by examining the stories written about World War One in Canadian newspapers in the 1920s and '30s. They have presented their findings at several conferences, and in *The Vimy Trap Or, How We Learned to Stop Worrying and Love the Great War* (Toronto: Between the Lines, 2016). An audio clip from one of McKay's presentations of this work can be found at: www.cbc.ca/radio/thesundayedition/remembering-alistair-macleod-sexual-assault-and-the-law-in-praise-of-the-theremin-ww1-what-for-and-vimyism-1.2905282
15. Ian McKay and Jamie Swift, "Alexander Boulerice: Another casualty of the Great War," *The Toronto Star,* May 5, 2013.
16. David Bernans, "Lest We Forget: Unarmed Canadians Killed by Soldiers in 1918 Anti-War Protests," *Montreal Media Co-op*, November 11, 2014.
17. "Don Cherry says Russian hockey team has no class," *The Canadian Press,* May 18, 2015. Quickly and consciously establishing himself as the Don Cherry of Canadian baseball is Sportsnet's so-called "man-alyst" Gregg Zaun, whose daily doses of patriotic machismo (ironic, given that Zaun is from California) regularly involve telling people to "man up," railing against players who are friendly with opposing teams' players, and in one case ostensibly inviting an opposing pitcher (Kansas City Royals' Yordana Ventura) to fight him in the broadcast booth.
18. The clip is available here: www.youtube.com/watch?v=-ka23Kgmac0
19. Josh Cooper, "NHL teams named in US 'pay for patriotism' report," *Puck Daddy*, November 4, 2015.
20. Natalie Stechyson, "Defence department spent $438,000 on pucks, balls and jerseys," *National Post,* July 4, 2012.

21. Randy Rose, quoted in Tom Ferda, "The Unbreakable Bond Between the NHL and the US Military," *USA Hockey Magazine*, November 2011.
22. "DND places rules around how Jets can use logo," *The Canadian Press,* November 19, 2011.
23. Kevin Engstrom, "Jets logo incites anti-war zealots," *Winnipeg Sun*, July 27, 2011.
24. A.L. McCready, *Yellow Ribbons: The Militarization of National Identity in Canada* (Winnipeg: Fernwood, 2013).
25. Government of Canada, Allocations from the Central Advertising Fund for 2012–13. Available at tbs-sct.gc.ca
26. Ibid.
27. Ibid.
28. Jason Fekete, "Conservative government spent millions on ads during NHL playoffs," *Ottawa Citizen*, September 18, 2014.
29. Gavin Drummond, quoted in Danny Kucharsky, "Canadian armed forces targets millennials with new campaign," *Marketing Magazine*, February 12, 2015.
30. Todd Gordon, "Positioning Itself in the Andes: Critical Reflections on Canada's Relations with Colombia," *Canadian Journal of Latin American and Caribbean Studies* Vol. 35, No. 70, 56-57.
31. An evocative illustration of this project can be found in Joseph Conrad's *Heart of Darkness*, in which the primary narrator, like Conrad himself, struggles with his own ambiguous position with respect to the colonial "idea." As the narrator famously remarks: "the conquest of the Earth, which mostly means the taking it away from those who have a slightly different complexion or slightly flatter noses than ourselves, is not a pretty thing when you look into it too much. What redeems it is the idea only. An idea at the back of it; not a sentimental pretence but an idea; and an unselfish belief in the idea—something you can set up, and bow down before, and offer a sacrifice to." Conrad struggles to understand how a belief in progress and human development can be expressed by the violent subjugation of one people by another, and this is the intellectual and spiritual problem that will increasingly face Canadians as the reality of Canadian imperialism becomes increasingly difficult to deny. Joseph Conrad, *Heart of Darkness* (New York: W.W. Norton & Co., 1988).
32. The long history of *post-facto* construction of imperial justifications has been touched on in a few different forms across this book. The process of constructing those justifications does psychological violence: to the colonized, of course, insofar as it writes narratives that denigrate or completely erase them from the history of human development; but also to the colonizers, who are encouraged to develop an obviously false consciousness—a necessarily self-deceiving narrative—of the world in which they live. This point is made eloquently by Frantz Fanon and Jean-Paul Sartre, among others, in the context of French colonialism in Algeria. See Jean-Paul Sartre, *Critique of Dialectical Reasoning: Theory of Practical Ensembles,* Vol. I (London: Verso, 1976). See also Frantz Fanon, *The Wretched of the Earth* (New York: Grove Press, 2004).
33. Christie Blatchford, *Fifteen Days: Stories of Bravery, Friendship, Life and Death from Inside the Canadian Military* (Toronto: Anchor Canada, 2008) 2.
34. Jon Hamilton, quoted in Blatchford, *Fifteen Days*, 7. (Emphasis added.)
35. Ash Van Leeuwen, quoted in Blatchford, *Fifteen Days*, 62–63.
36. John W. Warnock, "Afghanistan and Empire," in Jerome Klassen and Greg Albo, eds., *Empire's Ally: Canada and the War in Afghanistan* (Toronto: University of Toronto Press, 2013) 43–73.
37. This particular characterization fits into Edward Said's articulation of "Orientalism," or the creation of the colonized subject as something altogether different from the colonizer, an 'Other' that is necessarily pre-modern and backwards but simultaneously mysterious and intriguing. Edward Said, *Orientalism* (New York: Vintage Books, 1994). See also

Edward Said, *Culture and Imperialism* (New York: Vintage Books, 1994).

38. Albert Memmi, *The Colonizer and the Colonized* (Boston: Beacon Press, 1991) xvii.
39. Aimé Césaire, *Discourse on Colonialism* (New York: Monthly Review Press, 1972).
40. Wealth inequality in Canada is at an all-time high, with the 86 richest individuals possessing as much wealth as the poorest 11.4 million people. Jane Gerster, "Canada's richest 86 people have as much wealth as the poorest 11.4 million," *Toronto Star*, April 3, 2014.
41. Examples range from beer commercials that forcefully assert the statement, "I am Canadian," to the 2010 Canadian Olympic slogan, "Own the Podium," to the near-constant hammering of the language of toughness and Canadian-ness in the presentation of professional hockey. For more on this see Tyler Shipley, "National Game, International Shame: The NHL and the New Canadian Militarism," *Canadian Dimension*, Vol. 47, No. 4, July/August 2013.
42. Canadian Opinion Research Archive, Queen's University. Available at queensu.ca
43. The Canadian Press, "Trudeau won't back off Saudi arms sale despite warning from Amnesty," *Toronto Star*, April 14, 2016.
44. John Ackerman, "Mexico is massacring its citizens and nobody seems to have noticed," *Toronto Star*, June 27, 2016.
45. Drew Brown, "What Shirtless Justin Trudeau says about Canada," *Vice*, August 9, 2016.
46. "Caledonia Update: Peace, Order and Good Government, eh?" May 23, 2006. Available at: www.pogge.ca/archives/001135.shtml
47. Bev Sellers, quoted in Mining Watch Canada, "Canada has blood on its hands," Press Release, April 21, 2016.
48. Among the best remembrances of Berta's life and struggle is this short article by Karen Spring, in which she describes Berta thus: "I'll forever remember Berta's fierce, tireless, committed and determined activist side. On occasion, I saw her as a mother and a daughter as well. That's just how she was—she lived and breathed *la lucha*—the struggle. She was uncannily firm in her political positions, rooted in an anti-capitalist, anti-patriarchal, anti-imperialist and an anti-racist worldview. But she was much more than just an environmentalist or just an indigenous leader or just a feminist—she had a unique and rare political clarity that made her a well-respected leader in the wider Honduran social movement. This, of course, came with great personal sacrifice and difficulty." Karen Spring, "Berta Cáceres, the Murdered Honduras Activist, Did Not Die. She Multiplied," *Huffington Post*, March 23, 2016.

INDEX

Ablonczy, Diane, 84
abortion, 41–42
Acker, Alison, 11–12, 14, 17
Afghanistan, 1, 4, 147, 149, 152–54, 160, 162, 165, 168, 169–70, 172, 174n4; Strategic Advisory Team (SAT-A), 152
agrarian struggles, 19–22
ALBA. *See* Alternativa Bolivariana para los pueblos de nuestra América
Albo, Greg, 116, 155, 160
Allende, Salvador, 79
Almendares, Juan, 23, 99–100
Alternativa Bolivariana para los pueblos de nuestra América (Bolivian Alternative for the Peoples of Our America, ALBA), 37, 39–40
Alvarado, Martha Lorena, 41
Alvarado, Pedro de, 9
Alvarenga, Julian, 74
Alvarez, Oscar, 92
Alvarez Martínez, Gustavo, 21, 22, 42
Amadilia, María, 81
Amador, Carlos, 86, 99–101
Amaya Amador, Ramón, 14, 86
American Federation of Labour (AFL), 19–20, 179n75
Amnesty International, 73–74, 93
Amin, Samir, 175n10
ANAMINH. *See* Asociación Nacional de Mineros
Andino, Tomás, 38, 40, 61
Anduray, Fernando, 124
anti-mining activism, 41, 96
anti-sweatshop activism, 104
anti-union activism, 106
Anvil Knitwear, 105–6
Arbenz, Jacobo, 18
Argentina, 65–66, 128–29, 168
Argueta Santos, Eduardo, 76
Aristide, Jean-Bertrand, 149–50, 198n51
Arsenault, Daniel, 102
Arzú, Alvaro, 59
Asamblea Popular Permanente (Permanent Popular Assembly, APP), 36
Asociación Hondureña de Maquiladores (Honduran Association of Maquiladoras, AHM), 50–51
Asociación Nacional de Campesinos Hondureños (Association of Honduran Peasants, ANACH), 19–20
Asociación Nacional de Mineros (National Mining Association, ANAMINH), 96, 98
Aura Minerals, 98–99
Avro Arrow, 207n63

Bakan, Joel, 104
"Banana Coast," 109–15
banana industry/companies, 14–17, 20, 39, 116, 120
Banco Nacional de Desarrollo Agrícola (National Agricultural Development Bank, BANADESA), 28
Banda, Maria, 138
Barahona, Juan, 37, 88–89
Barrick Gold, 81
Batallion 3-16, 23, 42
Becerra, Longino, 7–8
Bell, Colleen, 205n21
Betancur, Father Iván, 20–21
Bird, Annie, 81, 127–28
Blackfire Exploration, 151
Blackwell, Adam, 123
Blatchford, Christie: *Fifteen Days*, 169–70
Blaut, Jim, 175n10
Bloque Popular (Popular Bloc, BP), 36–37, 89
Blue Energy, 162
Blu Rodriguez, Aquiles, 202n119
Bográn, Benjamín, 50
Bolívar, Símon, 12
Bolivia, 65, 89, 128

Bonilla, Manuel, 14
Borah, Woodrow W., 174n1(ch.1)
Borden, Robert, 145
Borgas, Marcelino, 182n145
Borjas, Maria Luisa, 121–22
Brazil, 128–29, 162, 168
Breakwater Resources Inc., 98, 102
British American Tobacco Company, 17
Brizuela, Claudia Larisa, 71
Brizuela, Pedro, 71
Brodhead, Frank, 60
Bulnes, Amílcar, 50, 59
Burgess, Bill, 140
Burns, Tommy, 164
Business Council on National Issues (BCNI), 149
Butler, Smedley D., 14–15, 116

Cáceres, Berta, 43–44, 92, 94, 161–62, 172–73, 193n95
Cálix, Álvaro, 58
Callejas, Rafaél, 25, 36, 43, 86
Campbell, Bruce, 141
Campero, Claudia, 197n31
campesino. *See* peasants
Canaccord Financial, 152
Canada: as beacon of freedom and democracy, 1–2; as chief antagonist in Central America, 174n4; Communications Security Establishment (CSE), 80; Conservative Party, 130, 136, 159; "Death to Canada" chants, 174n4; decline in development assistance, 135; Department of Foreign Affairs and International Trade (DFAIT), 156; Department of National Defence (DND), 156, 166–67; as economic dependency of US, 138–39; exclusion of from international organizations, 163; as force for good in the world, 2, 119, 135, 137–38, 162–63; foreign policy, 2–4, 79, 116, 130, 135–37, 141, 143–48, 149–50, 159, 168, 171; FTA with Honduras, 93–94, 97, 108–9, 119, 125; GDP of, 142; Green Party, 141; as "helpful fixer," 134–38; identity of, 171; investments in Honduras by, 95–129; Liberal Party, 136; militarism of, 136, 148–54, 163–65; national bourgeoisie, 142; New Democratic Party (NDP), 136, 141; as new imperial power, 3–4, 130–31, 138, 154–57, 168–73; as peacekeeper, 1–3, 135–36, 147–49, 173; place of in world today, 130–60; profit-seeking behaviour of corporations, 151, 153–54; reputation of, 2; as "rich dependency," 139; as second largest investor in Honduras, 95, 168; self-confidence of, 2; support of coup by, 35, 63, 65–94, 115, 129; trade with US, 142–43; as US ally, 147; Veterans Affairs, 167
Canadian armed forces/military, 124–27, 148–54, 156–58, 166, 171; "Operation Beyond the Horizon," 124–25; "Operation Martillo," 125
Canadian Chamber of Commerce, 149
Canadian Council for International Co-operation (CCIC): Americas Policy Group (APG), 96
Canadian Council of Chief Executives (CCCE), 149
Canadian International Development Agency (CIDA), 152, 156
Canahuati, Juan, 70
Canahuati, Mario, 70
Canahuati Larach, Jorge, 55
Canal 36, 54
capital: accumulation of, 27, 156, 159; Canadian, 3, 40, 95, 103–9, 115, 123, 129, 130–31, 134, 137, 140–42, 146–48, 150–51, 154, 159, 168; foreign, 12–13, 28, 30, 38–39, 65, 90–91, 119, 127–28, 142; global, 134; Honduran, 25; imperial, 134; over-accumulated, 133; political agents of, 133; private, 119, 123, 145; and the state, 148–49; US 138–39, 168
capitalism, 15, 88, 175n10; delinking Canada from network of, 160; "disaster," 196n4; dynamics of, 132–34; free wage labour and, 8–9; global, 7, 25, 140, 159–60, 206n32, 209n98; and imperialism, 131–34; industrial, 137; social relations, 7, 144; the state in, 148–49
Capote, Nieves, 203n148
Carías, Tiburcio, 6, 16–18
Carroll, William, 140; *Corporate Power in a Globalizing World*, 142
Cartagena Accord, 82, 84–87
Casco, Jorge Omar, 81
Castellanos, Julieta, 81, 121
Castillo, Lilian, 107
CEHPRODEC. *See* Centro Hondureño de Promoción para el Desarrollo Comunitario
Center for Justice and International Law (CEJIL), 81–82
Central American Free Trade Agreement (CAFTA), 128, 184n42
Centro de Estudio de la Mujer–Honduras (Centre for the Study of Women in Honduras, CEM–H), 77
Centro Hondureño de Promoción para el Desarrollo Comunitario (Centre for the Promotion of Community Development in Honduras, CEHPRODEC), 41, 97, 196n13
Césaire, Aimé, 171
Chamberlain, Robert S., 10

charter cities, 116–19
Chatfield, Frederick, 178n42
Chávez, Hugo, 39, 52, 65, 69, 82, 85, 128–29, 188n98
Cherry, Don: Canadian militarism and, 163–65, 208n76
Chile, 79–80, 123, 128, 147, 168
China, 201n102
Chrétien, Jean, 105, 123, 185n48
civil society, 22–23, 70, 72, 74, 99, 101, 148, 173
Clarkson, Stephen, 138
class, 11, 32, 137; capitalist, 33, 131–32, 139–44, 148–49, 154, 159; conflict, 19, struggle 134, 168
Clinton, Hillary, 126
CNRP. *See* Coordinadora Nacional de Resistencia Popular
Cocumba, 9
CODEH. *See* Comité para la Defensa de los Derechos Humanos en Honduras
CODEMUH. *See* Colectiva de Mujeres Hondureñas
COFADEH. *See* Comité de Familiares de Detenidos Desaparecidos en Honduras
Cohen, Andrew: *While Canada Slept*, 137
COHEP. *See* Consejo Hondureño de la Empresa Privada
Cold War, 3, 133, 146–47, 155, 173
Colectiva de Mujeres Hondureñas (Honduran Women's Collective, CODEMUH), 106–9
Colombia, 84
colonialism, 5–6, 151, 192n86; and imperialism, 171–73
colonization, 118, 169, 171
Columbus, Christopher, 5
COMAL. *See* Red de Comercialización Comunitaria Alternativa
Comando y Batallón de Reacción Antiterrorista (Anti-terrorist Commando Battalion, COBRA), 56
Comité de Defensa de Tierras Triunfeñas (Defense Committee for Triunfo Land, CODETT), 111
Comité de Familiares de Detenidos Desaparecidos en Honduras (Committee of the Families of the Disappeared and Detained in Honduras (COFADEH), 32, 52, 77, 79, 86–87, 92
Comité para la Defensa de los Derechos Humanos en Honduras (Human Rights Committee of Honduras, CODEH), 32, 62
Communications Security Establishment Canada (CSEC), 162
community organizing, 93
Compass Petroleum Ltd., 81
Comunidad de Estados Latinoamericanos y Caribeños (Community of Latin American and Caribbean States, CELAC), 163
Congo, 95
conquistadors, 7
Conrad, Joseph: *Heart of Darkness*, 212n31
Consejo Cívico de Organizaciones Populares y Indígenas de Honduras (Civic Council of Popular and Indigenous Organizations of Honduras, COPINH), 33, 36–37, 161–62
Consejo Hondureño de la Empresa Privada (Honduran Council of Private Enterprise, COHEP), 50, 70
constituyente, 42–45, 46, 48–49, 102
Contras. *See* Nicaragua
Coordinadora de Organizaciones Populares de Valle Aguán (Coordinated Popular Organizations of the Aguán Valley, COPA), 36
Coordinadora Nacional de Resistencia Popular (Coordinated National Popular Resistance, CNRP), 37, 51–52, 74, 96, 100; Manuel Zelaya and, 38–42
COPINH. *See* Consejo Cívico de Organizaciones Populares y Indígenas de Honduras
corporate social responsibility, 100, 103–5, 109
corporatism, 21
Corrales, Arturo, 70
Corrales Mejía, Victor, 53
Costa Rica, 11, 66, 152
counterrevolution, 25
Cristiano, Alfredo, 59
Cruz, José Miguel, 62
Cuba, 80, 147, 204n154
Cuffe, Sandra, 54–55
Cuyamel Fruit Company, 14
cyanide, 98–99
Cypher, Father Jerome, 20–21

D'Aquino, Thomas, 134
Dávila, Miguel R., 13
Defence Production Sharing Agreement (DPSA), 146
deforestation, 40, 99
Democracy, Diversity and Good Government, 135
Desarrollos Energéticos, SA (DESA), 161–62
Deutsch, Judy, 197n31
Diario Tiempo, 55
Dixon, Jari, 43–45, 84, 119–20, 129
Dobbin, Murray, 141
Dominican Republic, 104, 123
Dulles, Foster, 18
Dunkerley, James, 20
Dyer, Gwynne, 184n47

Ecuador, 66, 128
Eisenhower, Dwight, 18
El Salvador, 16, 18–19, 21, 24, 42, 66
Empire to Umpire (Hillmer and Granatstein), 136–37
Empresa Hondureña de Telecomunicaciones (Honduran Telecommunications Company, HONDUTEL), 27, 40, 92
Empresa Nacional de Energía Eléctrica (National Electrical Energy Company, ENEE), 40
encomienda, 8
Engels, Friedrich: *The Communist Manifesto*, 133–34
Espacio Refundacional, 86–87
Euraque, Darío, 47, 50

Faber, Daniel, 15
Facussé, Adolfo, 85
Facussé, Miguel, 71–73
Fanon, Frantz, 212n32
Federación de Organizaciones Magisteriales de Honduras (Federation of Teachers Organizations, FOMH), 74
Federación de Sindicatos de Honduras (Honduras Federation of Unions, FSH), 15
Federación Nacional de Campesinos de Honduras (National Federation of Honduran Peasants, FENACH), 19–20
Feministas en Resistencia (Feminists in Resistance), 41
Ferguson, Niall, 132
Fernández, Alejandro, 122
Fernández, Belén, 55
Fernández, Victor, 43–44
Ferrari, Rafael, 55
FIAN, 92–93
First Point Minerals, 98
Flores, Enrique, 87
Flores, José Manuel, 74–75
Flores Facussé, Carlos, 26, 30, 55, 86
FNRP. *See* Frente Nacional de Resistencia Popular
foreign direct investment (FDI), 95, 142–43, 168
Fox, Edward, 58–60
Frank, Dana, 17, 84
Freeland, Chrystia, 93–94
Freeston, Jesse, 46, 58, 85
free trade, 26, 134, 152. *See also* Canada: FTA with Honduras
Frente Nacional de Resistencia Popular (National Front of Popular Resistance, FNRP), 37, 51, 55, 57, 67, 72, 74, 84–85, 88; persistence of, 91–94
Fuerza de Refundación Popular (Popular Refoundation Force, FRP), 88–89
Fuller, Brandon, 118
Funes, Mauricio, 66
Fuñez Benítez, Julio, 71
"Futbol War," 27

Gabino Carvajal, Santos, 98, 198n41
Gálvez, Juan, 18
García, Nelson, 92, 162
Garífuna people, 35, 111–15, 117
garment industry, 103–9
gender, 32, 105, 137, 153
Germany, 206n32
Gifford, Kathie Lee, 104
Gildan Activewear, 103–9, 116
globalization, 26, 31, 88, 197n34; neoliberal, 142
Global North, 25, 31, 78
Global South, 3, 104, 129, 133, 139–40, 150, 155
Goldcorp, 41, 99–101, 116
golpistas, 50, 52, 55–57, 63, 66, 88, 121, 126
Gordon, Todd, 87
Gowan, Peter, 206n32
Granma International, 59
Granatstein, Jack, 136–37
El Gran Proyecto de Transformación Nacional, 26
Great Britain, 11–12; neo-colonialism of, 133; Slavery Act (1843), 177n38
Greenstone Resources, 98
Grinspun, Ricardo, 141, 146–47, 158
Guatemala, 16, 18, 21, 23, 42, 100, 125, 147, 151, 162
Gudiel, Enrique, 71
Guerra, Nahun Alexander, 76

Haiti, 4, 11, 105, 149–50, 168, 172
Ham, César, 61
Harper, Stephen, 5, 93–94, 108–9, 124–25, 159, 172, 185n48, 208n67
Harvey, David, 132–33; *The New Imperialism*, 154–55
Heap, Dr. David, 197n31
Heller, Henry, 175n10
Henas, Father Luis, 20
Heraldo, El, 55, 56, 102
Herman, Edward, 60
Hernández, Marlon, 52
Hernandez Juarez, Eliseo, 53
"Highway of Heroes," 167
Hillier, Rick, 1
Hillmer, Norman, 136–37
Hitler, Adolf, 207n55
hockey, militarism and, 163–66

Honduras: changes of government, 13; Citizen Participation Law (2006), 185n53; Constitution of, 42–48, 66, 82, 90, 98, 102; cost of living, 39; coup d'état (2009), 3, 33, 34–64, 65–76, 78–89, 91–97, 101, 105, 107, 109, 115–16, 120–23, 125–26, 128–29, 154, 162–63, 168; creation of, 7; destruction of organized left, 6; "drug war," 127; electoral fraud, 91; foreign domination of, 5–33; general strike (1954), 6, 17–19; independence of, 11–12; Indigenous peoples, 7–10, 33, 35, 95–97, 114, 117; insecurity state, 120–24; killing of children, 29–30; La Moskitia massacre, 125–27; land reform, 28; Ley Antimara (Anti-Gang Law), 30; Ley de Modernización Agrícola Agricultural Modernization Law), 28; Liberal Party, 35, 38–41, 45, 52, 60–61, 88; *maras* and vigilantes, 29–32; military and class conflict, 19; minimum wage, 38–39; mining code, 97, 99, 102–3, 123; National Party, 35, 89, 91, 124; oligarchy of, 35, 38–40, 42, 44, 46, 48, 50, 52–53, 63; pantomime elections, 57–64; Partido de Libertad y Refundación (Liberty and Refoundation Party, LIBRE), 87–91, 124; as "plutocracy," 55; Police Reform Commission, 122–23; Spanish colonization of, 7–11, 95, 118, 133; Toncontín Airport, 40; Truth and Reconciliation Commission, 183n17, 78–84, 85, 93; violence, 29–32, 59, 78, 108, 115, 119, 121
Honduras Brewery, 17
HONDUTEL. *See* Empresa Hondureña de Telecomunicaciones
Hong Kong, British control of, 117–18
human rights, 2, 52, 58–59, 62, 75, 77, 93, 101
Hurricane Mitch, 25, 29, 31, 36, 38, 96, 112
Hurtig, Mel, 141

Ignatieff, Michael, 2, 132, 136
imperialism, 120; Canadian, 3–4, 117, 125, 130–34, 138, 154–57, 160, 168–73; capitalism and, 131–34; and colonialism, 171–73; definition of, 132; dynamics of, 132; forms of, 133; "new," 133, 155; US, 125, 130, 134, 154
INA. *See* Instituto Nacional Agraria
Indigenous peoples: Canadian colonization of, 137, 143–44, 172; decimation of, 144, 174n1(ch.1); in Honduras, 7–10, 33, 35, 95–97, 114, 117
inequality, 26, 30, 52, 110, 128, 131–32
Infinito, 152
Innis, Harold, 138
insecurity state, 120–24
Instituto Nacional Agraria (National Agrarian Institute, INA), 28, 61, 72, 115
Inter-American Commission on Human Rights (IACHR), 71, 81; Declaration on the Rights and Duties of Man, 101
Inter-American Regional Organization (ORIT), 179n75
International Labor Organization: convention 169 (ILO-169), 101
International Monetary Fund (IMF), 25, 27–28, 32, 80, 134, 140
International Republican Institute (IRI), 59
international trade laws, 81, 134
Inversiones y Desarrollo El Triunfo SA (Investment and Development Triunfo, IDETRISA), 112
Iran, 147
Iraq, 4, 149–50, 168, 208n76
ISIS, 150, 171

Jackson, Andrew, 141
Japan, 206n32
Jorgensen, Randy, 113–14
Joyce, Rosemary A., 48

Kellogg, Paul, 146–47
Kent, Peter, 66–70, 79, 109
Kergin, Michael, 79–84
Kernaghan, Charles, 104
Kerssen, Tanya, 113
Keynesianism, 208n71
Kilo Goldmines, 152
Kipling, Rudyard, 169–70, 201n103
Kirchner, Cristina Fernández de, 65–66, 129
Klassen, Jerome, 142, 148
Klein, Naomi: *The Shock Doctrine*, 196n4

labour militancy, 20
labour relations, 179n74
Landa, Pedro, 41, 97, 196n13
Landaverde, Alfredo, 122
Lanza, Gladys, 77–78
Lara Fernández, Jorge, 44
las Casas, Bartolomé de, 8
Latin American and Caribbean Network for Liberty, 59
Latin American Community of Nations, 204n154
Laurier, Wilfrid, 145
left nationalism, 138, 140, 142, 159
Lempira, 9–10
Lenin, Vladimir, 133
Levitt, Kari, 138–39; *Silent Surrender*, 138–39
LIBRE. *See* Honduras: Partido de Libertad y Refundación

Libya, 4, 150
Life Vision Properties, 113, 116
Lobo, Porfirio "Pepe," 68–72, 74–76, 81–84, 87, 89, 92, 102–3, 107, 115, 121–22, 182n140, 185n48
Lockheed-Martin, 152
López, Blas, 74–75
López Arellano, Oswaldo, 20
Lugo, Fernando, 66, 129
Lupul, Joffrey, 166

Macdonald, John A.: National Policy, 144
Mackay, Cameron, 119
Maduro, Nicolás, 128–29
Maduro, Ricardo, 29–33, 37–38, 41, 86
Magana, Rafael, 106
Mali, 4, 150
maquiladora industry/laws, 25, 27, 32, 38–39, 50, 104, 106–8, 184n42, 204n150
Maquila Solidarity Network, 199n65
maras, 29–32
Marbella Tourist Corporation / Club Marbella, 111–12
Marin, Roger, 26
Martinez, Erick, 89
Marx, Karl, 7, 176n23; *Capital*, 150–51; *Communist Manifesto*, 133–34; Marxism, 132
Matamoros, David, 61
May, Elizabeth, 141
Maya Gold Company, 98
Mayan civilization, 6–7, 200n84
McCain, Greg, 126
McCormack, Geoffrey, 155
McCready, Alyson, 166–67
McDonald-Laurier Institute, 116, 118
McKay, Ian, 211n14
McKinnon, Hugh, 79
McLean, Ron, 208n76
McNally, David, 132, 140, 175n10
McQuaig, Linda: *Holding the Bully's Coat*, 141
media, 53–56, 57, 70
Mejía, Joaquín A., 43–44
Membreño, Delmer, 54
Memmi, Albert, 171
Menjívar, Omar, 43–44
Mexico, 11, 151, 168, 171
Meza, Victor, 93, 122–23
Micheletti, Roberto, 35, 40, 41, 49, 54, 58, 61–62, 69–70
militarism: Don Cherry and, 163–65; and imperialism, 148–54
military, Canadian. *See* Canadian armed forces/military
"military parasitism," 146–47, 154
military police. *See* Policia-Militar
mining, 13–14, 39, 41, 81, 123; Canadian, 95–99; cobalt, 95; diamond, 95; gold, 95; silver, 11
Mining Watch Canada, 196n3
Miranda, Miriam, 44, 76
mission civilisatrice justification, 118, 201n103
Molina, Felix, 58, 70, 76, 113
Moore, Steve, 139–40
Morales, Evo, 59, 65
Morazán, Francisco, 12
Movimiento Ambientalista de Olancho (Environmental Movement of Olancho, MAO), 36
Movimiento Democrático Popular (Popular Democratic Movement, MDR), 37
Movimiento de Mujeres por la Paz "Visitación Padilla" (Visitación Padilla Women's Peace Movement), 77
Movimiento Resistencia Progresista (Progressive Resistance Movement, MRP), 88
Movimiento Unificado Campesino del Aguán (Unified Campesino Movement of the Aguan, MUCA), 72–74
Murillo, Jose David, 51
Murillo, Isis Obed, 51, 55

National Endowment for Democracy (NED), 59
nationalism: anti-colonial, 139; left, 138, 140, 142, 159
National Labour Committee (NLC), 104
NATO, 140, 145–46, 149–50, 153
Necios, Los (The Fools), 37
Negroponte, John, 22–23, 42
neo-colonialism, 12, 133
neoliberalism, 4, 6, 24–29, 35, 36, 38, 45, 56, 96, 107, 128, 133–34, 142, 149, 153, 158–59; hyper-, 118, 127
Nicaragua, 18, 21, 24, 42, 128, 147; Contras, 22, 24, 27, 42; Sandinistas, 25, 182n145, 188n98
Niosi, Jorge, 140
NORAD, 140; Bi-National Planning Group (BPG), 156
Noranda, 98
Nuila, Andrea, 41
Nuñez, Gabriela, 184n42
Nyrstar, 98

Oliva, Berta, 79, 87, 124
Organización Fraternal Negra Hondureña (Fraternal Organization of Black Hondurans, OFRANEH), 44, 112–13, 115, 117–18

Organización Regional Interamericana de Trabajadores (Inter-American Regional Organization, ORIT), 19
Orlando Hernández, Juan, 89–91, 123–24

Padillo Sunceri, Rodolfo, 60
Palcios, Nahún, 71
Paley, Dawn, 113, 115
Panitch, Leo, 140
paquetazo, 25
Paraguay, 66, 128–29
Partido Innovación y Unidad Social Demócrata (Party of Innovation and Social Democratic Unity, PINU), 60–61
Pastor Fasquelle, Rodolfo, 204n154
patronato, 112–13
Patronato Regional de Occidente (Regional Council of the West, PRO), 36
Pavón, Andrés, 62
Paz García, Policarpio, 42
peacekeeping, 1–3, 135–36, 147–49
Pearson, Lester, 135, 145
Pearson Peacekeeping Centre, 125
peasants (*campesinos*): proletarianization of, 27, 33; social movements of, 18–21, 33, 35–38, 46, 56, 72–74
Peña Nieto, Enrique, 171
Perez Ambular, Evaristo, 114
Pestell, Debbie, 125
PetroCaribe, 37, 39
Pine, Adrienne, 31, 107, 195n124
"Pink Tide," 128–29, 158
Pinochet, Augusto, 80
Pinter, Julian T.: *Land*, 199n81
PINU. *See* Partido Innovación y Unidad Social Demócrata
Placer Dome, 123
"Plan Puebla Panama" preparations, 128
Plataforma de Derechos Humanos (Human Rights Platform), 52, 58–59
Plataforma de Lucha Hondureña (Platform of Struggle), 33
police corruption, 121–24
Policia-Militar (Military Police, PM), 90–91, 124
Popeye's Chicken, burning of, 187n83
popular resistance, 6, 15, 32–33, 47, 51–57, 96
Porter, William Sydney (O. Henry): *Cabbages and Kings*, 178n52
Portillo, Luis, 124
poverty, 27, 30–31, 39, 128, 131, 157
Prensa, La, 55
privatization, 25–28, 32–33, 36, 40, 133, 149

Quebec City: conscription protests in, 164

race, 137
Radio Globo, 53–54, 70
railroads, 12, 15
Razack, Sherene, 153–54
Reagan, Ronald, 24
Red de Comercialización Comunitaria Alternativa (Network of Alternative Community Development, COMAL), 56, 76
Reeder, Neil, 102
Regalado, Maria Luisa, 106
Reina, Carlos Roberto, 26
repartimiento, 8–10
requerimiento, 7–8
Reyes, Carlos H., 53, 60
Rios, Gilberto, 37, 89
Rivas, Joni, 74
Robinson, William I., 13
Rodenzo, Nectali, 121
Romer, Paul, 118
Romero, David, 53–54
Rosario Mining Company, 13, 17, 98
Rosenthal Oliva, Jaime, 55
Ross, Andrew, 80
Rotondo, Alberto, 151
Roussef, Dilma, 129
Rubí, Luis Alberto, 120–21
Russia, 150; Russian Revolution, 145

Sabillón Pineda, Ramón Antonio, 121
Said, Edward, 212n37
Salomón, Leticia, 121
Sanabria, Carlos, 16
Sánchez-Albornoz, Nicolás, 174n1(ch.1)
Sandinistas. *See* Nicaragua
San Martín mine, 99–101
Santos, Edwin, 40, 60
Sarmiento, Ulises, 53
Sartre, Jean-Paul, 212n32
Saudi Arabia, 163, 171
Schenn, Luke, 165–66
Seccarachia, Mario, 141
Secretaría de Integración Económica Centroamericana (Central American Secretariat of Economic Integration, SIECA), 203n145
Segovia, Alexander, 204n150
Sellers, Bev, 172
The Servant State (Workman and McCormack), 155
sex industry, 114–15
Shamsie, Yasmine, 141, 146–47, 158
Shanker, Thom, 126–27

Sindicato de Trabajadores de La Tela Railroad Company (Union of Tela Railroad Company Workers, SITRATERCO), 17
Sistema de la Integración Centroamericana (System of Central American Integration, SICA), 127
slavery, abolition of, 177n38
Smeaton, John, 41
SNC-Lavalin, 152
social justice, 86, 129, 158–60, 169–70
social movements, 18, 35, 40, 46, 48, 52, 95–97, 102, 173; breaking of, 72–78; genealogy of, 35–38
Somalia, 149, 153–54
Sosa, Roberto, 46
Soto, Marco Aurelio, 13
Soviet Union, 146
Spain, colonization of Honduras by, 7–11, 95, 118, 133
Spring, Karen, 213n48
Squier, Ephraim George, 12
SRK Consulting, 152
Standard Fruit Company, 17, 21, 179n75
Standard Mining, 98
Star S.A. factory, 105–6
Stein, Eduardo, 81
St. Germain, Gerry, 119
Stollery, Tom, 109–10
strikes, 15–16, 36–37, 45; general strike (1954), 6, 17–19
structural adjustment policies (SAPs), 25–27, 36, 38
Suazo Córdova, Roberto, 22–23, 42
sweatshops, 104, 106, 109
Swift, Jamie, 211n14
Syria, 4, 150

Tahoe Resources, 151
Tamayo, Padre Andres, 62
Tendencia Revolucionara (Revolutionary Tendency, TR), 37
Tilly, Charles, 195n128
Tomé, Rasel, 88
"torch marches," 91
Torobin, Jeremy, 117–18
Torres Calderón, Manuel, 55
tourism, 109–15
trade unions, 35, 38
Tribuna, La, 55
Tribunal Supremo Electoral (Supreme Electoral Tribunal, TSE), 52, 57–59, 90
Trinidad Cabañas, José, 12
Trinidad Sánchez, José, 56, 76
Trochez, Walter, 69
Trudeau, Justin, 93–94, 150, 159, 171–72
Trudeau, Pierre, 80
TSE. *See* Tribunal Supremo Electoral

Ukraine, 150
Unificación Democrática (Democratic Unification, UD), 60–61
Unión Nacional de Campesinos (National Union of Peasants, UNC), 21
United Nations Declaration on the Rights of Indigenous Peoples (UNDRIP), 101
United Nations Educational, Scientific, and Cultural Organization (UNESCO), 111
United Nations High Commissioner for Human Rights (UNHCHR), 75
United Fruit Company, 14, 16–18, 179n75
United Provinces of Central America, 11–12
United States, 2, 11–12, 16–17, 146, 155; armed forces of, 166; as Canada's "best friend," 137; Canadian economic dependency on, 138–39; Canadian identity as different from, 171; defence apparatus, 156; Drug Enforcement Agency (DEA), 126–27; and European imperial powers, 140; exclusion of from CELAC, 163; global power of, 131–32; imperialism, 125, 130, 134, 154; military and political hegemony of, 130, 132; neo-colonialism of, 133; presence of in Honduras, 14, 18, 21, 22–24, 36, 126; Republican Party, 59; Society for the Protection of Unborn Children, 41; support of coup by, 35, 126; Thirteenth Amendment, 177n38; trade with Canada, 142–43
UnoAmérica, 59
Uruguay, 128
USAID funding, 22, 24, 25, 27–28
"USS Honduras," 22–24, 42

Van Leeuwen, Ash, 170
Varley, Frederick: *For What?* 164
Vásquez Velásquez, Romeo, 31, 48–49, 53, 92, 185n53
Vega, Adelid, 56
Velázquez Rodriguez, Ilse Ivania, 75
Velez, Annarela, 76
Venezuela, 39, 65, 69–70, 84, 89, 128
Vietnam, 147
vigilantism, 29–32
Villeda Morales, Ramon, 18
Villeda Toledo, Manuel, 55
Vimy Ridge, 164

wage labour, free capitalist, 8–9
Walker, William, 120, 177n38
Washington Senior Observer Group, 59
Watkins, Mel, 138–39
wealth, 131, 213n40
Webber, Jeffrey, 87
Wells, Debi, 139–40
"White Marches," 51
WikiLeaks, 121, 126
Wilgress, Dana, 145
Willauer, Whiting, 18
Winnipeg General Strike, 164
Winnipeg Jets, 166
women, 35; and Constitution, 43–44; human rights abuses against, 77; Indigenous, 172; rights of, 170; violence against, 78, 108
women's organizations, 33, 77, 157
Wood, Ellen, 134, 175n10
workers' movements, 6, 18
Workers Rights Consortium (WRC), 105–6
working class, 15, 18–19, 39, 134, 148, 155, 157
working conditions, 107–8
Workman, Thom, 155, 179n74
workplace injustice, 15
World Bank, 28, 134, 140
World Health Organization: Ottawa Charter for Health Promotion, 101
World Trade Organization (WTO), 134

Yamana Gold, 98
Yaritza, Lesly, 100
yellow ribbons, 167
Yugoslavia, former, 149

Zaun, Gregg, 211n17
Zelaya, José Manuel, 20, 35
Zelaya, Lorenzo, 20
Zelaya Rivas, Maria Margarita, 61
Zelaya Rosales, José Manuel, 3, 20, 34–35, 37–38, 51–52, 56, 60–63, 66–67, 69, 73, 82–88, 91, 96, 102, 110, 115, 121, 128, 182n140, 204n150; and CNRP, 38–42; as popular figure, 35, 46; and referendum, 48–49
Zelaya, Xiomara Castro de, 87
Zepada Alonzo, Vanessa, 71